The Unfinished Liberation of
CHINESE WOMEN
1949–1980

The Unfinished Liberation of
CHINESE WOMEN

1949–1980

PHYLLIS ANDORS

Indiana University Press / Wheatsheaf Books
Bloomington *Sussex*

This edition first published in the United States in 1983 by
INDIANA UNIVERSITY PRESS
Tenth and Morton Streets, Bloomington, Indiana
and in Great Britain by
WHEATSHEAF BOOKS LTD
A MEMBER OF THE HARVESTER PRESS GROUP
Publisher: John Spiers
Director of Publications: Edward Elgar
16 Ship Street, Brighton, Sussex

Manufactured in the United States of America

Library of Congress Cataloging in Publication Data

Andors, Phyllis, 1942–
  The unfinished liberation of Chinese women, 1949–1980.
  Bibliography: p.
  Includes index.
    1. Women—China—History—20th centruy.   2. Women
and socialism—China—History—20th century.   I. Title.
HQ1768.A52   1983   305.4'0951   81-48323
1 2 3 4 5 87 86 85 84 83

ISBN 0-253-36022-6

        British Library Cataloguing in Publication Data
Andors, Phyllis
  The Unfinished Liberation
  of Chinese Women, 1949–1980.
  1. Women—China—Social conditions
  I. Title
  305.4'2'0951   HQ1738

ISBN 0-7108-0448-2

To Steve

CONTENTS

· vii ·

ACKNOWLEDGMENTS

This book began when I was a graduate student at Columbia Univesity, and I would like to thank the University for the financial support given to me. Further financial support by Wagner College helped me transform a dissertation into a book. I would like to take this opportunity to thank Stephen Andors, for without his love, support, and criticisms this book would never have been written, and my parents, whose loving encouragement sustained me over the years. I owe a special debt to the women's movement in the United States, which provided such wonderful intellectual stimulus and moral support, and to the many friends in the Committee of Concerned Asian Scholars.

Finally, I am indebted to the women of China, whose struggles, accomplishments, and persistent problems are, I hope, accurately described in the following pages.

The Unfinished Liberation of
CHINESE WOMEN
1949–1980

It's the same with women (the revolution is just beginning). Of course it is necessary to give them legal equality to begin with. But from there on everything still remains to be done. The thought, culture, and customs which brought China to where we find it must disappear, and the thought, culture, and customs of proletarian China, which does not yet exist, must appear. The Chinese woman doesn't yet exist either, among the masses; but she is beginning to want to exist. And then, to liberate women is not to manufacture washing machines.

Mao Zedong, in conversation with Andre Malraux

Introduction:
Theoretical Framework

The predominance of light industry and the lack of heavy industry [have] also resulted in another essential characteristic of Chinese labor that has affected the movement: the percentage of girls, women and children employed in factories and workshops. . . .[1]

At the turn of the century factory workers accounted for less than 1 per cent of the population [in Japan]. The majority were women who suffered from severe extra discriminations and oppression. Of the 422,019 people employed in the 7,294 factories in Japan in 1900, 257,307 were female. This reflects the preponderant role of the textile industry. As late as 1929 the cotton and silk spinning and weaving industries alone accounted for 54.7 per cent of all factory workers.[2]

At the time the Lowell cotton mills were started [Massachusetts, 1830s], the caste of the factory girl was the lowest among the employments of women. . . . It was to overcome this prejudice that such high wages had been offered to women that they might be induced to become mill-girls, in spite of the opprobrium that still clung to this degrading occupation. At first only a few came; others followed, and in a short time the prejudice against factory labor wore away, and the Lowell mills became filled with blooming and energetic New England women.[3]

Employers were quick to find that women and children were easier to subdue than craftsmen, proud of their trade and tradition. The existence of this reserve of cheap labour led factory owners to employ them—sometimes in preference to men—while congratulating themselves on not tempting women out of their traditional sphere because they paid them less than the men.[4]

Western modernization theory, taking the historical development of capitalism in Europe and the United States as the standard by which to measure both technological and institutional "modernity," has at times ignored women,[5] or, at other times, has assumed the universality and biological inevitability of certain "female" roles and family forms as modernization occurs and "traditional" society fades. The assumptions underlying this body of theory have far-reaching implications. By making these assumptions explicit, we can better understand the strengths and limitations of the theories, and in the process perhaps clarify alternative roles for women in the development process.

Many social scientists, perhaps influenced by Freudian psychology,[6] apparently have assumed that biological factors prevent women from successfully integrating their sexual biological roles with economic or political roles outside the family. These scholars frequently stress the continuity of maternal and housekeeping roles within a changing family structure in modernizing societies. As socioeconomic change occurs, these roles remain to provide "female fulfillment," albeit in a somewhat changed social or institutional context.[7] As wives and mothers, women are crucial socializing agents in this view, but since they supposedly have less contact with the modern sector, they usually transmit traditional values. Thus, women are likely to provide continuity in society; their roles are essentially conservative.[8] The perception of woman's role as confined largely to the family, and hence to the private sector, frequently led the early modernization theorists to underemphasize the often vital roles of women as active participants in the development process. Those trends indicating that women were developing fundamentally new and different economic, political, and social roles as a result of their participation were even less frequently if ever noted.

It is, however, precisely because the roles and functions of women within the institutional framework of the family are so important that it is necessary to point out certain problems with this approach. These problems become apparent when we examine the history of Western economic development.

It is widely recognized that the process of development effects changes in the traditional kinship system and alters the traditional pattern of the division of labor, including the sexual division of labor, that exists in every society.[9] In most traditional systems, the family is a self-sufficient unit that produces almost all it consumes. Women are important in making cloth, milling grain, and helping in the fields, in handicraft production, and in other vital productive activities. Once an economy passes beyond the stage of agricultural subsistence, many of these tasks are no longer performed within the family. This has profound implications for the role of women, not only economically but also in terms of social status.[10] Where women formerly played important economic roles vital to the subsistence of the family and performed functions that gave them respected status within the community, the development of urban industry and the market economy brought significant changes for women. The inability of the rural sector to provide employment opportunities had the effect of increasingly constricting the scope of female productivity to predominantly those sexual-maternal roles of childbearing, childrearing, and homemaking, except where urban migration was possible. In the urban sector, however, women were absolutely central to early urban industrialization efforts in market economies. And yet this has not often been reflected in development theory.[11]

The almost universal development of textile industries with their overwhelmingly female labor force during the early phase of industrialization points to the crucial role of women at this stage of economic development. That women workers predominate is hardly surprising, since spinning and weaving were also female tasks when performed as cottage industries in the home. The economic necessity that drove most women into the factories ensured their docility and manipulability.[12] Also characteristic of this female labor force was a high turnover rate. Many women quit work once they married, or were forced to leave when they became pregnant. This instability and reversion to "traditional" female roles centered around the home and family, even the more "modern" nuclear family, may account, in part, for the lack of any in-depth analysis of women workers as contributors to economic development. Moreover, the industries in which female labor dominated were not viewed as being as central to the development process as were the capital goods and heavy industries, from which women were largely excluded. Thus, the implications that working women had for the family and women's role within it were largely ignored. If our knowledge of the relationship between women and development generally remains partial and underdeveloped, so too does our understanding of the particular strains on families and of the problems of women as they are assimilated into the larger society.

The creation of educational opportunities, a crucial aspect of the process of modernization, has not always led to female participation. In certain countries and for a variety of reasons, women may be denied any education at all or, where available, the facilities may be qualitatively different from those enjoyed by men. Even where educational opportunities are the same, the potential for gainful employment by women is not as great as for men.[13]

That women may receive no education at all is not only possible but can be viewed as rational under certain conditions. In those societies where women traditionally play no public role, the acquisition of skills unrelated to home and the family is unprofitable and dysfunctional. Education is also expensive and unprofitable in those countries where the pace of industrialization is slow and the ability of the economy to absorb skilled workers is limited. In such situations the education of women and their competition with men for limited jobs, which in turn may create male unemployment and political disaffection, may be seen as a threat to overall development.[14]

Although modernization theorists have tended to view education as an essentially liberating process which leads to more rewarding employment opportunities, the experience of Western women raises some serious questions.[15] Working women, regardless of educational backgrounds, still tend to assume the responsibilities associated with the home and childrearing. Moreover, employment for women tends to cluster in clerical work, teaching, nursing, or other service-oriented areas.[16] Many of these occupations represent an extension of traditional female "private," sexual-maternal roles; thus, far from creating new roles, education may strongly reinforce and even add to the sexual division of labor. The mere possession of an education is not sufficient to guarantee women the same kinds of economic mobility that may be available to men, nor does it necessarily challenge past cultural and historical traditions.[17]

Education is not the only area in which modernization theory has been undeveloped and partial with regard to women. Technological development, and with it increased specialization of labor, and the creation of complex economic institutions have often been viewed as leading to societies that resemble, politically and economically, a very optimistic model of Western society.[18] For many development theorists, modernization on the Western model is seen as essentially a liberating, if not always immediately pleasant, process. These assumptions have not gone unchallenged; there are ambiguous implications, especially for women.[19] Whereas in "traditional" society women were crucial producers, in "modern" society consumption activities predominate and shape the female role played out within the narrow confines of the nuclear family.[20] When women have entered the labor force, they have tended to cluster in the lowest-paid, unskilled jobs. Where they have entered the professions, they rarely achieve positions of administrative and decision-making power.[21] In public life, the numbers of women elected to office, though growing, are nowhere commensurate with their overall numbers.[22] Thus, if contemporary "modern" society is any indication, the process of economic development and social change has no built-in guarantee of equality for women.

Modernization theory has pointed to the importance of attitudinal and value change in the development process,[23] but has not really investigated the roots of traditional attitudes toward women, which often are crucial variables in the development process. For example, the problem of population limitation is closely tied to traditional attitudes toward women. Many poor societies have traditionally encouraged large families with several *male* children, who, it is held, will provide income and security in old age. Clearly, in this case, traditional attitudes toward women have their roots in poverty and insecurity. Since the family cannot be replaced as the provider of social services in the early stages of development, traditional female roles are reinforced by economic realities, since families with many able-bodied male workers have greater incomes. Moreover, when development does occur, it might occur in a way which reinforces these attitudes about the importance of the female childbearing role and the superiority of male children. This is especially true where high degrees of inequality accompany development.[24] Development, then, does not automatically mean that traditional attitudes that narrowly define legitimate roles for women will disappear.

In recent years, however, the "woman question" has assumed a new and increasingly respectable place in development theory, and the inadequacy of earlier "modernization" literature regarding the role of women in the development process has become clear. As the development needs of Third World nations assume greater urgency, and as a varied but influential women's movement has gained prominence in the West, women are no longer being ignored, and in fact their role in development is being emphasized. The United Nations has declared a decade for women (1976–1985), and regional agencies to deal with issues of women and development have been created.[25] In the United States, a Women in Development Office has been created within the government.[26] The impact of these changes on the perception and reality of women's roles in development remains to be seen.

If the present state of traditional development literature is in flux with regard to the "woman question," Marxist analysis remains a promising though undeveloped approach. For Marx, women, while never a dominant theoretical concern, were considered full participants in human society, and the reproductive function made the relationships between male and female a central part of what Marx considered the material foundations of social reality. Marx himself never developed this aspect of his historical materialism, but unlike non-Marxist theorists, both he and Engels considered female oppression a reality, a part of the larger and more general problem of exploitation and inequality in human society. Sexual oppression was viewed essentially as part of class struggle, struggle that would be progressively transformed and ultimately transcended; indeed, the male-female relationship was itself potentially a symbol of the perfect human relationship. Nevertheless, women could only achieve liberation and equality in a classless society.

Both Marx and Engels included the female component of the nineteenth-century British working class and its prominent role in the textile and millinery industries within their analyses of capitalism.[27] They were quite aware also of the implications a female working class held for the nuclear family, and of the differential impact of industrialization on different classes. Engels pointed to the disintegration of working-class families where women were out of the home twelve to thirteen hours a day. However, in including the "woman question" within the larger problem of class struggle, Marxists have generally maintained that, in the long run at least, women as women would not have special interests against men, that class conflict, and not sexual conflict, was the primary dynamic in society. Thus Engels argued that women's emancipation must be predicated upon mass participation in labor and a sharp reduction in the amount of time spent on domestic chores:

> We can clearly see that to emancipate woman and make her the equal of men is and remains an impossibility so long as the woman is shut out from social production and restricted to private domestic labor. The emancipation of women will be possible when women can take part in production on a large social scale, and domestic work no longer claims anything but an insignificant amount of her time.[28]

Engels's argument implied clearly that domestic work was still woman's work, and he left unresolved the implication that women would have a special historical burden to bear until somehow "domestic chores" disappeared.

Marxists have, however, pointed out the exploitation of female labor and sexuality under capitalism,[29] and Marxism has identified the economic role of the family as the almost universal factor in female subordination. Engels stressed that it was the family's *economic* role in society as a provider of necessary but unpaid services that made it the basis of special female oppression and inequality:

> Then it will be plain that the first condition for the liberation of the wife is to bring the whole female sex back into public industry and that this in turn demands the abolition of the monogamous family *as the economic unit of society*.[30] (emphasis added)

Even though Marxist theory has pointed to the role of women within the family as a crucial factor in sexual inequality, the theory has not developed a coherent view of the process by which the family and women's role within it are transformed. Marx and Engels saw a close relationship between capitalism and an oppressive family system, but left unresolved was the contradiction between woman's participation in production outside the family and her responsibilities for what traditional Marxism either implicitly or explicitly condemned as a degrading, boring, and exploitative division of labor based on sex. Socialism, the revolutionary transition period between capitalism and communism, was to be the way out of this dilemma. And it was in this period, Marx implied, that the question of sexual equality could, for the first time, be directly and effectively confronted.

The issue of the relationship between female liberation and socialism was of course first confronted in the Soviet Union. Whether one wishes to identify Soviet development as "socialist" or not, there can be no question that Lenin and other early Bolshevik leaders looked on women's emancipation with favor, and saw the path to this in terms of enlarging the number of women engaged in productive labor outside the home. Equally important as a support for these new roles was the radical family legislation of the Leninist period. At that time, the family was considered the institutional embodiment of tradition and hence counterrevolutionary. Laws were enacted which granted women freedom in marriage and divorce, inheritance rights, and the right to abortion as a form of birth control. Children born out of wedlock were recognized as legitimate. However, with the passing of Lenin and most of the Old Guard, the pendulum began to swing in the opposite direction in the 1930s under Stalin. The reproductive, social services, and housekeeping functions of the family emerged as crucial to the success of the new economic development plans. Policies toward women created the "double burden." Low wages made it necessary for women to work outside the home to meet the subsistence needs of the family even though they still bore the prime responsibility for the family and housekeeping.

By the 1930s, the development strategy of the Stalinist leadership made large-scale female participation in production outside the home an economic necessity. During the 1940s, both war and development plans meant jobs for women. Today, there is a very high level of female employment in the Soviet Union.[31] While new fields and opportunities for women have opened up with industrialization, a large proportion of the female labor force is still engaged in agriculture and the service industries, such as teaching, medicine, child care, and food processing. In the professions, women tend to cluster at the lower levels and their representation at the decision-making levels is minimal. This reflects the greater difficulty women have in acquiring an advanced education. By 1971 only 4 percent of Soviet women had advanced degrees, as opposed to 31 percent for men.[32]

Party membership, the basic requirement for a political career, illustrates the limited abilities of Soviet women in transforming economic participation into political power. While the percentage of female Party members went from about 8 percent in 1922 to 23 percent by the 1960s and to 22.6 percent in 1971,[33] the Party's highest organs remained resistant to female inclusion. Women did appear to play important roles in both Party and government organizations on the local level.[34]

The Soviet experience has shown that large-scale female participation in production outside the home under a noncapitalist development process can occur without fundamentally altering women's sociopolitical place. While levels of participation in the labor force and in the political system have increased significantly for women, they are not equal to those of men. Nor has there been any significant redefinition of the sexual division of labor within the family. The increasing economic role of women has not transformed the structure of male authority and the male hierarchy within the economy, nor has it forced a substan-

tial change in male-female roles outside the economic sphere. The Soviet experience clearly indicates that economic development and women's participation in
social production outside the home are not guarantees of equality for women.

The emergence of radical feminist and other women's movements in recent
years, not only in the industrialized nations of the West but all over the world,
has made it necessary to address with new effort the theoretical problems raised
by Marxist theory, and the experiences of those countries taking a noncapitalist
development path.[35] Many people heir to both a Marxist tradition and a feminist
experience are actively attempting to create a synthesis of the two traditions. One
tradition, the feminist, has focused on the role of patriarchy as the decisive
variable in structuring female roles. Marxism, however, has identified oppression
of women as part of the wider context of class relations and as a function of
society's mode of production and reproduction.[36] Significantly, whether we are
analyzing the situation of women either in the advanced industrial nations[37] or
in Third World countries,[38] the salient role of women in the family as housekeepers and mothers emerges as most crucial to understanding the lack of transformation in women's social status even when women work outside the home. Thus,
both Marxists and feminists seek to build on the original Marxist insight articulated by Engels: that the family is the root of female oppression.

Investigations into the human reproduction process and into the role of the
family in providing the means of subsistence have led Marxist analysis to new
insights into the nature of traditional "female work." Reasons have been advanced
as to why housework is usually neglected by socialist planners even with increasing socialization of the means of production.[39] One hypothesis concerns the
important role of women as major consumers in the private sector.[40] Other writers
have focused on the reproductive roles women play within the family as the key
element in their oppression. In order to better understand the ways in which
childbearing and childrearing shape women's self-images as well as their opportunities, one theory argues that it is important to study the psycho-emotional
factors in the process of reproduction, in addition to economic factors. This
insight is especially valuable in predominantly poor countries, but recent analyses
of richer societies have also stressed psychological factors and exploitation. In one
extremely provocative Marxist analysis it is argued that "the oppression of women
is based on the role of women in the exploited class as the reproducers of laborers
in class society, i.e., laborers who are the performers of exploited surplus labor."[41]
Institutional and societal relationships between men and women are determined
by the economic resources provided to women during childbearing and childrearing, resources which constitute part of the material base of any society. Thus, the
family has been moved from the previously ignored private sector into the center

stage of recent Marxist analysis of women in society. Yet although this analysis recognizes that psychological factors are important and that relationships between men and women do have inherent contradictions, these insights are explored in terms of class relations in the wider society.

Building on the idea that class oppression involves psychological and emotional oppression, some writers have attempted to integrate the insights of Freudian psychoanalytic theory with their Marxist orientation to understand how childbearing and childrearing roles have structured both the familial and nonfamilial roles of women.[42] Such insights into the continued importance of the family unit, even as it loses many of its economic, educational, and political functions, are important.

The persistence of traditional discriminatory attitudes toward women both in the industrialized nations of the West and in the revolutionary societies of China, Cuba, and elsewhere has made the insights of feminist scholars relevant and valuable. Historical patterns of patriarchy have been decisive in determining social reality in many countries.[43] The controversy regarding "patriarchy" as an analytical category[44] should not obscure the value of pointing out the continuation of patriarchal patterns of male dominance in societies that, like the Soviet Union, have undertaken a noncapitalist development path. However, none of these noncapitalist societies are replicas of the Soviet Union, and many of them claim to have transformed the concept of socialism with the reality of their own development experience. China, of course, is one such society, and in the history of the Chinese revolution a fascinating variety of approaches to development has been tried. This mighty Asian country therefore offers a way to test the validity and usefulness of some of the theoretical approaches put forth by recent Western theory and provides perhaps a large and important source of information that can be used to continue the process of building up a theory that adequately addresses itself to a consideration of the status of women in the development process.

Although this study is not primarily a theoretical analysis, but an attempt to describe and understand the reality of Chinese women's experience, nevertheless, I hope that it can make some contribution to the debates and developments described above. The experience of Chinese women especially during the period from the Great Leap Forward through the Cultural Revolution and into the post-Mao era, a period characterized by at least two discernibly different approaches to development and two different definitions of socialism, is useful in several ways. Since the Chinese accept the basic Marxist view that sees the relationship between the sexes as a function of relationships between classes, the shifting policies of the Chinese Communist Party regarding class struggle were bound to have an impact on women.[45] Moreover, given the central role of the family in traditional China, and the particularly oppressive conditions under which women lived, the resolution of the "woman question" has clearly been a central factor in determining the intensity and the scope of social revolution.[46] The precise relationship between class and sex conflict has therefore been uniquely important in the practice, if not necessarily the theory, of Chinese Marxism.

The particular period chosen is of interest because between the Great Leap Forward and the Cultural Revolution the Chinese consciously attempted to develop their own model of industrialization. In previous industrialization efforts in other societies, female labor was used at the initial stages of development, but the factors that significantly altered female economic dependency and led to changes in status on a society-wide scale were a function of urban-centered industrial development which allowed for the production of labor-saving devices that reduced the domestic burden to the point where home and career were, at least theoretically, compatible. However, in China, beginning really with the Great Leap Forward, there was a conscious attempt to limit the growth of urban areas, to develop rural industry, and to invest in areas other than those that eliminated labor in production. Because this development strategy differs, the Chinese case offers a unique opportunity to see the degree to which women's roles are shaped by development strategy rather than determined by "female" characteristics or biology.

Certain major themes and questions will appear and reappear in this book. How did the experiences of urban women differ from those of rural women? How did the different approaches to economic development and social change handle or even generate uniquely female interests in Chinese society as distinct from the interests of other groups? What were the advantages and the costs of particular development strategies to women? How did development policy change the structures of male authority and hierarchy, and what impact did changes in authority relationships in general have on the particular power of women in Chinese society? Consideration of these questions will provide a basis for evaluating the relationships between class and gender.

Another set of questions will focus on the family. How have new productive roles for women affected the nature and functions of the Chinese family? Has the division of labor within the family changed? How do changes in the traditional marriage system reflect and reinforce changes in attitudes toward women, and how do changing job opportunities reflect and reinforce patterns of marriage?

Another major concern will be the degree to which levels of female political participation have changed over time. What have been the key obstacles to and promoters of such participation? With which issues and at what levels were women involved in public life? What has been the role of women in the powerful Communist Party, and what has been the organizational and ideological relationship between the Chinese Communist Party (CCP) and the women's movement, particularly the organized Women's Federation? All of these considerations make the politics of women's emancipation in China quite complicated and have enormous implications for people, male and female, struggling with these matters in their daily lives.

Women in Pre-1949 China

THE PROCESS OF RAPID SOCIAL CHANGE THAT HAS CHARACTERIZED POST-1949 China and was dramatically intensified by the Great Leap Forward (1958–1961) and the important innovations of the Cultural Revolution must be understood in the historical perspective of the often contradictory influences at work in pre-1949 China. This is especially true in the case of women, for the traditional order put females in an extremely unequal and oppressed situation, and yet women were often the first to feel the effects of change that began to accelerate in the middle of the nineteenth century. In this chapter we will summarize briefly but critically the traditional attitudes, the influence of the emerging capitalist sector and women's role within it, and pre-1949 Communist Party policies toward women. All of these factors shaped the material and psychological context in which post-1949 and, most importantly, Great Leap Forward policies were implemented.

Traditional Ideal and Reality

By the beginning of the twentieth century, the actual roles of Chinese women had begun to deviate widely from an ideal of female behavior based on a Confucian value system. Internal decay of a dynastic system based largely on a subsistence agrarian economy and the increasing exploitation of China by the Western imperialist powers created new opportunities for some women.[1] The vast changes wrought in China from the 1840s on met their greatest resistance in the basic social unit of society, the traditional family. The family was a crucial unit of economic production and socialization. It was also hierarchal, authoritarian, and patrilineal, embodying a strict sexual and generational division of labor. Ironically, while women were strictly subordinate within the Chinese family, they had the key role of providing for its continuity. The enormous undertaking of emancipating women in twentieth-century China must be understood in this context.

The functional importance of all women in traditional China lay in their reproductive role. In a patriarchal and authoritarian society this reproductive function took the form of reproducing male descendants. Thus, female subordination was a central feature of the traditional Chinese family system. The ideal of female behavior was embodied in the concept of the "three obediences." In youth a girl was obedient to the wishes of her father; when married, to her husband; and in widowhood, to her son. In addition, the "four virtues" demanded propriety in behavior, speech, demeanor, and employment.

Since descent was patrilineal, a woman's position within her natal family was temporary and of no great importance. The predominant patrilineal household model in combination with early marriage meant that a young girl often left home before she was of significant labor value to her natal family. Hence, education or development of publicly useful skills for a girl was not encouraged in any way, and was viewed as "weeding another man's field."[2] Marriage was arranged by the parents with the family interests of continuity (that is, bearing male children) and efficient household management in mind.

The custom of paying a bride price and a dowry likened the marriage arrangement to a commodity exchange. After marriage a woman literally belonged to her husband's family, which had claim to all of her children as well as to her labor. Her natal family's obligations ended, except to see that she was not excessively mistreated. Even if there was mistreatment, they were restricted in their ability to prevent it, unless they were willing to risk a divorce with its attendant disgrace and wealthy enough to assume the obligation of taking care of her.

Thus, a woman retained only the most distant of ties to and claims on her natal family. She had to turn all her attention, wit, and abilities to securing a position within her husband's family. Moreover, her position and security within this new group remained ambiguous until she produced male heirs. In addition to the wife's reproductive duties, the strict sexual division of labor demanded that she undertake total responsibility for child care, cooking, cleaning, and the like. These household chores were lightened in families well-off enough to hire servants. However, even in such cases, responsibility for efficient household management and supervision of help was woman's work. In the early years of marriage, in addition to being subordinate to all the adult male members of the household, a woman was usually under the direct supervision of her mother-in-law, who was in charge of socializing the new bride into the routines of her husband's family. Thus, a Chinese bride could not even count on support from her husband, since the demands of filial piety forced him to side with his mother in any conflict with his wife.

This situation ameliorated somewhat in middle age as the younger woman took over more of the responsibilities of household management. In old age, though still nominally subordinate to male authority, a woman usually enjoyed a certain amount of the respect accorded to age. In this period, women usually retired from active management of household affairs and were able to enjoy some leisure and the grandchildren. This was only true, of course, if they had borne sons and if the family were not living on the margin between starvation and survival, as a large part of the peasant population lived.

While the family dominated the role of women in traditional China, women did play one public role legitimately and openly: the role of matchmaker. In a culture where male descent was so central to the preservation of the traditional family, it is perhaps ironic that the question of marriage and the selection of a suitable mate was almost entirely handled by women, usually the mothers in the families concerned.[3] The delicate process of negotiating an acceptable marriage contract involved the exercise of great sensitivity, tact, and patience. The match-maker compromised the demands made by both parties in a formula acceptable to all.

This brief, and by no means exhaustive, description of the role of women in traditional Chinese society represents the "ideal." The ideal was realizable, how-ever, only among the scholar-officials and landed gentry classes that could afford to keep women secluded within the family, confined to their reproductive and child care roles. The majority of women who have participated in mass move-ments of social change in China, from the Taiping Rebellion to the Communist Revolution, did not come from these classes, but from the lower classes, most often the peasantry.[4] The ideal of feminine behavior created a dependent being, at once inferior, passive, and obedient. However, the reality of harsh economic conditions often demanded female labor participation, and resulted in widespread deviations from what was obviously a class-based idealization of female behavior. Peasant women throughout China, but particularly in the south, not only worked in the fields but were responsible for making cloth, gathering firewood, drawing water from the village well, laundering the family wash in the river, and other tasks related to daily life in a preindustrial agrarian society. Performance of these chores resulted in continual contact with nonfamily members of both sexes. Such women, while bowing to public norms of feminine behavior, often were the dominant forces in their own homes.[5]

Even where women did not dominate, they of necessity learned the skills associated with tact and diplomacy. If a young bride intended to live peacefully with her mother-in-law, she had to learn how to avoid provoking her and how to initiate changes in the management of household affairs in a manner acceptable to the older woman. Even young girls very early acquired the skills of persuasion, the use of threats, and the knowledge that the same words spoken by men or boys carried more weight. These skills were developed within the context of the family, but, as we shall see later, many women were able to use them in the very different context of participation in the liberation struggle and in mass campaigns after 1949.

Even though the family was the dominant institution and the Chinese emphasis on the seclusion of women excluded the possibility of formal social organizations for women, there apparently did exist in most villages an informal community of women.[6] Peasant homes were smaller and less secluded than those of the gentry, and since lighting was poor, women often worked in their doorways talking with one another. Some tasks, such as washing clothes, were performed outside the home in a group setting.[7] These encounters were often used to discuss the latest village happenings. They also provided women an informal court of appeal in the instance of excessive mistreatment. Since community discussion of private family matters was considered a loss of face to the family concerned, daughters-in-law had some means of mitigating the harsh rule of mothers-in-law. Criticism by other women and nonacceptance by the local community could be severe sanctions in a system that denied any legal recourse. These informal groupings of women often were the basis for Communist-led revolutionary women's associations in both pre- and post-1949 China.

Thus the legacy of tradition was ambiguous; for while the position of women in traditional Chinese society was undeniably subordinate to that of men, and often extremely oppressive, some of the skills in managing human relationships and the behavior patterns developed by women to make life bearable were to become relevant in post-1949 society.

Influence of Early Industrialization and the Emergence of a Women's Movement

While China remains predominantly an agricultural society even today, the emergence of an urban industrial sector was very important for women. Changes in the economic mode of production occasioned by early industrialization created new opportunities for women beyond the walls of their rural courtyards.

Beginning in the middle of the nineteenth century, Chinese cities, particularly in the coastal areas, became the site of nascent industrial development. Before this, wealth had been predominantly in the hands of a rural landed gentry whose position was based on land ownership, moneylending, and bureaucratic position. The family and the village were twin pillars of this socioeconomic order. Nonagricultural production was typified by home and family-based handicrafts.

The development of Chinese industry began within the framework of the unequal treaties imposed on China by the Western nations, a system under which native capital and entrepreneurship competed on unfavorable terms with the

more technologically advanced nations of the West.[8] This situation was ameliorated for a short time during World War I. The preoccupation of the foreign
powers with European matters provided an opportunity for the development of
Chinese-owned and Chinese-controlled light industries, particularly textiles, tobacco, matches, grains, and food processing. The establishment of banks transformed the money and credit system. While the agrarian sector of the economy
remained by far the larger, a pattern of bureaucratically modified urban capitalist
industrial development began. In addition to commercial and industrial development, the early decades of the twentieth century also saw the rapid growth of
modern, Western-influenced educational institutions.[9]

Both the industrial development and the expansion of educational opportunities in this period had important implications for the traditional family system
and for the role of women within it. The attractions of a city life and freedom
from onerous family responsibilities proved irresistible to many ambitious and
discontented young women.[10]

The urban experiences of most Chinese women were clearly defined by their
class background. For the most part, education and, subsequently, political and
social participation were limited to women of the middle and upper classes.[11] For
many of these women, traditional familial obligations and ties placed severe
restrictions on their activities. For women from poorer rural or urban families,
jobs in factories at low wages, long hours, and under abysmal conditions were
the only alternative to rural farm life.[12] The Chinese women's movement that
emerged from the ferment of the May 4th era (1917–1921), with its student
unrest and the beginnings of an organized labor movement, was a product of
both kinds of female urban experience.

Organizations of women had been politically active before the May 4th Movement. However, from the turbulence of these years emerged a new revolutionary
movement that eventually united the various feminist, nationalist, and socialist
forces.[13] The May 4th Movement was characterized by a blend of nationalism and
desire for economic development and political modernization. Under the influence of Western liberal and various socialist and Marxist ideas, the movement
was above all an intellectual rejection of traditional Chinese social and political
institutions, values, and ethics, which were perceived as being responsible for a
weak and exploited China. The problems inherent in the traditional concepts of
women's place in Chinese society came to the fore as part of a critical evaluation
of the family as a pillar of the old oppressive social order.

The "woman problem," in China as in the West, was at this time defined
primarily in narrow institutional political terms. Moreover, the necessity for far-
reaching social reforms to support even these changes in women's roles was very
poorly understood by most Chinese intellectuals and by Chinese women in par-

ticular. During the 1920s a variety of organizations and associations appeared pursuing purely feminist concerns. On July 22, 1922, the Women's Suffrage Association was established, quickly followed, on August 23, by the Women's Rights League.[14] The development of these kinds of groups was accompanied by a split in the women's movement between those concerned with narrow political and legal rights and more radical women who began to see the "woman question" as part of the larger problem of social and economic reform.

Among the group of radical students who would turn to organizing the urban working class in the 1920s were some of the most important early women leaders in the Communist movement. Xiang Jingyu, Cai Chang, and Deng Yingzhao all were students and activists in the May 4th period.[15] Their participation in the myriad study groups organized at this time afforded them the opportunity to meet and unite in efforts aimed at mobilizing other women. Several, like Xiang and Cai, went abroad, where they joined Marxist study groups, while others, like Deng, who remained in China, also were exposed to Marxism through the impact of the Russian Revolution on Chinese intellectuals. As the high tide of the May 4th Movement receded, both groups of radical students agreed on the necessity of organizing the workers if China was going to be strengthened.

The Chinese industrial labor force in the 1920s consisted of about 1.5 million workers, over half of whom were employed in foreign-owned enterprises.[16] Light industry predominated over heavy industry in China at this time. The textile industry, mainly cotton and silk production, was the leading industry in terms of the value of its output, the amount of capital invested, and the numbers of workers employed.[17] Women constituted an extremely important part of the labor force, not only in textiles, but in light industry as a whole.

> A typical feature of Chinese industry at this time was the sizable proportion of female and child labor employed. Women and children were paid at lower rates than men, but had to endure the same long hours and harsh treatment. . . . The tobacco and match factories were another sector in which the employment of female and child labor predominated.[18]

In spite of their large numbers and the oppressive conditions under which they worked, women played a secondary role in the labor movement. This situation changed somewhat as a result of the extensive efforts of the Women's Department of the young Chinese Communist Party (CCP) during the 1920s.[19]

The increasing political activism of the urban labor force during the 1920s is explainable, in good part, by the organizing efforts of the CCP.[20] The Women's Department, under the leadership of Xiang Jingyu, was given the task of organizing women workers. This separate department for women illustrated both the Party's attitude toward women as a special part of the labor force and the reluctance of men to cooperate organizationally with women. It also pointed to the special practical difficulties involved in organizing women inherent in the conditions under which women sought factory jobs.

Most women viewed factory employment as the means to survive. In some areas female contributions to total family income were crucial. Single women, bereft of family, had few other occupations open to them, the most widespread alternative being prostitution. Thus, loss of factory employment could have dire consequences for both the woman and those dependent upon her. General reluctance to unionize was reinforced by traditional socialization patterns which presented male authority as unchallengeable. This hardly conditioned women to rebel in a work situation in which all persons in positions of power, from supervisor to factory owner, were male. Moreover, most workers were only recently peasants, unsophisticated in urban ways and industrial organization, and very young.

In face of the obstacles confronting women, the Women's Department under Xiang had a formidable task. Yet, throughout the period of the 1920s, the number of organized women rose and the incidence of strikes increased.[21] The first significant women's strike action came in the wake of the highly successful Hong Kong seamen's strike in 1922.[22] Although the women were unsuccessful in achieving their demands, the experience of collective action was a valuable lesson. An appreciation of the need for organization and effective leadership resulted.

Although the Hong Kong seamen's union strike in 1922 and the May 30th Strike Movement in 1925 (which began at a Shanghai cotton mill in which many women were involved) dominate the period, the Nanyang Tobacco Company strike in 1924 was also important. Xiang Jingyu and other women cadres participated in this strike, which ended only after management enlisted the community's police power.[23] Worker demands focused on increased wages, shortened workdays, and restriction of managerial power, especially physical abuse. Special protection for female and child labor appeared as general slogans in May Day demonstrations, but was not itself a cause of particular strikes. Feminist concerns do not appear to have been a pressing issue for women workers in the 1920s, and the questions of wages, hours, and working conditions were more important than matters of social welfare and services provided at the workplace.

Female participation in the industrial labor force had significant implications for traditional concepts of the family and women's roles. The receipt of individual wages by women weakened dependence on the family.

> To an increasing degree, especially in the cities, and in the case of factory
> workers, their political status in the family is coming to depend upon the
> size and importance of their contribution to the family income on the one

hand, and whether or not it is sufficient to support them independent of the family on the other.[24]

For other women, work provided the means by which to escape an unhappy marriage or to prevent an arranged marriage.

In one case, this developed into a little known but fascinating antimarriage movement among young girls from certain silk-producing areas near Guangzhou employed by the Guangzhou silk factories.[25] This particular area had a history of female employment outside the home, and many peasant families in this area evidently were dependent on the earnings of a wife or daughter.[26] During this movement, many of the women refused to marry or, if married, refused to live with their husbands. They joined girls' houses (apparently similar to modern-day sororities) and even reimbursed their families from their own earnings for their dowries or for other moneys necessary to buy their freedom. Although never developed beyond Guangdong, the movement illustrated how far women might be willing to go to escape the oppression of traditional marital and familial roles. It also points out the possibilities inherent in the relationship between economic change (in this instance, a factory job and wages) and the changing role of women.

The traditional childbearing role was also influenced by the rise in female factory work. Traditional Chinese family life encouraged large numbers of children, especially males. But as the number of working women increased, a lower fertility rate also occurred among these women, and one observer noted that "women workers bear children later and less frequently than non-workers of the same class."[27] Moreover, there was a change of attitude on the part of the family toward a woman who worked. Wages gave her some status and independence within the family and ameliorated the harshness of the mother-in-law/daughter-in-law relationship.

Thus, the confluence of political and social change in urban China that culminated in the May 4th Movement, and the rising importance of an urban-based industrial system that relied so heavily upon female labor, served to integrate the "woman question" with the larger question of economic development and social change. This seriously undermined the traditional view of women as a marginal and unimportant segment of the population. But the situation in the countryside was not nearly as dynamic, except for those areas of rural China where the CCP had established itself in "border region"[28] base areas.

Pre-1949 CCP Policy and Women's Participation in Rural Areas

Before 1927, the organizational efforts of the young Chinese Communist Party focused on the urban proletariat. In that year, the Guomindang offensive against the urban left and the Communist movement necessitated a retreat into the countryside and a drastic reorientation of the movement toward mobilization of the peasantry. For the next twenty years, until victory in 1949, the rural base areas were the locus of the Communist movement. Throughout this period the base areas (about fifteen in the earlier period and about twelve later on) were subject to either Guomindang or Japanese attack and saw constantly fluctuating borders. At times they maintained only tenuous contact with their capitals in Ruijin (up to 1934) or Yanan (1937–1945).[29] Serious disagreements among the revolutionary leadership arose (particularly in the earlier period) and military emergencies often led to the neglect of less urgent socioeconomic matters.

The development of policies aimed at furthering female progress and the creation of institutions that supported women's struggles must be viewed against this wider political and military reality. That such policies and institutions were developed at all reflected both the ideological commitment of the Communists to sexual equality, and a practical political recognition that many of the issues involved in the "woman question"—such as the family, marriage, and divorce—potentially undermined the old social order. Of course the question of women's role in society was also potentially divisive of peasant unity and peasant-Party relations in a still largely tradition-bound countryside.

The positive and negative experiences gained by the Party in attempting to initiate social change in the Jiangxi Soviet period (1931–1934) served as a base upon which successful, mass-supported policies were created during the later Yanan period (1936–1945). In the case of women, sharp resistance emerged from male peasants and the traditional family in Jiangxi when the political ideals of female emancipation and equality were pursued. Moreover, the military crisis forced the attention of revolutionary cadres elsewhere, making efforts at organizing women haphazard at best. Serious rethinking about how to achieve the goals of women's liberation and equality occurred when the Communists reached Yanan. Here policies were formulated and implemented that avoided the direct confrontations that had occurred in Jiangxi,[30] but using the practical experience gained during that time.

The laws of the Jiangxi Soviet marked a break with tradition. The Constitution of the Soviet Republic (November 7, 1931),[31] the Land Law of the Soviet Republic,[32] and the two marriage laws promulgated by the Central Executive Committee of the Soviet Republic in 1931 and the revised edition in 1934[33] all dealt directly with the "woman question." Article 4 of the Constitution granted citizenship "irrespective of sex." Article 11, however, forcefully and directly stated the policy and commitment of the CCP:

(11) It is the purpose of the Soviet Government of China to guarantee the thorough emancipation of women; it recognizes freedom of marriage and will put into operation various measures for the protection of women, to enable women gradually to attain to the material basis required for their emancipation from the bondage of domestic work, and to give them the possibility of participating in the social, economic, political and cultural life of the entire society.[34]

Article 1 of the Land Law, in reference to confiscated lands of landlords that were to be distributed, stated:

Hired farm hands, coolies, and toiling labor-owners shall enjoy equal rights to land allotments irrespective of sex.[35]

Full and rapid implementation of these legal provisions, which represented goals toward which to strive, would probably have undermined support for the small Communist movement. The overriding peasant concern of this period was rent reduction, an issue of basic survival. The particular manner in which women participated in the rent reduction movement brought to the surface a contradiction between Party policy and the prevalent traditional marriage system, a contradiction that clearly illustrated the limited applicability of the Jiangxi Soviet's legal provisions regarding women.

Female participation in the peasant movement was often through women's unions, organized by women activists.[36] The tasks of these groups were to mobilize and educate women peasants to participate in the larger peasant movement. However, these efforts were, in many cases, thwarted by the prevalence of traditional attitudes toward women's capabilities and proper roles, and by the system of arranged marriages. The newly organized women's groups, however, seized quickly upon the legal provisions of the Marriage Law and demanded free marriage and divorce, but the Party was unable to respond without jeopardizing male peasant support for the land reform and the revolutionary movement generally and for the army's needs specifically. Many male peasants had gone into debt to afford the bride-price, and if wives were allowed to divorce their husbands, clearly the implications could be disastrous.

This problem of free marriage and divorce, however, struck at the heart of the traditional family system and was to surface repeatedly wherever women were organized. It was a crucial problem, for as the Communists recognized, oppression of women was part and parcel of other oppressive systems of authority in Chinese society. As Mao pointed out:

As to women, apart from being dominated by the three systems mentioned above, they are further dominated by men (the authority of the husband). These four kinds of authority—political authority, clan authority, theocratic authority and the authority of the husband—represent the whole ideology and institution of feudalism and patriarchy, and are the four great cords that have bound the Chinese people and particularly the peasants.[37]

The Marriage Law of the Jiangxi Soviet, and later marriage laws, attacked the traditional system by attacking its basic institution, the family. Mao expressed the rationale behind this:

As to the authority of the husband, it has always been comparatively weak among the poor peasants, because the poor peasant women, compelled for financial reasons to take more part in menial work than women of the wealthier classes, have obtained more right to speak and more power to make decisions in family affairs. In recent years rural economy has become even more bankrupt and the basic condition for men's domination over women has already been eliminated. . . . In a word, all feudal and patriarchal ideologies and institutions are tottering as the power of the peasant rises.[38]

The Jiangxi marriage law specifically granted women freedom of marriage and divorce and gave them rights to underage children and to inherit property, all of which amounted to an attack on the traditional family and social order. Freedom of marriage between two individuals favored the development of the nuclear family, whose hope for economic well-being placed it in direct relationship to the state rather than to the extended family. The registration of marriage did more than ensure the free choice of the union; it was a political act which helped to transfer loyalties to an entity larger than the family. Even though the marriage law was not immediately and widely implemented in the base areas, it did embody goals which transcended the law itself and thus gave women an ultimate stake in achieving those goals as part of a larger revolutionary movement.

In addition to the marriage laws, policies toward women were implemented through women's organizations closely allied with and directed by the Soviet's cadres involved in women's work. For a variety of reasons, these cadres were almost invariably women. It is unclear how widespread or well organized these women's associations were. Mao's report on Changgang District[39] suggested that women's groups were common but did not always include all women, especially those from the poorer peasant families, and without Party leadership and participation these groups often concentrated on issues concerning marriage, divorce, and family matters. Even though these issues were important, they were precisely the ones that contained the potential for creating divisiveness among the peasants, whose support the Party and the army desperately needed. Thus, women's political and organizational efforts were guided into other areas that would strengthen the movement.

The main task of the women's movement in this period was support of the army. Although the war effort assumed overriding importance, few women were actually involved in combat. However, women were organized for production that supported the military efforts of the Communists.[40] For most of the women involved in production, work meant farm work. Since male peasants were recruited for the Red Army, the women had to replace them in plowing, planting, and harvesting. And, while it is clear that traditional household and child-care burdens prevented the most efficient use of female labor in this area, nevertheless by 1934 the contributions of women to the labor force were such that they received public acclaim.[41] Women leaders of the period developed farm skills previously possessed only by men.[42] In addition to performing field work, women were also organized into sewing groups to make uniforms and especially shoes for the army. While the war production efforts of the women were stressed, their participation in civilian economic and political affairs increased significantly.

As more men joined the army, female substitutes appeared in production work and then in political assemblies. In one township, Caixi in Fujian, Mao recorded the dramatic increase of women delegates from 30 percent in 1931 to 62 percent in 1932 to 64 percent in 1934.[43] Caixi may have been unique in this respect, but it is clear that in a relatively prosperous area in which women had begun to work outside the home and where male absence had increased this trend, female political participation resulted.

The Jiangxi Soviet experience yielded valuable lessons. It became clear that unless institutional and material conditions changed in the poor and traditional countryside, the demands some women raised for emancipation and equality threatened not only the social fabric of traditional society but also the success of Communist attempts to rally peasant support in other areas. However, it also became evident that in a precarious military situation in which men were occupied with army and security matters, more visible and alternative political and production roles for women could emerge. Yet, in comparison to the way in which women lived in Yanan in Northwest China (the city that was soon to be the new sanctuary of the CCP), the advances of women in the Jiangxi Soviet represented an advanced stage of revolutionary transformation.

The north Shenxi base with its capital at Yanan was a poor and backward region.[44] For women, the tight bonds of tradition remained strong. Footbinding, already disappearing in much of China, was still a strong part of everyday life.[45] Footbinding and the influence of traditional ideas about the proper role of female labor accounted for the fact that only about 5 percent of the female population engaged in agricultural work with any regularity.[46] The traditional and secluded existence of Shenxi women made the home and courtyard the sphere of their activities. The use of women to help at harvest time was considered a family disgrace and was resorted to only by poorer peasants. This conservative atmosphere presaged a slow and difficult course for the Party's work among women. However, the harsh realities of civil war, the Japanese invasion, and the creation of strong Communist base areas favored social change.

As the collapse of the United Front (the Chinese Communist Party and the Guomindang) became increasingly evident in 1940–41, the Communist areas were subjected to economic blockade. The entire Communist movement focused on formulating and implementing policies that would guarantee survival. After the *zhengfeng* (rectification) campaign of 1942, CCP policy toward women reflected the new priorities of production and the tasks of the Anti-Japanese War.[47]

In the early Yanan period Party policy toward women changed only slightly from the Jiangxi Soviet period. The earlier marriage law was at first reprinted for all base areas, but then the individual bases produced variants of their own.[48] The conservative attitude toward women's work and the burdensome household chores of women created difficulties for mobilizing women in the new base areas. A women's organization was established in 1936[49] with the job of encouraging women to participate in the wartime effort at the local (village) level. It appears that most efforts were aimed at supporting the army by mobilizing women to sew uniforms and shoes and to collect food, and, to a lesser extent, by involving women in farm work.

The issue of political rights, and especially the thorny question of implementing the marriage laws, was kept alive by a group of Western-educated women who had come to Yanan from the urban areas. Products of the May 4th Movement and beneficiaries of urban exposure to ideas of social justice, these women contrasted sharply with the poor peasant women of Shenxi.

Within the Party, feminist goals characterized the concerns of some but not all of the leading female activists.[50] These women concentrated their efforts on the implementation of the marriage laws and favored an all-out Party effort on behalf of women's rights. In 1942, the conflict between Party policy and these feminists came into the open with Ding Ling's article "Thoughts on March 8," written ostensibly for International Women's Day and published in the *Liberation Daily*.[51]

In her attack, Ding Ling pointed to the contradictory demands made by the Party on women. On the one hand, women were to participate in production and social activities; on the other, they still bore prime responsibility for household management and children. If a woman failed in either role, criticism followed. Many of Ding Ling's observations were accurate descriptions of reality. Her feminist perspective, combined with her position as a member of a small intellectual elite of emancipated women, however, probably reflected the frustrations of that social group more than it did the more immediate needs of the masses of peasant men and women in the border region villages. At any rate, during the *zhengfeng* movement of 1942, the Party responded by declaring Ding Ling's feminism outdated and its implications detrimental to revolutionary mobilization. It was not until the post–Cultural Revolution period that many of the issues Ding Ling spoke to received serious attention.[52]

Party policy toward women after 1942 concentrated on involving women in production both within and outside the home. The Party Central Committee Resolution on Women's Work reflected the urgency of the economic situation in the border regions and the orthodox idea that female liberation would depend on participation in social production.[53] Since Shenxi was poor and its women isolated, economically dependent, and hence oppressed, this insistence on broader participation by women made both economic and political sense. Furthermore, the Jiangxi experience showed that increased political and social involvement came if women worked. The directive criticized the lack of a mass viewpoint that had prevailed previously and insisted that raising the political status of women and achieving liberation depended on their achieving economic independence by their own efforts.[54]

Women activists were instructed to mobilize the female peasant masses into local women's associations. These associations were to become the vehicle for organizing female labor to increase both agricultural and industrial production. The military situation in Yanan was not as precarious as in Jiangxi until the Civil War period (1946–1949), when the shift from guerrilla to positional warfare demanded greater male peasant recruitment. Until then, the daily household chores of women, the traditional lack of female labor in the fields, and the greater incidence of footbinding in Shenxi meant that men performed most of the farm work. But by 1949, Deng Yingzhao, vice-chairman of the women's movement, claimed that in the older liberated areas 50 to 70 percent of the women were involved in farm work.[55] The significance of female labor in the fields became evident in the land reform movement, in which many women actively participated.

In 1938 approximately 5,150 workers in public factories, private factories, and the home constituted the textile industry in the border regions. The overwhelming majority of these workers, about 5,000, were women working at home. Moreover, these workers were responsible for 76 percent of textile production in the border region areas.[56] By 1943, the number of women engaged in home cloth production reached 41,540, and they continued to be responsible for most of the cloth produced in these areas. Production in public and private factories, a program supported by the Communists in the years 1938–1941, had proven insufficient, costly and vulnerable to enemy attack.

Production organized at the village level obviated the need for large-scale investment and, though inefficient in comparison to modern means of production, was valuable to the industrial effort in several ways. The decentralization movement in 1943 made the villages ideal production sites for cloth manufacture. As part of the *xia-xiang* movement,[57] Party cadre and other political and economic workers were sent to villages to organize local industrial projects, and although many of these undertakings were primitive, they nevertheless created a source of income for women workers. The Central Committee directive on women emphasized participation in industrial work for wages (a first for most peasant women). Traditional female skills used in a new context made this an acceptable but quite revolutionary change in the social relations of production. The increased contact between women, valuable in itself, was more significant. Women learned to work together effectively and to organize their time, and were stimulated to establish collective childcare projects. Greater contact between women also led to wider participation in public affairs.

In addition to working in cloth production, many women organized sewing groups to produce uniforms and cloth shoes for the army. Not only did this activity produce income for women, it linked their efforts with the national struggle against Japan, an important political step. While cloth production and sewing were perhaps the most common efforts, women also began developing subsidiary occupations, such as making vegetable oil or raising pigs and chickens. Some helped in the curing of leather and the making of paper. All of their efforts at production led to visible increases in village standards of living. And as women contributed to the collective economic welfare in the villages, the groundwork for change in women's status and role was being laid.

Production was not the only theater of female involvement. Although the armies were dominated by male soldiers,[58] women were organized into local village militias responsible for gathering intelligence, acting as couriers, and, in rare instances, backing up regular troops.[59]

The experience of the Chinese Communists in the base areas did indicate that women's progress was dependent upon participation in production. Clearly, the mobilization of female labor in wartime China, where male labor power was continually called upon to serve in the military, had led to the creation of new sociopolitical roles for women, as well as new roles in production. Moreover, women themselves commonly began to challenge traditional roles and status, especially as the land reform campaign was instituted in 1946–47.[60]

The victory over Japan in 1945 and the subsequent Civil War beginning in 1946 saw a dramatic change in Chinese Communist policy toward women. As the Civil War progressed and landlord support was viewed not only as no longer necessary but in contradiction to the direct interests of the peasants whose support was crucial to a Communist victory, a new land reform campaign was instituted. In conformity with Party policy, the 1948 Central Committee directives concerning women aimed at the mobilization and organization of women for participation in land reform.[61] In contrast to the 1943 directives, this document argued that progress for women, while based on labor participation, had to be reinforced by laws prohibiting footbinding, female infanticide, and child marriage, and by implementation of the marriage laws.[62] Furthermore, it was necessary to fight the general prevalence of traditional attitudes toward women, but this form of struggle was manifestly different from that waged against the landlords. The potential for conflict between women's demands and social revolution was dramatically revealed in many areas during the course of the land reform campaign.

Traditional attitudes restricted female participation within the peasant associations, where women rarely spoke out. Experience in mobilizing women for production and social participation had been based on the creation of separate women's associations, and these groups became the vehicle through which women participated in land reform. The numbers of women and the levels of participation in these associations apparently varied greatly, and depended on such factors as the degree of male opposition to women attending political meetings, the degree to which women had participated in production, the attitudes of Party cadres responsible for the land reform work, and the strength of the local women's association.

In some cases, strong local women's associations provided support for peasant women in their efforts to ameliorate familial oppression. In other places, the women who were most independent and outspoken and who became influential in organizing other village women were often categorized as disreputable and immoral because past poverty had forced them to break traditional codes of behavior, both social and sexual. As one cadre put it, "The virtuous women weren't militant and the militant women weren't virtuous."[63] In still other instances, local cadres did not implement reforms, especially when their personal interests were involved.[64] Thus, while Party policy gave women the right to own land in their own name, many women were unable to realize the full benefits of land reform because it raised issues concerning women's proper role within the family and society that were unresolvable at the time. However, the shift to positional warfare and the further recruitment of men to serve in the army resulted in more women having prime responsibility for home production. This increased the legitimacy of women's demands, but in a way that eschewed open conflict among the peasants. Interestingly, where women formed the majority of the labor force, the incidence of mutual-aid teams and agricultural cooperatives was highest.[65]

The problem of women's rights often brought out contradictions within classes.

Among the poorer peasants there appeared to be basic agreement on the question of women receiving their equal share of land, but there was considerable lack of unity when the problems of marriage, divorce, and inheritance arose. Older women, fearful of losing control over their daughters-in-law, did not welcome the marriage laws. Generational differences among the women, reinforced by the traditional family structure, projected conflicts of interest. Even many young women did not protest arranged marriages, since the social setting offered few opportunities for male-female contact and hence few chances for women to find husbands. These kinds of problems were to arise more dramatically in the marriage law campaign of the early 1950s.

Conclusion

By the close of the Civil War period, the Chinese Communists were heir to a mixed legacy of policies toward women. The early urban experience had amply demonstrated the potential of a female labor force that could achieve a high level of organization and political consciousness in addition to performing economically important work. The liberated base areas had illustrated just how intricately the problems of poverty and tradition were related, especially when social change regarding women threatened to undermine the mass mobilization required to overthrow the institutional roots of both poverty and women's oppression. This experience in the base areas had revealed potential conflict in the short run between women's emancipation and other, more general socioeconomic transformation, even while it had demonstrated how closely the two were related and dependent on each other.

Reconstruction and the First
Five-Year Plan

PRE-LIBERATION POLICY TOWARD WOMEN HAD, OF NECESSITY, FOCUSED on the crucial productive roles of women and was consistent with the theoretical assumption that liberation would come through struggle and especially through female participation in social production. The 1949 Communist victory in China reinforced this emphasis on production as the focus of attention shifted from the rural bases to urban centers. The particular problems of women paled in comparison to the necessity to reconstruct and develop the war-torn economy. Nevertheless, the relationship between women's progress and other kinds of socioeconomic change that had been revealed so tentatively during the previous years of violent military conflict and civil war was to be revealed more starkly in the ensuing years, which focused on economic reconstruction and development. Encompassing both continued radical social reform (up to 1953) and a Soviet-modeled development strategy in the First Five-Year Plan (1953 to 1957), these years were to provide valuable lessons concerning the potential of female participation and the problems this raised. Thus, even though the period up to the Great Leap Forward did not consciously put women's concerns or participation as a central priority, the impact of this period on women and on the woman question was significant.

1950–1953

Recognition of a new stage in the women's movement came at the First Congress of the All-China Women's Federation (henceforth referred to simply as the Women's Federation) held in 1949. Deng Yingzhao, vice-chairman, outlined "new tasks" for women, including participation in the land reform and marriage law campaigns; women were also to be prepared for tasks in construction and in economic reconstruction.[1]

The Women's Federation was the mass organization responsible for the channeling and development of female participation in economic development and sociopolitical reform, and was not a feminist group either in theory or in practice. From its creation,[2] the Federation was organizationally a part of the larger social movement under the supervision of the Party and did not either formulate or reflect a totally autonomous or particularist woman's viewpoint. And while the women's organization was responsible for increasing female political consciousness and participation, this was conditioned, at any one time, by the Party's definition of the relationship between women and social revolution. Changes in this definition were reflected in the different development policies and provided the ideological context in which women's struggles were joined.

In the early post-1949 period the older liberated areas had the strongest women's organizations. But throughout the 1950s the national press was full of references to women's meetings and Federation branches established at the provincial, county, village, and district levels, indicating a fairly widespread development of women's organizations.[3] These local organizations differed in structure, in their levels of activism, in their relationship to the parent organization, and in their ability to affect the progress of women in their areas.

The Women's Federation from the beginning was involved in a variety of issues: land reform, the Marriage Law campaigns, political study, education, agricultural development, street industry, and the development of social services. The development of women worker, peasant, student, teacher, and political cadres also integrated women into the larger polity. On issues relating to their relative positions of power and privilege in society, including the female role in the social division of labor, the Women's Federation as often promoted Party policies toward women in places of work or residence as it acted as a promoter of specific women's interests within the Party itself or between the Women's Federation and the CCP. It is in this broader context that the role of the Women's Federation must be viewed.

Urban Women 1950–1953

In the four years from 1949 to 1953 the female proportion of the urban labor force increased from 7.5 percent (about 600,000) to 11.0 percent (about 2,132,000).[4] Most women workers could be found in the light industries— textiles, tobacco, matches, food processing. At a national conference on women's work held in 1950, Liu Ningyi, head of the All-China Federation of Labor and a prominent member of the Communist leadership, pointed to the important role of women workers in urban industry, which at that time was dominated by light industry.[5]

The rapid increase in the number of female workers was not to be sustained.

In 1952, a State Council directive made it clear that all women who wanted jobs would not find work.[6] The Women's Federation was instructed to concentrate on mobilizing those women who were "suitably qualified" and on helping them to find jobs.[7] This relatively small group of skilled female workers, who had been recruited for work and political activism, were primarily urged to expend all efforts on increasing production.[8]

In spite of the gradual expansion of industry and the difficulties of employment for women, certain advances were evident, mainly in those sectors which had a history of female employment. The textile industries expanded, especially the cotton mills, where women constituted about 70 percent of the work force.[9] Expansion of all service industries, but especially primary education and health, accounted for an increasing portion of the total female working force. In the period 1950–1953, articles about individual women technicians and engineers employed by heavy industry regularly appeared in *New Women of China,* but these were not nearly as numerous as the articles about women in textiles, match production, and the service industries.

The traditional female-labor oriented industries historically had lower wage scales than the few heavy industries which existed in pre-1949 China. While the continued predominance of women in light and service industries implied institutionalized discrimination against female labor, this should not obscure the fact that more and more women were working outside the home for wages. Moreover, it is in these industries where day nurseries, clinics, and study classes for workers to increase skills and technical ability were established most frequently. While undoubtedly the necessity to provide for the special needs of female workers was a disincentive for other industries to hire large numbers of women, more importantly, in the long run, it implied an acceptance by the government of the social overhead costs of an increasing female component of the labor force.[10]

Some urban women who could not find regular employment organized themselves into local handicrafts and service shops. The local level of the Women's Federation, located in urban neighborhoods, supported these efforts. Production was the most important task and emphasis was placed on the development of street industries. A movement to start street production begun in 1950 would later assume enormous importance in the Great Leap.[11] During the 1950s these enterprises remained undeveloped, appearing and disappearing sporadically.

The Women's Federation, in addition to encouraging and organizing production efforts, was also involved in literacy and other cultural projects that would overcome the officially recognized "backwardness" of Chinese women. The oppression women suffered under the feudal system, and their consequent lack of skills and low level of political consciousness, were root causes of their inability to enter production or to take on any jobs involving skill.[12] Thus, while formidable

problems faced women in urban areas, particularly those who remained housewives, there were possibilities for change within the neighborhoods. The urban
priority for national investment and development contained at least the potential
for greater female participation.

Rural Women, 1950–1953

The land reform and marriage law campaigns dominated rural politics from
1950 to 1953. Both were meant to lay the groundwork for far-reaching social
change. The two campaigns were closely associated, with the marriage law campaign usually following closely behind the final stage of land redistribution and
organization. And, in both campaigns, women's active participation was considered necessary for success.

Land reform, begun in 1946–1947 in those areas then under Communist
control, continued throughout the early 1950s as the Party consolidated its
power. The tasks of the women's movement were clearly outlined by the Party.[13]
In many places the absence of female cadres or even female activists meant that
men would be responsible for Party work among women. Party policy demanded
unity between male and female peasants in the class struggle against the landlords.[14] The "special oppression" of women was to be subordinated to "the oppression both men and women shared" under the old system. However, in practice
many women seized upon their oppression in the family as the main target for
struggle, with husbands and mothers-in-law rather than landlords singled out
for especially harsh criticism.

Still, female peasants were urged to participate in peasant meetings organized
by the cadres of the Party. In the women's associations, comprised entirely of
women, this was not a difficult task, and women gained confidence and experience in public speaking; but it was an entirely different matter for women to
speak out in meetings where men were present. Yet Party policy at this time
clearly stated that if women could not obtain their lawful rights by their own
efforts, and instead were given them by others, the results would be a short-lived
sham.[15]

By 1950, one of the most successful areas for land reform was Henan Province.
In July 1949, the Women's Association, quite strong throughout the province,
called a province-wide meeting as a preliminary step to organizing women to
participate in the coming land reform campaign.[16] This meeting revealed a strong
awareness of and sensitivity to problems to be faced, many of which were seen to
be related to still persistent traditional attitudes held by both sexes toward
women. A strong women's association independent of male participation or leadership was emphasized, but also at issue were conflicts between mothers-in-law

and daughters-in-law and between the older more conservative generation and the younger more change-oriented women. The influence of the old system of child brides, arranged marriages, and female infanticide continued to be strong. Women liberated from this system did not yet have a lot of experience in organizing or in assuming public roles. The struggle for women's liberation was hard and generated intense personal and interpersonal conflict filled with deep emotion. Murder and suicide were not unknown, and in some places women dared not struggle for fear of bodily harm.

The success of land reform was uneven, but even in highly successful areas the real benefits to women were questionable. Actual control over the land allotted to women often remained in the hands of the family or the male head.[17] Divorced or remarried women, or those who left the area, could not easily dispose of the land they had title to since the whole process of sale and disposal of privately owned land remained legally ambiguous. Even more important, as long as the system of agricultural production remained individual rather than collective, and women still lacked important skills and were still confronted with traditional familial relationships and responsibilities, owning their own land in itself meant no substantial change. Thus, many rural women, even after getting their own land, desired to marry factory workers and move to the cities.[18]

The close relationship between land reform and the Marriage Law was based on the view that land reform established a basis for the reforms stemming from the Marriage Law by enabling women to become economically independent.[19] Moreover, the Marriage Law also attacked aspects of the family system that supported the domination by rich peasants and landlords over the economy of rural China. But the Marriage Law was also intended to benefit women specifically. Individual articles in the law gave women specific rights of economic and social equality, and indirectly attacked the traditional family for denying these.

In early 1953 a nationwide campaign was launched to thoroughly implement the Marriage Law. It began with great fanfare, but by the end of the year publicity had substantially lessened as other issues clearly seemed to take priority for both Party and government.[20] Much of the responsibility for the marriage law campaign thus devolved on the shoulders of the Women's Federation, and the Federation faced a truly formidable task for several reasons.[21]

First of all, there was often deep-seated and violent opposition to the Marriage Law. Women cadres were not always united in their views or in their methods, and confusion and misunderstanding resulted. Generational differences between women, and the resistance of mothers-in-law, were particularly important. Mothers-in-law, faced with a challenge to their whole concept of selfhood developed over years of emotional and often physical pressures, formed an opposition that put them into alliance with men against young brides or unmarried daughters.

Physical abuse often resulted. Indeed, the level of violence was indicative of how deep-rooted and institutionalized was the opposition to change in women's status, and how much education and propaganda were necessary. In many cases, the cadres or activists who assumed leading roles were ill-suited to these terribly difficult tasks. They were young women who had no status in rural society and against whom the full force of the traditional code of proper behavior was leveled. All the preparatory efforts the Women's Federation had expended were of no avail given these circumstances.

Secondly, problems with implementing the Marriage Law in many areas revealed the potential for conflict between the woman question and other aspects of Party policy. Some cadres were fearful of implementing the Marriage Law, for then "all would be chaos"; still others simply could not resolve male peasant opposition, especially against the divorce provisions. Reports from Hunan and Henan highlighted the plight of poor peasants in particular, men who had supported the Party only to have their wives divorce them. The relationship between implementing the Marriage Law and constructing a socialist society was not evident at this stage, and the issues concerning values and attitudes toward women were not ones everyone agreed on. As the resistance to the Marriage Law increased, the willingness of the government and the Party to push the campaign decreased. The high incidence of divorce and the consequent growth of social instability threatened to lead to political disaffection, and this was hardly a desirable outcome in the early postrevolutionary years when political consolidation was so important.

Moreover, in the context of a still poverty-stricken China, maintenance of the family system was terribly important. Aside from providing old-age security, child care, and medical facilities, the family, as an economic unit, engaged in subsidiary production, providing food, clothing, and shelter. Thus, although the Marriage Law was intended to weaken the traditional extended family and to correct the most glaring abuses against individual women, when it began to threaten the nuclear family and promised to risk political disaffection, its implementation slackened off.

The record of the land reform and the marriage law campaigns in the early years after 1949 was a mixed one. In some places there were definite gains for women, especially where there were experienced women cadres or where previous social change had taken place during the Civil War and the Anti-Japanese War period. Areas that were liberated zones under Communist control before 1949 were of this type. But regional and geographical factors (proximity to a large city, for example) also produced variation. It is difficult and would be misleading to attempt to generalize concerning the results of the land reform and marriage law campaigns for the entire country.

Political Gains, 1950–1953

If the early years of social and economic transformation revealed important contradictions between women's emancipation and other forms of change, female political participation progressed in a less ambiguous context. Basing itself on Lenin's notion that "In order for working men and women to be equal not only in law but in reality, we must have more women participate in the work of public bodies, the party and government,"[22] the Women's Federation mounted an intense propaganda campaign aimed at getting women not only to cast ballots but to stand for election themselves. Participation in decision-making bodies was seen by women cadres as an important form of struggle.

National statistics are scanty on the numbers of women who were successful candidates in the 1953 elections for the National People's Congress, but admittedly impressionistic data gleaned from a survey of the press suggest that women did better in urban areas than in rural areas. In Beijing, for example, women deputies constituted 13.0 percent of the district people's congress in 1950, 24.0 percent by 1952, and 26.7 percent by 1954.[23]

Women in Dongdanju, Beijing, a district which included a large number of women who worked prior to 1949, were particularly active.[24] A typical delegate from Dongdanju was Xiao Dama. Her work as a peddler, ironically, had provided her with those skills necessary to operate in the new society. The huge amount of time spent in the street talking with people, soliciting opinions, and ameliorating conflictual situations made her an ideal candidate.[25]

The Women's Federation claimed that 84 percent of Chinese women voted in the 1953 elections.[26] A total of 17.3 percent of delegates at all levels of government were women.[27] The majority were located in urban areas. The general situation suggests that sex discrimination, at least in urban areas, was not an insurmountable obstacle preventing participation in representative bodies, especially on the local level.

The First Five-Year Plan Period, 1953–1957

Employment Opportunities and Participation of Urban Women

The traditional roles of housewife and mother continued to characterize conditions for women in the early post-1949 years in urban China. In contrast to the strong emphasis on female participation in production embodied in both the 1943 and 1948 Party directives on women's work, the period of the First Five-Year Plan, begun in 1953, emphasized a contraction of the number of women in the urban labor force.

The question of working women was an extremely difficult one throughout our period (1949–57). The demand to participate in the work force was considerable and the Party's experience of economic administration in wartime had convinced it of the potential value of women workers. . . . Whenever the urban labor market contracted, the whole apparatus of persuasion and propaganda had to be mobilized in an effort to keep women out of the labor force.[28]

The shift in emphasis concerning female participation in the labor force was occasioned by the particular economic development strategy of the First Five-Year Plan.[29] The emphasis placed on heavy industry at the expense of agriculture and light industry militated against the recruitment of large numbers of women into the work force. From 1953 to 1957, the percentage of the Chinese nonagricultural labor force that was female increased only slightly from 11.7 to 13.4, or from 2,132,000 to 3,286,000, while total nonagricultural employment rose by slightly more than 34 percent, from 18,256,000 to 24,506,000. Table 1 shows the yearly trends.

The number of women workers increased, but remained a small minority within the labor force. Women continued to cluster in the same industries they had worked in before the First Five-Year Plan: textiles, food processing, handicrafts, and the lower levels of education and government administration. However, the expansion of these sectors did not necessarily lead to increased female employment, because men began to make inroads into the traditional female labor industries. Perhaps more important, the industries in which female labor predominated were precisely *not* those that the economic priorities of the First

TABLE 1

Female Workers and Urban Employees in China, by Year, 1949–1957

	Total workers and employees (in thousands)	Female workers and employees (in thousands)	Females as percent of total
1949	8,004	600	7.5
1950	10,239	n.a.	n.a.
1951	12,815	n.a.	n.a.
1952	15,804	1,848	11.7
1953	18,256	2,132	11.7
1954	18,809	2,435	12.9
1955	19,076	2,473	13.0
1956	24,230	3,266	13.5
1957	24,506	3,286	13.4

Adapted from Joint Economic Committee of the U.S. Congress, *An Economic Profile of Mainland China* (Washington, D.C.: Government Printing Office, 1967), page 539.

Five-Year Plan made crucial to capital formation. Hence, they had a low priority in terms of capital investment.

Capital, created through increased production, was to lead to the future expansion of employment. An initially high rate of male unemployment was tolerated, but as jobs became available in the expanding heavy industry sector, as well as in other sectors, they were to be allocated to men. Thus, the development strategy of the First Five-Year Plan radically changed the nature and composition of the urban labor force. In Shanghai, for example, in the early part of the century women formed the majority of the industrial labor force,[30] and this presumably had not changed decisively by 1950. But by 1957, women only accounted for 21 percent of Shanghai's work force.[31]

Nevertheless, urban unemployment, a serious problem inherited by the Communists when they came to power in 1949, remained at fairly high levels until the Great Leap. A Chinese source in 1957 claimed that in one area the number of unemployed who registered for and were actively seeking jobs was 1.15 million and, of this total, 517,000, or almost one-half, were women.[32] If this percentage is at all representative of the situation elsewhere, and there is no reason to assume that it isn't since development strategy was nationally uniform, it is obvious that women formed a substantial portion of the urban unemployed.

In 1954, *Xin Zhongguo Funü (New Women of China)* published a series of articles addressing this problem and suggesting an answer for women, many of whom might have begun to wonder about their roles in the "new" society. The series was entitled "How Housewives Can Serve Socialism." The forum suggested that even if women were unable to hold jobs, they could feel a sense of participation in national construction because there was a relationship between doing a good job at housework and contributing to socialist construction.[33] Where economic independence (i.e., a job) had previously been considered necessary for male-female equality, now doing a good job in keeping the home and caring for children would lead to harmonious, democratic families wherein husband and wife were equal. This view of women as dependents whose main task was to arrange home life well so men could devote all their energy to the (more?) important tasks of constructing socialism was to surface again and again.

This theme, with numerous twists and variations, dominated the women's literature up to the Great Leap. In 1956, the Women's Federation mounted a "five goods" campaign to illustrate how most women could support socialist construction. The campaign was directed at housewives,[34] who were urged to be good at:

(1) uniting with neighborhood families for mutual aid;
(2) doing housework well;

(3) educating children well;

(4) encouraging the family in production, study, and work; and

(5) working well themselves.

However it should not be assumed that domestic bliss was ever considered a proper goal for all women, even when the responsibilities charged to women easily led in this direction.

The mid-1950s found the women's movement in a difficult position. All during these years the Women's Federation conceived of itself as a united front group whose basic objective was to organize women from all walks of life.[35] This included urban bourgeois women from advantaged backgrounds who were the most educated among Chinese women. This urban middle class almost certainly made up the majority of the audience for the Women's Federation journal, *New Women of China*. Thus, not surprisingly, the magazine contained differing attitudes in regard to female roles in Chinese society. Perhaps more importantly, it also revealed the contradictions of a women's movement committed to revolution and social change in an increasingly unsupportive socioeconomic context.

The Women's Federation and its journal were not, however, the totality of the women's movement in China during these years. Women's participation in local political activities was very important, and the leading activists were often outspoken and direct:

> We [women] are not willing to spend our lifetime in household chores. We possess infinite potentialities which we want to dedicate to the new society. We expect to take part in work like our men comrades. . . .[36]

With the economy only able to absorb a fraction of the women who wanted to work, this energy and talent needed channeling.

The adoption by the National People's Congress Standing Committee in December 1954 of the order to establish urban residents' committees was probably the most important institutional development for unemployed city women in the pre–Great Leap Forward period.[37] The committees had jurisdiction over an area encompassing anywhere from 100 to 600 households and were staffed, in the main, by housewives. Women were ideal recruits for the committees because of their great familiarity with the affairs of neighborhood inhabitants, their physical presence for most of the day, and the specific charge to the new committees to take care of "women's work." The committees were responsible for health work, sanitation, keeping the peace, mediating minor civil disputes, and organizing the masses for participation in national campaigns. In at least some cases, this led to a feeling of contributing to a national undertaking. As one woman activist exclaimed, "Street work is not a small job in contributing to the construction of socialism."[38] Women thus gained experience in local politics and became intimately familiar with neighborhood problems, needs, and resources, experience that proved all the more valuable as street committees later became the basis for the development of urban communes.[39]

The residents' committees increased the numbers of women active outside the home, but they did not involve the majority of housewives. Since these committees did not organize people for production and had little influence on consumption other than establishing some child care facilities, most women continued in the traditional housewife role. The ability of local units to affect production and consumption and to thus open radically new alternatives for women would have to wait until the Great Leap Forward.

Employment Opportunities and Participation of Rural Women

As limited and restricted as urban employment opportunities and other alternatives to the traditional roles of urban women were in the early 1950s, even these did not, for the most part, exist in the vast Chinese countryside. However, land reform had laid the basis for the collectivization movement of the 1950s, which contained the potential for radically transforming women's role in production. This potential was to be more fully developed in the Great Leap Forward.

The limitations for the development of agriculture posed by the urban-industrial orientation of the First Five-Year Plan were beginning to be questioned by 1955.[40] In that year, Mao's speech "On the Socialist Upsurge in China's Countryside" signaled a greatly accelerated pace in the collectivization movement.[41] The agricultural sector thus experienced two different approaches to the question of collectivization, both within the period of the First Five-Year Plan.

In the original plan, agricultural collectivization was to be dependent upon technological developments in the form of mechanized production techniques. Collectivization was to proceed slowly because the technical transformation of agriculture was to follow the development of heavy industry. Women's labor, therefore, was not perceived as a real target for mobilization by the planners. The change in policy occurred when collectivization, which had proceeded more rapidly than originally planned, revealed the potential of female labor for increased production even before mechanization was available.

As early as 1954, the Women's Federation was heavily involved in efforts to mobilize rural women for agricultural production, a task more consistent with the 1943 and 1948 work directives on women than the simultaneous urban efforts emphasizing the traditional housewife and mothering roles of women. However, the tone of Federation directives, mindful of the recent abortive marriage law campaign, was circumspect; the directives argued not that collectivization would create new opportunities for women so much as they argued that the use of female labor would lead to increased production that would benefit the community as well as the women involved.[42]

Thus, the economic aspects of female participation emerged as most salient. Stories such as that of Zou Yuzai were characteristic of the period. Zou Yuzai, a young daughter-in-law, insisted upon working in an agricultural producers' cooperative in Zhuanbei xian, Hunan. "Since Tsou Yu-tsai {Zou Yuzai} proved that she could earn much more than what she actually consumed, her position in the family changed and her mother-in-law took quite a different attitude toward her."[43] Zou was married, but it appears that many of the active young women were not. Judging from the model young workers whose stories appeared in most issues of *Women of China* (*Zhongguo funü*), it was the unmarried girls whose work was praised and who even received a modicum of recognition from male leaders.

The potential of collectivization for increased production and construction (dams, dikes, irrigation works) even in the absence of mechanization was becoming evident by 1955. By the end of the year, the possibilities of cooperativization for the expansion of agricultural production and the use of female labor were reconsidered. The result was that Party efforts now reinforced those of the Women's Federation in mobilizing peasant women in collective agriculture.

The increased pace of collectivization in 1955–56 stressed the importance of female participation in agricultural production. With the development of the agricultural producers' cooperatives, the traditional patterns of work could be transformed and projects such as large-scale irrigation works, difficult if not unthinkable before, were now possible. The emphasis and tone of some of the propaganda toward women changed again, now more directly linking collectivization with women's progress toward liberation and not just emphasizing their contribution to production. As a *People's Daily* editorial quoting Engels stated, "The first prerequisite for the emancipation of women is that all women participate again in social labor: to achieve this individual families are required to be no longer units of the social economy."[44]

The high tide of agricultural collectivization before the Great Leap Forward came with the Party's "Draft 1956–1957 National Program for Agriculture,"[45] revised in 1957 and then discarded with the coming of the Great Leap Forward. However, the provisions regarding female employment remained operative even into the Leap, and these provisions were contained in a 1956 Women's Federation proposal issued on March 8, International Women's Day and traditionally a day for promulgating new policy for women. The New China News Agency published the "National Women's Draft for Realizing the 'National Program for Agriculture.' "[46] The Federation claimed that the "realization of this program is the fundamental promise for the complete emancipation of rural women and the achievement of genuine equality between men and women."[47] The directive consistently urged women to be active in the cooperatives, at whatever levels they could manage. Participation need not await either mechanization or the solution of all traditional role problems that fettered women. Very significantly, the tone of this document aimed at rural women differed in a fundamental way from much of the propaganda directed at urban women.

Limited industrial opportunities led to the idea that full employment of urban women was to await the expansion of modern industry and was not a present possibility. In the countryside, however, the collectivization drive and the mobilization of women went hand in hand. The Women's Federation insisted on the necessity of women participating and becoming an integral part of the development process in the countryside. And because the Party now wished to push a radical policy of collectivization, the disruption that female participation would cause to old values and institutions was viewed as a positive contribution rather than as a threat to solidarity.

Basically, the draft aimed to have every able-bodied woman give a significant number of days each year to production efforts. Because much of agricultural labor is seasonal, the greatest contributions were to be at harvest and planting time. Many of the traditional skills of women were to be utilized, albeit in the new context of collectivized agriculture. Most of these tasks did not require the acquisition of new skills or intensive training and, for the most part, were menial. They included sideline occupations or subsidiary production, most often raising pigs and chickens, tending vegetable plots, or the care of certain crops and their processing, such as cotton, tea, or silkworms.

While the labor force participation of Chinese women increased during the First Five-Year Plan, the extent of the increase depended not only on development strategy in terms of investment priority, but also on the organization and scale of production, especially in the rural areas. The tendency to project women as workers, whether as peasants or as technicians, was impeded, however, by the existence of generic problems common to all women.

Influence of and Change in Familial Roles of Women

The viability of extrafamilial roles is determined by the social context, which transcends the individual family. Nowhere is this more evident in China than in the early campaign to implement the Marriage Law. The Marriage Law was not designed to effect a revolution in female roles very quickly. The emphasis was on gradual change. But it was also clear, from the Civil War and Anti-Japanese War days and from the collectivization drives of 1954–1956, that changes in female role patterns could also act as a catalyst for further sociopolitical change, as a threat to the political stability of established institutions. The understanding of the concept of social production during this period and the views concerning the sexual division of labor within the family in no way led to a questioning of the basic sexual-maternal role definition that was so much a part of traditional Chinese society. Lack of employment and of extrafamilial roles for the majority of urban women thus led logically to a glorification of the housewife and mother rather than to an analysis of how these very roles reinforced the organization of production and the division of labor in the wider society.

Biology decreed that women were the bearers of children, but traditional Chinese society, like most societies, also decreed that women must be the child-rearers. While it is logically and practically possible to separate these two functions—and indeed it was part of Marxist theory that they would be separated—throughout the period of the First Five-Year Plan these responsibilities were viewed as belonging uniquely to women. Almost without exception, each issue of *New Women of China* and its successor, *Women of China* (the name changed with the first issue of 1956), contained a special section on child care.[48] The Children's Bureau of the Women's Federation assumed the task of getting factories to provide crèches and nursery facilities for their female employees and making sure women received time off for pregnancy and for nursing of infants. Moreover, the Children's Bureau was responsible for training women workers to staff these facilities. Judging from the Federation's efforts and the continuous articles appearing in the women's press, it is clear that child care was considered a female job, in the home, or at work. The urban orientation of the First Five-Year Plan lessened the contradictions between familial and extrafamilial roles for women in ways simply not possible for peasant women.

In rural areas the amount of time spent in child care and home management severely limited women's ability to work outside the home. Nevertheless, the increased emphasis on participation in production (in 1955–56) virtually made it an obligation for women to shoulder two burdens. An editorial in the *People's Daily* flatly asserted that this double burden was what made women women:

> Participation in agricultural production is the inherent right and duty of rural women. Giving birth to children and raising them up as well as preoccupation with household chores are also the obligations of rural women. *These things set women apart from men.*[49] (emphasis added)

In case anyone felt burdened by this, the *People's Daily* editorial continued, "While farm production is the principal form of labor in the countryside, good housekeeping and proper care of children are also labor of social significance." Housework may have been "labor of social significance," but no labor points were accorded it and hence it had a lower value both in the eyes of the community and for the women who did it.

The ideological climate of the 1950s did not stress the issue of equality between male and female so much as it emphasized production, female contributions to collectivization, and, in rural areas, male-female unity.[50] Thus, the traditional discriminatory attitudes concerning female inferiority in general naturally carried over into the workplace. Factories were reluctant to hire women because of the expense and effort of providing social welfare services that had to be made available; women were used as unskilled laborers who could be shifted from job to job and were most expendable in any contracting labor market situation; women did not receive equal pay for equal work, and educated and experienced women workers were often not promoted.

Employment was not the only way in which women's activities carried them beyond the courtyard. Many women, especially the young, benefited from the increase in educational opportunities, particularly in urban areas. This did not have an immediate impact on employment, but it was important for later developments. The training necessary for a technical job required at least a middle-school education. It was not until the later 1950s that even a sizable minority of women had acquired this level of education. And the effects of more advanced training are not evident until the 1960s. Moreover, the small numbers of women attending middle, technical, and higher educational institutions at this time suggested that discrimination toward women was greater where male-female competition for the limited spaces available was high.

While ideology, development strategy, and half-hearted, limited support by the Party restricted women's progress during the First Five-Year Plan, the organizational problems of the Women's Federation were also a factor. Since 1949, the Federation had concentrated on urban organizational development, neglecting the rural areas where some pre-1949 local associations remained active never-

TABLE 2

Percentage of Female Students in Total Number of Students

	Institutions of Higher Learning	Technical Middle Schools	Middle Schools	Primary Schools
1949	17.8	21.1	20.0	25.5
1952	19.8	24.9	23.5	32.9
1957	23.9	26.5	30.8	34.5
1958	23.3	27.0	31.3	38.5

Source: Zhang Yun, "Report to the Third National Congress of Chinese Women on September 9, 1957," (Beijing) *People's Daily*, trans. in *Current Background* 476:14.

theless. Significantly, many of the most highly trained women cadres, particularly those prominent in pre-1949 women's work, lived in the cities and resisted efforts to send them out into the countryside where their talents were very much needed. Li Jing, chairwoman of the Ance xian, Inner Mongolian Women's Federation, probably spoke for many who felt negative about an assignment in the rural areas. "After arriving in the countryside, while my body was in the countryside, my heart was still in the city."[51]

Where rural unmarried female activists had been elected to responsible posts, a disturbing phenomenon developed once they married. Family and home responsibilities led to decreased activism and loss of leadership. The traditional pressures still had a strong influence on women. In some cases it was a mother-in-law or husband who objected to an activist wife. One woman's husband complained that her duties took her to far-off places during the day and her preoccupation with planning the next day's activities at night led her "to boil oil in order to mend the seat of trousers," a clear case of domestic neglect![52] While the woman finally convinced her husband of the importance of her work, there were probably more numerous instances where women activists were forced to curtail their activities.

Complaints regarding the low level of ideological consciousness among women cadres abounded. However, it was more than just a lack of familiarity with Marxism that created problems; the messages received by women were contradictory. This is nowhere better illustrated than at the Third National Women's Congress in 1957. When speaking of the tasks facing women, Zhu De (a prominent national leader) stressed the importance of women's participation in revolution and of the elimination of exploitation of women by the traditional system.[53] Guo Morou, a leading cultural figure, emphasized the Chinese family and the role of women within it, stressing the caretaking tasks of women as they worked hard and thriftily as housekeepers.[54] The contradiction between ideology and practice was evident; the tasks for women, however temporary they were viewed, stressed household management, child care, and study over revolutionary and participatory roles that some women had already assumed in production and administration.

The choice of women as role models reinforced the idea that women were doing double duty in the creation of socialism. In addition to the articles extolling the virtues of women as workers, there was a continuous flow of articles praising women who successfully combined domestic duties and a full-time job, or women whose desire to work and contribute led them to surmount incredible obstacles. For example, Zhi Wenjiao, a factory worker employed by the Beijing Shilushan Electronics factory, was a full-time worker and mother of six children.[55] In addition to her job and household tasks, she somehow found time to study and to head a newspaper reading group. Her dedication to and hard work for socialism carried over into her home management, where she was economical and thrifty, kept the family healthy, and brought up her children. In all this, the father's contribution was conspicuous by its absence. Excelling in traditional roles lent legitimacy to a woman's new worker status.

Urban women predominated as models in the press, but with the collectivization of agriculture, more peasant women were written up as exemplary workers. Li Yushi, from Chinghua xiang, Jieho xian, Shenxi Province, was portrayed as a representative of the new peasant woman.[56] A poor peasant with enormous responsibilities, which included a sick mother-in-law, a weak husband, and a small child, Li Yushi took it upon herself to learn new skills with the agricultural cooperativization movement. She became a model worker who worked 264 days in 1955, surpassing the average for male workers. Nevertheless, Li illustrates that conformity to traditional roles was necessary even while undertaking new ones.

Conclusion

Certainly one of the most important and far-reaching achievements of the Chinese Communist government during the 1950s was an assault on the traditional role of women in Chinese society. While the record is far from one of rapid, even development, achievements by women in such diverse areas as legal rights, job opportunities, education, health care, and political power were significant enough to make a decisive break with the pre-1949 period.

Not only were more women working, but they were entering fields like heavy industry formerly considered open only to men, and although their numbers were small, they were breaking down age-old barriers. Women were even entering the prestigious scientific fields. By 1957, one-seventh of the researchers in the mathematics research institute were women.[57]

In rural areas, more women were entering farm production, especially with the advent of the agricultural producers' cooperatives. By 1957 over 100 million women ages 16 and over were members of these collectives.[58] Of the farm labor heroes attending the 1957 National Conference of Model Farm Workers, 80, or 8.4 percent, were women.[59] Women were active in local rural producers' co-ops, where some served on management committees and others even became deputy directors.

In spite of this progress, and partly because of it, the picture for women during the First Five-Year Plan was fraught with contradictions. The experience of the 1950s demonstrated that economic development and change was important in improving women's condition. However, a development strategy that was unable to provide growing employment opportunities for *the majority* of women led in China to a reemphasis of those traditional roles that were the embodiment of women's oppression. This was made even clearer just prior to the Great Leap Forward.

With a contracting labor market in the period from late 1956 to the Great Leap, attention focused on women's domestic role. Pressure was even exerted on women cadres to retire, although they were reluctant to do so.

> There are women cadres who consider "the taking up of household work as a dishonor and a job below their dignity" and therefore feel reluctant to go home. This obviously is incorrect. As we all know, a home is not only a cell of the society, but also a basic part of our life. . . . Family and State are interdependent and interrelated. For this reason, in China home work and social labor are mutually geared together, and home work is just a part of social labor and plays an important part in socialist construction. . . . If a woman can integrate what *little* she can do into the great cause of socialist construction and if she has the ideal of working for the happiness of future generations, she would be a noble person, a woman of benefit to the masses, a woman of Communist morality.[60] (emphasis added)

This "correct approach to the problem of retirement of women cadres" appeared in *Women of China* in February 1958. That confinement to the domestic sector was not well received by women is reflected in the enthusiastic response to the complete reversal of this policy scarcely six months later as the Great Leap Forward gathered momentum.

· 3 ·

Women in the Great Leap Forward

THE GREAT LEAP FORWARD, ENVISIONED AS A RAPID MEANS TO BUILD socialism in China by mobilizing masses of people, including millions of women, brought out the relationship between socialist revolution and women's liberation in a way unprecedented in Chinese or world history. Western patterns of industrialization and technological change, with the exception of industries like textile manufacturing, have precluded mass recruitment of women into the labor force until the level of technological development was sufficient to introduce labor-saving devices in the home that freed some women from some of the burdens of household tasks. But in the Great Leap, the Chinese sought to emancipate women from traditional roles long before the use of labor-saving devices in the home. In a mammoth effort of politically induced social change which encouraged—even demanded—that women enter into production and engage in political activities, the Great Leap called into question traditional institutions and historically given roles in the division of labor. Many of the tasks which kept women tied to the home were collectivized and, especially in urban areas, have become an integral form of social production in Chinese society.

Great Leap Forward policy toward women was a logical outgrowth of the mass mobilization of labor which was at the bottom of this development strategy. It implied a radical change in policies of the pre-Leap period. A 1958 conference on women's work set the revolutionary tone of the Great Leap Forward.

> To cope with the needs of production and to push it forward the conference pointed out that women's federations must, under the unified guidance of Party Committees, and in the midst of the developments in production, organize the life of the people on a cooperative basis thereby transforming household chores gradually into social labor, so that women who wanted to take part in socially productive labor could do so and those who had already taken part could successfully solve the contradiction between their work and household chores.[1]

For those in the Chinese leadership who were concerned about the problems of an increasingly impersonal and unresponsive bureaucratic system, the growing disparities in living conditions between urban and rural areas, and the inability of the agricultural system to achieve significant breakthroughs in levels of production under conditions of low capital investment and lack of mechanization, women were to be a key political resource in the development policies of the Great Leap. The mass mobilization of women for participation in economic production was viewed as one way to create additional alternatives for increasing production in both agriculture and industry. Women's labor was a substitute for capital investment. "Women substituting for men" freed men to undertake new projects, such as the development of rural industry, and allowed already skilled male labor to concentrate on even more complicated and advanced technology.

Politically and socially, Great Leap policies were to foster female participation and struggle, allowing women to contribute to China's rapid modernization while moving toward equality—two oft-repeated rhetorical goals of the CCP regarding women. But the goal of equality was more often emphasized in women's magazines and Women's Federation directives than in labor mobilization directives issued by the Party or government.

However, just as the Leap addressed itself in a meaningful way to the crucial problems of economic development and women's emancipation, it created a whole new set of problems. The rapid and widespread mobilization of women called into question traditional roles and institutions in ways that created resistance, and hence threatened the very economic development it was also promoting. The Great Leap thus unintentionally and objectively raised the issue of special female interests in a particularly direct and dramatic way.

The Great Leap Forward in Rural Areas

The main purpose of Great Leap Forward policy in both industry and agriculture was to achieve breakthroughs in levels of production given the limitations of technology and the availability of capital goods. Labor, the one factor of production thought to exist in overabundance, was thus mobilized, recruited, and reorganized in an attempt to obviate the necessity of large-scale capital investment, especially in rural areas. As part of this effort, local industrialization was encouraged to take advantage of local human as well as natural resources. Local rural industry aimed at serving agricultural needs, and large-scale, modern urban industry, now complemented by small-scale urban local and collective industry, would continue to command scarce capital and skilled manpower.

As a "high tide" of agricultural cooperativization swept the countryside in 1956–57, it merged with the communization current leading to the Great Leap. From the very beginning of rural collectivization, even before the Leap, the labor power of women was a major target of mass mobilization. In his 1955 speech "The Upsurge of Socialism in the Countryside," Mao had pointed to the necessity of women being mobilized for production:

> In the case of many localities where production scope has expanded, operating departments multiplied, labor scope extending toward nature broadened, and work more meticulously done, labor forces will become insufficient. This situation is still only beginning and will develop year after year in the future. . . . Women of China constitute a great source of manpower. This source must be tapped.[2]

The Great Leap's mobilization of rural women differed from previous attempts in two distinct ways, however. First, it was on a much larger scale, an attempt to involve some 300 million women.[3] Secondly, it was accomplished under new institutional arrangements—the communes—which could absorb and utilize their labor.

The agricultural producers' cooperative movement had illustrated the capacity of collectivization for undertaking large-scale irrigation and water control projects, and certain projects had revealed the feasibility of even larger collective units than the agricultural cooperatives. Even before the communes became officially sanctioned units in the countryside, the participation of women in these projects gave rise to the demand to further harness female labor power. "Women's dams, women's dikes, March 8 reservoirs, March 8 forests, and so on, have appeared everywhere in various provinces and *xian* areas."[4]

The first communes were formed before the Party's August 1958 Beidaihe Resolution, which officially sanctioned the establishment of peoples' communes in the rural areas.[5] Initially, women were to substitute for men mainly in agricultural production.

> In many areas where the menfolk departed to take part in large water conservancy projects, women took over most of the productive tasks such as manure collection, field management, building of small irrigation facilities, afforestation, and sideline production.[6]

As the Leap unfolded in its enormous variety of activity, labor, once perceived as an abundant resource, quickly became a scarce one. As a result, even more emphasis was placed on recruiting female labor and providing conditions to facilitate this. The Women's Federation urged women to substitute for male workers wherever feasible. The *People's Daily* reflected this new perception of female labor in an editorial on a new institution in rural China, the public mess halls.

> The most conspicuous advantage is that the labor power of many women is
> set free from heavy household work and thrown into productive labor. This
> partially solves the serious shortage of labor power in the rural areas.[7]

While the government, the Party, and the women's organizations all expended
great efforts to set women to work outside the home, there was a discernible
difference in their appeals. The government and Party were clearly concerned
with the economic aspect of the mobilization policy and reflected the economic
imperatives of the Great Leap generally. By contrast, the Women's Federation,
while acknowledging national needs, was also quick to point out tangible benefits
to women in terms of their progress toward liberation and equality.[8]

In spite of official policy and the combined efforts of the Party and the Wom-
en's Federation, the mobilization of female labor engendered a significant amount
of opposition. Traditional superstitions were cited to oppose women doing work
outside the home. "If women go to the fields, it won't rain" and "If women go to
sea, the boats will overturn." Families were often reluctant to have women go
into the fields. In many cases field work was considered improper for women,
especially because it involved contact with males outside the family and because
it was deemed ill-suited to women's capabilities. Grandmothers who were forced
to shoulder a greater burden in housework and caring for children, and who had
reached the age where they traditionally gave up many of their household responsibilities, were opposed to their daughters-in-law working. The Women's
Federation, more keenly sensitive to these kinds of problems than were the
male-dominated governmental organizations, mounted an intensive campaign
to explain to the entire family the benefits of working women.[9]

But opposition from traditional sources was not the only problem. With the
entry of large numbers of women into agricultural production, it became necessary to establish collectivized services such as mess halls, child care facilities, and
other welfare services that would free women for labor outside the home. And
while temporary mess halls, nurseries, and kindergartens had been used previously in peak seasons, they now had to be permanent institutions if women were
to work on a regular basis.

The pace of communization was very rapid throughout the fall of 1958. The
Central China province of Henan emerged as a leader in the new movement and
as a model for utilizing female labor. In the space of little more than six months
it was reported that "6,000,000 women in the province were thus emancipated
from domestic labor."[10] Certain communes and even whole counties throughout
Henan achieved national prominence as leaders in the national "backyard" steel
movement and in the establishment of welfare services for their members.

Weixing Peoples Commune in Suiping xian, which had been organized as a commune even before the Party's call in August 1958, was not only producing iron and steel, but women were producing 40 percent of it.[11] Chiliying Commune was one of the earliest to strive for mechanization, and since mechanization helped minimize differences in strength between men and women, it was considered an influential factor for women's progress.[12] But the Great Leap did not stress mechanization nearly as much as it did mass mobilization of female labor. Women were active in the cotton fields and small commune enterprises at Chiliying.

> The commune now has 450 women workers constituting 21.2% of the total labor force, while of the staff in the community dining rooms, 40% are women. There are not only many women brigade leaders, but also quite a number have positions of leadership as factory directors, heads of workshops and animal or poultry farms.[13]

As more women entered production their demands for services went beyond the rudimentary social welfare services already established (mess halls, nurseries, etc.) to include literacy classes and primary education, cultural groups, sewing classes, and technical study groups. The relationship between services like mess halls and child care centers and the ability of women to work was becoming quite evident.

> The people's communes have transformed most household work from petty irksome drudgery into socially run large-scale undertakings. Each has, on the average, 300 dining halls where whole families can take their meals and 200 nurseries and kindergartens where kids are cared for. Clothes and shoes are made by the commune tailoring workshops which exist in every production brigade, instead of being made laboriously at home by each family.[14]

The Leap's emphasis on institutional experimentation within the communes, combined with a political atmosphere that encouraged both the pursuit of social goals and increased production, favored female progress in Henan. By 1960, the effect of women's more public role was being felt in priorities of social policy. New rural institutions emerged to accommodate the masses of working women. Henanese women reportedly had access to 100,000 "maternity centers" and were allowed 45 days maternity leave. Spare-time schools had enrolled 2.7 million women and there were 180,000 women serving as chairmen, vicechairmen, or brigade or deputy brigade leaders.[15] While the extent and quality of these services were uneven and probably more often than not quite rudimentary in the countryside, the services did represent an important political gain for women. Much of this change was attributed to the communes' advantages over the agricultural cooperatives in enlarging the scope of activity and responsibility of rural collectives.

At first, the intensive efforts to mobilize women were largely successful. In

1958 women accounted for 50 percent of the labor force in agriculture, and in certain areas—where men were being used in industrial projects—this figure went as high as 70 to 80 percent.[16] The majority of women were engaged in field work or related jobs such as manure collection. Those women whose "household burden" was especially great were encouraged to engage in subsidiary production near the home. This usually entailed raising pigs, chickens, and ducks and/or tending vegetable gardens.

While household chores and subsidiary production appear to have had a major claim on female labor time in addition to field work, there were women engaged in irrigation, afforestation, and some construction projects. For most of these special projects women were organized into all-women work groups with women leaders. Judging from the media and particulary those articles that appeared in *Women of China,* the all-women work groups did a better job in utilizing women's labor power properly than did teams led by men. Old women were sent to get rid of insects and worms and to tend vegetables, pregnant and menstruating women were given dry, light work and proper care, and women with several children had work arranged to accord with domestic schedules. This contrasted with previous experience under the agriculture producers' cooperatives, where female labor was used at harvest time but where lack of proper attention to women's needs frequently resulted in physical hardships and accidents. Women leaders, often local activists, tended to be more familiar with the skills and special needs of their team members than were the male leaders.

The benefits of participation were several. Reports of bumper harvests in 1958 and 1959 underscored the importance of women's work in the fields. Large numbers of women were accorded workpoints and thus shared in the distribution of income and were responsible for increased family income. The psychological impact of remuneration for labor should not be underestimated.

> There is no question as to what the work-point does in terms of its possible effect on interpersonal relations. For example, some women prefer to earn work-points instead of having more children who tend to tie them down, in spite of creches and nurseries. Even more important, for the first time, women have come to appreciate their own labors, in terms of some standards other than as wife, mother, or daughter-in-law, so that the importance of their contribution is economically and therefore more objectively measured.[17]

During rest periods, production groups were often converted into study groups primarily concerned with teaching women to read. Literacy acted as an integrative mechanism for women, linking them with the wider society. Thus, compensation for labor participation plus the acquisition of literacy skills gave women a vested objective interest in the new society and, at the same time, created active, subjective support among them for the experiments of the Leap period. Participation by women in collectivized "women's work," in canteens, nurseries, and maternity clinics, helped to increase knowledge of technology. Operating noodle machines, sewing machines, and simple electrical equipment required the acquisition of technical knowledge and some basic mechanical skills. And in the fields and kitchens this led to certain simple innovations in tools.[18]

In the rural areas, the women seemed to have achieved some success in accomplishing the goals set by the Women's Federation. Commune leadership positions for women included director, deputy director, brigade leader, deputy brigade leader, team leader, and deputy team leader. Although there were no national statistics to determine what proportion of each level's leadership was female in the Great Leap period, available evidence indicates clearly that women were a minority. However, it was clear that the political power and social status embodied within these positions flowed from participation in labor production. Thus, the path to power for women had to be labor participation even if the low technological levels of production meant that much labor remained manual and heavy. In those communes where women were deputy directors, their chief responsibility tended almost always to be woman's work, and their backgrounds, while "activists," were also in women's work. Further, it seems that many of the women who did emerge as leaders either were rather young[19] or were over forty and activists from pre-1949 days.[20] Those women who were too young to have participated in the pre-1949 revolutionary activity or too old to have been educated under the Communists were undistinguished in the Great Leap. Whole generations of women thus seemed to be living more or less traditional lives.

The number of young, enthusiastic but relatively inexperienced women, and of older activists, was limited in rural areas. There was, therefore, an attempt to recruit urban women cadres for work in the rural areas, where their intellectual, organizational, and manual skills were needed.[21] Several of the communes where women had achieved positions of commune level leadership were, therefore, located near large cities. Moreover, in these communes men were often recruited for industrial projects, thus creating a proportionately larger female labor force. For example, in the 169 communes surrounding Shanghai in 1959, 33 either had female directors or female deputy directors.[22]

Problems of Rural Women's Participation

Changes in women's roles during the Great Leap revealed several serious contradictions, however, and brought the woman question to the fore even though it was, by itself, not a central focus of Great Leap policy. The evident lack of basic institutional and attitudinal change in the pre-Leap period and even during the Leap led to problems that seriously threatened the very policy of mass labor utilization, a major premise of the Great Leap's developmental strategy. The question of woman's mobilization for labor outside of traditional channels seemed to have far more radical implications for Chinese society than many of the other policies that were first experimented with during this period.

Health care was probably the most evident illustration of how far-reaching were the effects of female labor mobilization. The rural agricultural collectivization drives of 1956–57 that developed into the commune system demonstrated the importance of an adequate health care system. To mobilize female labor there had to be a system which provided for the "special needs" of women workers— maternity facilities, gynecological supplies, education in and facilitation of birth control, and so on. Even prior to the communes there were alarming reports of a "rash of accidents."[23] The Women's Federation, through its principle organ, *Women of China,* had been stressing the importance of developing adequate health care since agricultural collectivization had begun in 1954. National recognition did not come until the Great Leap graphically illustrated the relationship between health and development, with the matter of female health an especially significant factor.

During the 1950s, rudimentary medical knowledge and facilities developed in most areas in the course of health campaigns to eliminate the "four pests" (mosquitoes, flies, rats, and sparrows, and sometimes bedbugs) and to develop sanitation. However, almost all of the medical schools, health institutes, and modern hospital facilities were located in urban areas. In the countryside, old, small hospitals, usually located in the county seats, left most rural dwellers devoid of meaningful clinical or hospital services. The health burdens of the rural areas were largely shouldered by practitioners of traditional Chinese medicine. Even the establishment of the communes did not see the transfer of medical personnel and services to the countryside, or really change the *quality* of health care in rural areas.[24] Individual communes were expected to develop their own health facilities without either financial help from higher administrative levels or recruitment of urban doctors. Under this arrangement, traditional doctors staffed the meager commune medical facilities and medical expenses were met by the collective's scarce funds. It was not until the Cultural Revolution that the development of communal health facilities became a major priority.

By 1960 the lone voice of the Women's Federation was joined by others in pressing for the development of rural health facilities. The concentration of facilities in the urban areas, with the subsequent neglect of peasant diseases specifically and rural health needs generally, was criticized. An attempt to rectify this situation focused on building up the county-level hospital and making it the center of rural health care. The emphasis on self-reliance meant that the county hospital provided both medical training and health care for cases which the local communes could not handle. There was to be more intensive use of existing resources,[25] but no new commitments of major capital and human resources were made at this time. The failure of this system to provide for the needs of the population was most apparent in the case of women.

To compound matters, by 1959 the abuse of women in the labor force was widespread. The chairwoman of the Women's Federation of Hebei Province, Lin Xiao, complained that the special needs of women laborers were largely ignored.[26] The pressures on women to work were enormous, and male leaders often assigned pregnant women heavy labor and work that necessitated squatting. They did not allow nursing mothers time off to feed their children, and assigned menstruating women work in cold, damp places. These practices too often resulted in injuries to women and children and permanent health damage. Not until 1961 did the costliness of these abuses lead to some concessions to the "special needs" of women, but by that time the intense labor mobilizations of the Leap were fast disappearing in the wake of serious problems.

> The cadres agreed that in arranging work, the women's team heads should be consulted first. In accordance with the strength of female labor, their technical skills and their home care burdens, work should be developed rationally according to individual and local conditions and in keeping with agricultural chores.[27]

Still complaints of improper use of women in the labor force continued.

Health Minister Li Dejuan, an outspoken proponent of safeguarding women's health, pointed out the underlying problems. Resistance to developing an adequate health care system was closely related to traditional attitudes toward the role of women, summed up simply in a popular saying: "You women are a lot of trouble." Moreover, the media, especially the women's media, reinforced this attitude by concentrating on the health care needs of women during the "four periods" of menstruation, pregnancy, postpartum, and lactation. There was a failure to see the relationship between healthy women workers and increased production. Underlying and reinforcing these traditional attitudes was a material reality. Investment funds were scarce, and the male leadership tended to view investment in health protection as a threat to successful completion of pressing production quotas. They said, "protecting women's health means not completing production responsibilities."[28] In actuality, those areas of China that have traditionally used women in the fields attest to the physical strength and stamina of women agricultural laborers. When women "substituted for men" in the fields, they did all the field work that was necessary. The contradiction assumed larger proportions as the necessity for healthy women workers to carry out Great Leap policies became more urgent.

Thus, the health question for women focused most sharply on the reproductive role of women, not on weakness or fatigue, and relating as it did to pregnancy, birth, and child care demands for health facilities, it directly challenged the traditional cultural attitudes toward the maternal-sexual role of women within the family.

The communes, in breaking down the patriarchal nature of the family, were the key to freeing women from their position of inferiority. "What we want to destroy is the patriarchal system, not the family system." For the commune would take over the family's traditional role not only in production but also, and for women just as important, in consumption. The institutional and historical role of the family in its consumption activities relied heavily on continuation of the traditional female role.

An attempt to implement a birth control program met opposition from several unrelated sectors. In a country striving to increase its capacity for production, a large population was deemed an asset. Thus, the perception of labor shortages undercut the validity of a birth control program prior to the Great Leap, and the media became noticeably silent on the subject. The contradiction, however, became apparent very early in the Great Leap when the effort to mobilize women's labor was hindered precisely because many small children tied women to the home. A policy shift was detectable by mid-1959, when the necessity for birth control measures was again discussed in the media outside of women's magazines. "The promotion of planned births is, first of all, to protect the health of women and children. . . ."[29] But the ideological premise that a large population was an asset was never publicly refuted, and although birth control programs became acceptable, even necessary, in theory, they failed in fact.

The main form of birth control (apart from abstinence) was the male condom. The pill, developed by the early sixties, was not available. Even when modern birth control measures became available in the countryside, there was widespread resistance to the very idea of limiting family size. Many were embarrassed even to discuss the subject.[30] The traditional cultural emphasis on large families, and especially on male children to provide labor power for income and for security in old age, militated against the ready acceptance of birth control.

Pressures to bear male children came from other sources.[31] First, most girl children usually left their natal family and village once they married; hence, the family could not count on their continued contributions. Second, "male work" tended to earn more workpoints than did "female work," and even where women engaged in "male work" they were not accorded equal workpoints. Third, since women were still responsible for housework, which was not accorded workpoints, working in collective agriculture would only contribute to their burdens, and even then sons would be able to make greater contributions to family income than could any woman. As long as production was collectivized and consumption was tied to the income of individual peasant households, the traditional pressure for large families had a basis in economic reality. Hence, any rebellion against numerous pregnancies might face severe opposition from the family, as well as from a woman herself.

Thus, economic inequality in terms of workpoint remuneration (based on sex-role division of labor), and the fact that female labor, although it contributed not only to family income but also to collective production, lasted only as long as a girl remained single (and then, after marriage, became either a double burden or disappeared), were crucially important obstacles to women's emancipation. In affecting none of these realities very significantly, the Great Leap left untouched major sources of antagonism to female emancipation from both males and females. To have dealt with these problems frontally would have required far greater material resources than were available, would have meant a challenge to deep-rooted ideas and traditional images of women's role, and would undoubtedly have antagonized male supremacists. This in turn might have threatened economic development, and even political stability.

Throughout the Great Leap, the Chinese press publicized the efforts of women to contribute to socialist construction. However, traditional attitudes toward the proper division of labor between men and women, and the limited capabilities of the women themselves, based on their lack of education or experience, placed limits on the kinds of participation and the achievements of working women. This was clearly illustrated by the "skill revolution," a mass campaign during 1959 centering around technical innovation and technical revolution.

In the "skill revolution," campaigns were organized to produce "bumper crop maidens," "women Red Flag holders," and "women innovators."[32] Women were especially urged to develop advanced farming methods. The pressure to perform well and produce did lead to changes in work patterns. Many women's teams realized the necessity to train women technicians and to maintain close relationships with other female work groups to trade information and technical knowledge. While the "skill revolution" increased the scope of women's contacts and created the possibility of new jobs, it nevertheless glaringly pointed out that lack of basic technical knowledge or experience on the part of women severely restricted their ability to do more than develop simple innovations on basic tools. Given the conditions of female participation historically, it was remarkable that as many as 20 to 30 percent of the women participated in the skill campaign.

The Chinese blamed the overall poor results of the campaign on the low cultural levels of women, their self-deprecating attitudes, and the burden of household chores.[33]

The establishment of the communes, with women forming a large component of the work force, made the problem of workpoint allocation central when previously in the agricultural cooperatives it had had only marginal importance. The ramifications of the problem went far beyond the simple distributional question of equal pay for women; it challenged the traditional attitudes of male supremacy in production and brought out contradictions in the very definition of the term "work" as used by the Chinese.

Work in the communes was evaluated in terms of complex wagepoint systems that differed substantially from commune to commune. The maximum for a day's labor was ten points, with the minimum usually set at three or four. Workpoints could be assigned for the task or for the individual, or for a combination of the two. Women rarely achieved the maximum, regardless of the task or their ability. It should be noted that the very definition of what constituted productive labor worked against women. The exclusion of all those tasks performed in the home and largely by women—cooking, cleaning, clothes making, subsidiary production—and which placed time-consuming demands on women's labor power, denied women the possibility of working equal hours with men, much less receiving equal wages. Yet, these very tasks when performed "collectively" in mess halls or child care centers were eligible for workpoints. The fact that mostly women performed these tasks not only perpetuated the prevailing definition of what constituted productive work, but channeled most women into a permanently unequal position in the division of labor. Throughout the Great Leap Forward there was no evidence that suggested a recognition of this problem.

Where women performed "productive" work, the struggle for "equal pay for equal work" was complicated by the lack of national guidelines and the lack of support of commune officials, most of whom were male. In some areas certain tasks were designated "women's tasks"—for example, weeding, afforestation, small irrigation projects, and subsidiary production—and were accorded anywhere from three to seven or eight (mostly five or six) workpoints. Female resistance to this system existed, but was often passive and unorganized.[34]

The Great Leap thus raised the problem of a new sexual division of labor, which, like the old but on a very different level, was both separate and inherently unequal. If a situation arose in which women could earn more workpoints than men, attitudes of male supremacy would not allow such a condition to continue. In the interesting case of the Dachangsheng Production Brigade of Xinchiao Commune, the brigade assigned eighteen women to handicraft production, making bamboo baskets. Remuneration was on the basis of piecework.

At first the workpoints from handicraft work were added to the workpoints from farm production for unified distribution (where men performed both). But some complained later because some *women* workers were fast in handicraft work and they accumulated more workpoints from handicraft work than others from farm work. In order to solve this problem discussions were held among members and a democratic decision was made. It was decided that the workpoint accumulation by those engaging in handicraft production cannot exceed the highest workpoint accumulation by those same type of labor engaging in agricultural production.[35]

If women were only able to earn seven or eight workpoints in their field tasks then that would be their limit in handicraft production, regardless of the output or the quality or contribution to collective income. The national media and the women's publications printed several articles which weakly tried to counter this kind of situation by emphasizing that "Numerous facts gleaned from the big leap forward show that women, particularly those in their youth and prime, can do anything and do it well."[36]

In addition to unequal pay based on sex-role division of labor, there was also clear evidence that even where women were doing the same jobs as men, they were receiving fewer workpoints. The practice in Fenglin Peoples Commune, Yingshan xian, Hebei, was widespread. Here the disparity in wages between men and women (ten workpoints for men, seven for women) had an adverse effect on the activism of women. In a competition between a male worker, Cai Huabo, and a woman worker, Wu Xiuning, it was discovered that both accomplished the same work but Cai was given ten points for his efforts and Wu received only seven.[37]

The commune, with authority over this matter, thus was an important arena of political conflict for women. The existence of a local and well-organized women's federation was a significant element in the ability of women in some rural areas to raise if not solve the issue of "equal pay for equal work" and to achieve a reevaluation of the workpoint system. In these areas, women cadres first organized the female workers to discuss the problem, then carried out an investigation, and only then met with the commune's (usually male) leadership and eventually called for a mass meeting. When the commune's leadership was faced with the results of the investigation and with statistics on the contribution of women to overall production, pressure to revise the system was strong. In many cases this did not lead to overall equal wages, but it did lead to an upgrading of the average wage for women's labor: "As a result of the adjustment, the average basic wage points allowed to a woman were raised from 4.5 to 6.5"[38]

In some communes the question of workpoint allocation rested with a lower level of collective life, or even with the production team. In these smaller groups pressures against sexual equality were stronger. If the production team was based on a village and many male members of the women's families participated, the "equal pay" issue could have had ramifications within the family. Since many Chinese villages were dominated by a few families, production teams and brigades often had a kinship base. At this level women were at a distinct disadvantage. From the evidence available, it seems that women were more successful in pressing their demands at the brigade or commune level, where change of status did not present such a direct challenge to male family members.

One of the arguments raised to oppose allocating women a greater number of workpoints was the inconsistency of women's labor. A monthly average for women could range anywhere from twelve to twenty-three days depending on the intensity of household burdens. Household tasks were and have remained largely the responsibility of women and receive no workpoint allocation. The collective institutions that sprang up in the course of the Great Leap to socialize some household work (for example, mess halls, nurseries, sewing groups) were not part of every commune, and even where they existed serious problems of efficiency and quality arose. In addition, transfer of fuel and food to the mess halls was awkward and difficult given the level of development of the transport network. Other problems relating to scarcity and a low level of technological development arose. For example, peasant households which gave up their cooking fuel to the mess halls had nothing left to heat the *kang* (a brick bed with fire space beneath it) or their homes in the wintertime. Thus, while collectivized services undoubtedly freed women from some of the burdens of running a house, as soon as the economic situation tightened up seriously in 1960–61, these institutions were the first to be abandoned. It was only the women's organizations that urged the maintenance of the rural mess halls and child care facilities, noting however that "there are people who fail to see the great role community welfare services play in the emancipation of women, and the women's strong demand for the collective way of doing household chores."[39]

The Great Leap Forward showed just how far the emancipation of women would take rural China, and just how far rural China had to go before technology and economic growth, along with new evolutions and changes in attitudes, could accommodate the drastic changes that would be necessary.

Pre-Commune Urban Participation in the Great Leap Forward

While rural communes were organized by local and national political leaders for the purposes of production breakthrough, with the woman question largely peripheral until it revealed itself as crucial, the urban commune movement grew in part from the initiative of women, mostly housewives. The urban commune extended the production sector into consumption-oriented residential neighborhoods and involved urban women previously identified primarily as agents of consumption. Its accomplishments in terms of production, especially in the development of light industry, were largely unforeseen. Where the process of rural communization had been fairly uniform in terms of its broad organizational and production goals, that of urban communization was vastly more complex and diverse. Cities varied greatly in size, level of industrial development, and functional relationship to the national and local economy.[40] And the separation between work and residence that was often part of urban life necessitated a qualitatively different form of organization from that which characterized rural communes.

Urban communes developed around places of work—a large factory, a school, a government office—as well as in residential areas. In the former, the functions of the commune included production, whereas in the latter, meeting local neighborhood needs was the commune's main function.

The initial recruitment of women in cities was related to the "backyard steel movement," rural labor shortages, and the expansion of industry. Many urban women, particularly those in suburban districts of Beijing, went to rural areas to participate in agricultural production. But as urban industrial expansion commenced, many enterprises found it necessary to recruit new workers.[41]

The Great Leap produced two patterns of female employment in urban areas. One was characterized by entry into regular industrial positions. Factory managers were interested in recruiting women to take over the basic and simpler tasks, thus freeing men for other tasks. The movement to "substitute women for men" was an attempt to solve an anticipated labor shortage in a rapidly expanding industrial sector, and allowed women to enter regular industry, especially light industry, services, and commerce. Examples below indicate the rationale behind this development.

> Replacement of men by women in light industry, commerce, and the service trades is one of the major measures being undertaken in the urban areas to solve the manpower shortage and usher in a new forward leap in industry and agriculture. It is estimated that if the proportion of women workers in the textile mills under the Ministry of Textile Industry is raised from the present 58 to 70 per cent, more than 100,000 men can take jobs in heavy industry. In commerce, if all the work which can be done by women is handed over to them, possibly raising the proportion of women in this field to 70 per cent, millions of men can join heavy industry.[42]

or

> In such districts as Jiangning, Changning and Penglai, housewives were
> organized to process toys manufactured by the Kangyuan Toys Manufactur-
> ers; within the past two months, the factory has been able to detach nearly
> 100 competent, male laborers to the iron and steel front and the machine-
> building industry.[43]

and

> Over the past three months, over 15,300 housewives have been drawn into
> commercial and grain departments which have sent over 5,300 men workers
> below the age of 30 to industrial production. The number of women workers
> in the commerical, grain and service enterprises of the city has risen to over
> 80 per cent of the total number of workers employed.[44]

In many cases urban residents' committees helped recruit women, but there was
also a great deal of recruiting by individual factories from among the dependents
of their own workers. For example, the families of workers in the Shijingshan
Iron and Steel Works organized themselves into units of auxiliary labor.[45] More
than 1,500 women workers were given simple processing jobs by the Beijing
Hat Factory to allow men to take on more complex tasks. Most of the new
women workers were family members of regular workers and did not, therefore,
require additional living quarters or other welfare arrangements.

As logical as this policy was in terms of economic development, it did bring
women into the urban labor force on a clearly unequal basis. It provided limited
participation and acquisition of only the most elementary skills. The men who
previously performed these tasks were to be trained for the more complex, more
prestigious, and higher-paying skilled jobs. In other words, the advancement of
a large sector of the male labor force depended on the new female role. Both
groups advanced in absolute terms, but their relative positions remained largely
the same.

Street industry provided the second pattern of female urban employment. The
accelerated pace of the Great Leap and the stigma attached to "idleness" increased
enormously the numbers of women who wanted to work and changed former
official attitudes toward "housework," which was now described as "trivial and
burdensome enough to make people stupid."[46] Regular industry was limited in
its ability to absorb the masses of women whose lack of education or even literacy
severely restricted the kinds of tasks they could perform. The skills most women
possessed were related to their homemaking role, and these women were now
mobilized to form small "street industries" centering on the production of daily
consumer items. Housewives, working in small makeshift workshops, produced

cloth, made cooking implements, or processed simple foodstuffs. They set up neighborhood "service centers" also. The movement grew rapidly in most major Chinese cities.

In the Zhangjiazhai area of Xincheng district of Shanghai, over 90 percent of the housewives organized themselves into eight production and processing teams involved in sewing, embroidery, and manufacturing electric switches, vacuum lightning arresters, paper boxes, and other articles.[47] The Changan Residents' Committee in Wuhan, Hubei, under the leadership of Zhou Chunchiao organized 48 percent of the able-bodied women in the district. They raised funds, searched for raw materials, built workshops, made household repairs, and, in addition, they began producing spray paint, packing cases, leather shoes, clothes, paper bags, and fiber products, turning a consumer area into a production site. Of the twenty chairpersons and members of the resident's committee, sixteen women became managers of these small factories and workshops.[48] Preliminary statistics appeared in early 1959 claiming that the number of women workers had more than doubled in 1957–58, from 3 million to 7.5 million. By March of 1959, in twenty-two cities alone 530,000 housewives had set up 40,000 small plants and workshops.[49]

The development of street industry was not limited to the East China coastal cities either, for reports of "former housewives" involved in new production poured in from Harbin (Heilongjiang), Chengzhou (Henan), Daiyuan (Shanxi), and other areas.[50] As in rural areas, as more women left the home to join in factory work or street industry, the need for certain collective services became evident. Nurseries, kindergartens, and mess halls appeared.

The experience of Hongxunli Lane, Tianjin, underscores the close relationship between female participation in production and the need to collectivize services, especially child care. Hongxunli had only seventeen women workers before the establishment of the First Tianjin Producer Cooperative, which was staffed entirely by women. The cooperative, formed by workers' wives, supplied the additional manpower needed by the local electric wire factory for expansion of production. The women in Hongxunli Lane got together to support those women who went to work outside the home, by setting up a nursery, a kindergarten, a community restaurant, and tailoring services. These were staffed by women whose household burdens or health prevented them from becoming full-time "outside" workers. As these services expanded, more women went to work, until the Lane boasted 11,000 women workers. Hongxunli became a model for others to follow.[51]

The accomplishments of these women are even more significant considering the conditions imposed on the development of street industry by official policy. All neighborhood or street industries were guided by the "five basic principles."

They would not apply to the government for (1) funds, (2) raw materials, (3) machines, or (4) buildings, and (5) they would not recruit workers in state-owned factories to work in their factories.[52] The development of street industry was a real "Operation Bootstrap." Women were encouraged to participate and help in socialist construction but, being outside the planned or "official" industrial system, they were given no help or training. Street factories had poor equipment and low-grade resources and material—much of it the discards or waste of regular industry and most of the rest built by the women themselves. Production methods were labor intensive and technologically unsophisticated at the beginning. Successful enterprises were incorporated into the larger industrial system, usually by regular contracting with state-owned industry or by becoming a satellite or a subsidiary of a state-run plant.

Former housewives benefited by the acquisition of skills and, if their project was successful, they were paid. In the initial stages of production, wages were often deferred due to the necessity to accumulate capital for reinvestment. However, even when paid, street industry wages were much lower than in regular industry and, because capital accumulation was so slow, the luxury of a welfare fund to provide services such as child care, sick leave, or maternity pay was almost totally absent.

Workers in street industry were not accorded the status of regular workers. Street industries were subsidiary production that added to the income of the state, especially in the light industry sector and in the production of consumer articles, and they provided an important means by which the female labor force attained skills and education and even new attitudes. Their status, however, in the overall economic structure was ambiguous and subject to change.

Street industry provided undeniable benefits to wage-earning women. For those families whose income was not large, or for large families, the additional money earned by women was clearly useful. But this was not the only benefit. As the women's press was quick to point out, the effects of women wage earners on the relations between daughters-in-law and mothers-in-law were significant.[53] Indeed, the ability to work for pay both increased the status of women in the family and lessened the degree of family control over women.

The establishment of service industries provided jobs for women who would not have been able to work otherwise. This included old women whose failing strength and lack of industrial skills largely precluded their entry into the regular labor force but whose traditional skills of home management made them ideal for neighborhood welfare services. Young women with several children and others with heavy household burdens could work in shifts, especially in neighborhood services, at hours convenient for their home schedules. Thus, work in mess halls, kindergartens, nurseries, laundries, tailoring, food processing, repair shops—in short, almost any work done mainly by service teams—led in many cases to a massive entry of "former housewives" into social labor. As one report noted from a city in Gueizhou:

> 80% of all those people with laboring capacity in the city who did not take part in labor in the past (of whom the overwhelming majority were women) have begun to take part in production or in the work of the service centers (teams).[54]

Their work allowed women a feeling of participation in socialist construction and added to their family income. Urban local industry centering around services came to be uniquely a province of women workers. A comparison to the sweatshops of Japan or America must take into account two important differences. Chinese women, for the most part, were not driven to work by economic necessity, and the ideological motivation of participation in a national endeavor was very high.

Urban Communes

The urban commune incorporated the street committees, which were staffed mainly by resident housewives. As basic-level administrative organizations, street committees played an important role as agents of socialization. They organized the residents for participation in political and cultural studies and for participation in national campaigns, they generally oversaw the welfare services of their areas, and, most importantly, they mediated local disputes. These disputes often involved the support of women's rights against the opposition of husbands and mothers-in-law.[55] Mediation committees are part of the legal process in China. If they are unable to resolve the conflict, a formal court hears the case. In cities the mediation committees were usually staffed by women, while men predominated in the countryside. The Women's Federation appeared to play an important role in mobilizing urban women for street committee work,[56] since many of the functions of the street committees directly concerned women. Chinese women regarded their role in these committees as having great social and political importance.[57]

Street committees represented both an organizational and an ideological basis for the development of the urban commune movement. Together with the rapid development of street industry, they formed the backbone of these new, but short-lived, experiments in China's major urban centers. Beijing, since it had the greatest percentage of female workers in neighborhood street industry, provides a good study of the movement and its impact on women.[58] The urban communes did not survive the Great Leap, but many of the production sites and welfare services they fostered did, and for this reason the communes are of direct relevance to urban women.

Although several of Beijing's urban communes were supposed to have started between August and October 1958, press coverage began only in April 1960. By this date thirty-eight urban communes had been established throughout the city.[59] Although communes organized around a factory, school, or government office did appear in Beijing, the most numerous and important in terms of production were those situated in residential areas and based on local street industry. The five most important urban communes in Beijing were the Zhongsuyiyu Commune of Shijingshan district, established in August 1958; the Zhunshu Commune of Xuanwu district; the Erlung Road Commune of Xizheng district; the Beixinjiao Commune of Dongzheng district; and the Diyuguan Road Commune of Chungwen district.[60] All but the Zhongsuyiyu Commune were supposed to have been established in September–October 1958.

Many of the communes were known for their most successful enterprise. For example, the knitting factory of the Erlunglu Peoples Commune, though only one of eighteen small enterprises in the commune, was started in 1958 by 12 women and grew to employ 130 women making 5,000 dozen pairs of industrial gloves per month by mid-1960.[61] Although official policy with regard to street industry prohibited it from absorbing regular workers, it was apparent that many of the workshops arranged training programs in regular factories or used regular workers as teachers for the "former housewives." The Xuanwu Glass Plant (25 workers trained) and the Yanjing Paper Mill (18 workers trained) trained enough women for the creation of a small glass factory and a small paper mill.[62] Though the use of regular workers to help local industry might be considered a departure from the "five principles," by 1960 there was a recognition of the possible importance of local industry, and hence a greater willingness to support it at its inception. In addition to these larger production efforts, many smaller workshops developed. The success of the factory often acted as a catalyst for others, as the development of Zhunshu Peoples Commune in Xuanwu district illustrated.[63]

Xuanwu was a working-class district in which some women held jobs outside the district. Under the increasing pressure of the Great Leap the residents of Zhunshu Commune in the Xuanwu district collectively worked first on establishing an iron and steel works and then a chemical plant. Apparently the first project, part of the "backyard steel" campaign, was abandoned. However, the chemical plant galvanized other residents into setting up workshops for production of articles ranging from plastic raincoats to glass tubing.

The nine women of Zhunshu Lane who started the chemical works were members of worker or cadre families. The women wanted to produce an insecticide needed in rural areas, thereby supporting a national endeavor to increase agricultural production. As with most street industry, the women started with few resources (a fund of 2.40 yuan and two pairs of bellows and two pots). They received outside help from bricklayers, who built two ovens for them. Persistent experimentation with the waste of a local state-owned nail factory and the advice of some skilled workers finally led to successful production of the insecticide. Since the women were illiterate, they had to memorize the formula and devise simple methods to replace the use of even simple instruments, like thermometers, which they could not read. Their success led other factories—among them the Electrolite Copper Factory, the Beiyuan Chemical Factory, and the Xinhua Dyestuffs Factory—to contract for the removal of their waste materials for reprocessing. As more factories contracted, they agreed to "loan" some of their workers to the women for short periods to train them and help improve their production technique.

The chemical factory was a real success story, creating a total value of 7 million yuan in less than six months. From an original staff of nine, the factory's employees grew to number three hundred workers in four workshops producing ten different products. Other women, noting the development of the chemical works, began a glass factory, which grew to three hundred workers, and a plastics factory, which ultimately employed five hundred workers. Still other women established small workshops and small production teams which operated out of the home and produced daily consumer items. The experience and links with local industry illustrated the potential for economic development that existed in spite of the lack of capital. Thus, urban street industry was clearly an increasingly important element in the decentralization of industry.

Street industry under the urban commune was considered vital in terms of the contribution it made to the social well-being of the community as well as to economic growth. When the urban organization in Zhunshu was established, one of its first tasks was to attempt to unify and rationalize this form of production. The commune reorganized hundreds of small production teams into two general factories to process articles of daily use for the market. Commune administration over distribution and marketing of the products was strengthened also.

By 1960, urban commune administration had become involved in the creation of collectivized welfare and social services. The emphasis on production, so evident in 1958 and 1959, now shifted to the political, ideological, and educational effort necessary to mobilize the masses of urban dwellers to initiate collective services such as mess halls, child care, and neighborhood service centers.

Mess halls were introduced in 1958, but were not used by large numbers of people until 1960 at the height of "housewives' " involvement in industry. By that time, Zhunshu was an advanced model, boasting a network of mess halls that included three mechanized and semimechanized public dining halls, located in Shanxi Street, Houxun Park, and Haibeishi, the site of Zunshu's major factories. Each could accommodate 1,000 persons. In addition, several "satellite" mess halls serving individual workshops and production sites were started.[64] The limited capacity of many of the mess halls, the use of ration cards, and the traditional preference for family dining probably made the mess halls more popular for meals other than the evening one.

But aside from custom, the mess halls had serious problems that ranged from inefficiency and poor management to economic scarcity. In Zhongjing complaints focused on the low quality of food preparation and on lack of hygiene, problems due to the inexperience and ignorance of women workers accustomed to preparing food for a family, not a community.[65] Tianjin's mess halls, subjected to a vigorous investigation, indicated that proper management and supervision necessitated skills such as accounting and finance which women as "former housewives" did not possess.[66] The poor harvests of 1960–61 and the shortages that ensued compounded the problems that already beleaguered mess halls throughout China.

The Women's Federation had always placed great emphasis on the mess halls, for in addition to freeing working women from the time-consuming chores of cooking and food preparation, the mess halls were also used as cultural and educational centers, for classrooms, conference sites, and meeting halls. Where these extra activities were available and women used them, they reinforced new patterns of behavior and attitudes on the part of the new workers.

The child care facilities of Zhunshu Peoples Commune do not seem to have been extensive. Hallways, courtyards, and spare rooms (if any were available) were used to create very simple nurseries. The largest, Sezhuanying, cared for one hundred children. This nursery and the Shanxi Street kindergarten appear to have been the largest and best facilities in this model commune.[67] It was evident that most families still relied on "grannies" and older children to provide childcare. Zhunshu also had service centers that supplied women workers to clean homes, leave thermoses of hot water, do laundry, and complete errands for people (mostly women) who were at work. By 1960 Beijing boasted 370 service centers serving local neighborhoods throughout the city.[68]

The necessity for the service centers, and hence their impact on transforming women's condition in Chinese society, was very much related to the fate of street industry during and after the Leap. The change in female roles was not, after all, enormous. Many of the centers made use of traditional homemaking skills without disturbing the household routines of the workers. The uniqueness of the Great Leap period lay in the collective nature of the work and in the fact that it earned compensation. The emergence of service centers allowed many women alternatives to the "housewife role" narrowly defined. But women still were unequal participants in the industrial sector as a whole, and the social division of labor in regard to home responsibilities remained in female hands.[69] In extending the sphere of collectivized activity to include services that formerly were the sole responsibility of the household, the Great Leap made an important departure from the past, but one that was an amelioration of the traditional sexual division of labor and not an attack on it.

The neighborhood residents' committee, usually staffed by women, worked with local male-dominated Party committees and commercial and financial departments in government to help organize and supervise the service centers. Although women provided almost all the labor in these undertakings, management of them remained a male province with few women rising to posts of leadership other than on the residents' committees. But the Great Leap did illustrate the intimate relationship between work and the transformation of political and social roles. Working exposed women to political study groups, lectures, literacy classes, and skill training, and gave them opportunities to take on political and administrative responsibility. The urban communes seemed particularly important.

> In Beixinjiao commune, . . . 32 persons have been accepted by the Party as members and 56 persons were taken in by the Young Communist League. Some 451 members of the Zhunshu commune have been rated "red flag hands" and "skillful girls" and 40 of them have been appointed factory managers, nursery chiefs and mess hall managers.[70]

To the extent that the urban commune provided for the educational and cultural development of working-class women it marked a significant departure from previous street and service undertakings.

Although employment within the urban commune's own enterprises predominated, the communes also served as organizations from which women could be recruited for other kinds of work, particularly as men left for new construction jobs and women were called upon to replace them. For example, young unmarried women, female students, and shop assistants were recruited from Beijing's communes and trained to direct the city's traffic. The Beijing Bus Company recruited and trained over two hundred women as taxi drivers and others as bus operators.[71] The number of women trained in these kinds of jobs strongly suggests this was not mere tokenism.

The experience of Beijing was not unique in the Great Leap Forward. There was a marked increase in the number of women workers in regular industry during the Great Leap. In 1959 women constituted slightly over 15 percent of all workers and employees, and by 1963 the expansion of heavy and light industry had increased this percentage to 25 percent, even with the severe economic

problems of 1959 to 1962.[72] The Anshan Iron and Steel Works, which had
employed no women in 1949, by 1962 had six hundred women engineers,
managers, technicians, and designers.[73] All were educated in post-1949 China.
Although the increase in women workers was significant, it was confined mainly
to the light industrial sector and the traditional cotton, wool, silk, and clothing
industries. Anshan was clearly an exception. The industries most resistant to
hiring women were iron and steel and machinery, where the prestige and wages
were highest. Resistance to hiring women workers was largely the result of
traditional attitudes toward the capabilities of women. Many supervisory personnel would not teach female workers because they did not think women capable
of mastering the skills necessary for participating in industrial labor.[74] This kind
of discrimination often kept women in the lowest level jobs and reinforced their
own sense of inferiority, even when they entered heavy industry. In many cases
women had to contend with on-the-job discrimination in addition to familial
dissatisfaction with the decision to work.

Women in urban China were also active in areas outside industry. By 1960,
women constituted 25 percent of the researchers in the Chinese Academy of
Sciences and 50 percent of those in the Chemical Industry Research Institute and
in the Light Industry Research Institute. Women also constituted 40 percent of
the doctors in Beijing and about 30 percent of the student body in such key
universities as Beijing, Chinghua, Beijing Union Medical College, and the Chinese
University of Science and Technology.[75] That most of the students came from
urban families is indicative of the greater ability of those in cities to receive an
education. The advances made by women in the cities did not necessarily influence the ability of peasant women to do the same. Peasant girls were still needed
for housework and care of younger siblings, and the limited educational facilities
available meant they were passed over in favor of their brothers.

Conclusion

In claiming that there was no conflict, only mutual reinforcement, between
the emancipation of women and socialist development, the Chinese were echoing
the standard analysis that had come to them via the Soviet Union's interpretation
of the "woman question" begun with Lenin. This analysis held that women's
emancipation depended on two things, their participation in production outside
the home, and the socialization of domestic labor, and that since both of these
were socialist goals, women's emancipation and socialism were mutually supportive.

The economic development policies adopted during the Great Leap Forward
in many ways initiated precisely the kind of "general struggle" Lenin spoke of.
Great Leap policies were aimed at the rapid creation of socialist institutions,
primarily to mobilize female labor for economic development. But in the process

it raised the issue of sexual equality in a direct and unavoidable way that was neither anticipated nor even admitted by the Chinese.

In short-run terms there were clear indications that there was a real contradiction between economic development and woman's liberation, especially in terms of capital investment. In a capital-poor country investment in services often must be made at the expense of investment in productive and reproductive capacity, and this clearly emerged during the Leap. In a poor country with a huge labor force in which men have historically and generally occupied the leading positions, it therefore may make sense to forego massive investment in those institutions which provide the real basis for significantly changing the role of women in society in favor of investing directly in productive facilities. Nevertheless women as a class did make important advances during the Great Leap period. The very large increase in the numbers of women in educational institutions and working in industry, agriculture, and the service establishments represents important advances. But this did not diminish the reality or immediacy of the contradictions that had been raised. Even where the opportunity for female employment and participation was pursued within the context of simultaneous increase of production and expansion of social services, there emerged a clear pattern that tended to perpetuate *relative* status inequalities between men and women.

Of all the policies adopted in the Great Leap, the attempt to change the role and status of Chinese women probably resulted in the most widespread, consistent and far-reaching opposition. It was both qualitatively and quantitatively different from other problems, for it involved questioning traditional cultural values and institutions that had structured and reinforced concepts of self, the sexual division of labor, and people's daily lives and routines. The Great Leap revealed three crucial areas where conflict emerged within the goals of economic development: health, education, and the role of women in the family.

In the post-Leap period, the health problem, especially in rural areas, was closely tied to matters of pre- and postnatal care, birth control, and female sexual rights vis-à-vis husbands and other family members. The rural areas of China had always lacked medical facilities and personnel to deal with these matters as well as many others, but until collectivization and the vast recruitment of women into the labor force the urgency of the rural health problem was not recognized. The lack of attention by the authorities to rural health therefore reflected the weakness of feminist issues in policy planning. While the Great Leap showed the relationship between adequate medical service and the creation of productive human beings, the Chinese did not begin to deal intensively with this problem until Mao's famous critique of the Ministry of Health in 1965. The whole problem of health care remained an important and controversial issue that emerged most dramatically in the Cultural Revolution.[76]

Women were also members of an educationally disadvantaged group whose contribution to the construction of socialism would be necessarily limited by their lack of skills. Even the familiarity with modern techniques that basic literacy brings was absent. Mass mobilization and intense politicization could get many women into the labor force but could not guarantee the success of their attempts at production. While the Great Leap experimented with new kinds of education programs, mainly spare-time study groups, which many women joined, these seemed to have decreased significantly in the early 1960s.

The extreme conservatism of the Chinese regarding the proper role of women within the family (especially in the countryside) and the apparent reluctance to force change in this sphere of life during the Great Leap pointed to the traditional biosexual role of women as most in need of change and most difficult to change. The potential threat to the stability and maintenance of the Chinese family, in which the female role was pivotal, was of greater import than the desire to alleviate objectively visible female oppression and inequality—except in its most extreme forms, such as forced marriage and physical abuse. The necessity to develop new institutions supportive of new roles for women was quickly grasped, but the economic and "cultural" cost of the attempt was not understood nearly as well. Once attempted, during the Great Leap, the development of these supportive institutions provoked the sharpest conflict with economic development goals because of the demands it placed on limited economic, technical, and human resources. While mess halls, nurseries, and service centers sprang up everywhere, there was no overall planning for these institutions or training of personnel to staff them. In large part this was because the tasks they performed were considered "woman's work" (and women were the majority of workers) and hence not worthy of capital investment or any particular attention. Yet, these very institutions directly affect the quality of life of all the people, and their efficiency and satisfactory management were essential to releasing women from home responsibilities. The failure or simple inability of the Chinese at this stage to develop these basic institutions so that they became qualitatively acceptable substitutes for the family's role in fulfilling these same functions only catered to the conservative concepts of "woman's proper place" in the home.

In general, the experience of urban women in the Great Leap did not raise the specter of conflict between women's liberation and economic development in as intense a manner as the experience in the countryside, though there was clearly a trade-off between the two, especially in terms of the division of labor, occupation, and worker classification. The urban sector, having been favored during the 1950s, was the site of most major medical facilities and almost all the Western-trained doctors. It had the largest educational institutions, and most technical and part-time schools were in the cities. More important, perhaps, the cities were where women had made the greatest advances in industry, education, and as representatives in government. The Women's Federation was strongest in the urban areas and was more experienced and successful organizationally. In short, the advantages of past modernization and urbanization presented a wider range of alternatives to women who wished to enter production.

In both rural and urban areas women emerged as a significant political force on the local level. The role of local urban women in the neighborhood residents' committees expanded to include production, and the production team and brigade levels in the communes saw an enlarged role for women. The urban street committees, staffed by housewives, were responsible for many functions directly affecting the quality of life in the community, for men as well as for women. Sanitation, health, primary and part-time education, and the service industries fell within their province. The continued development of these facilities—where they were maintained—sometimes involved necessary investment by district or municipal government and this was at the initiative of women. Thus experience began to extend into the legal and coercive instruments of society.

In rural areas it was common to have a woman as deputy director of the commune, as deputy leader in a production team, or as leader on an all-female team. While it appears that these women most often were responsible for "work among women," it nevertheless legitimized and institutionalized women as public leaders. In many areas, many teams were all female, and women assumed responsibility for organizing work and, with it, developing a relationship to the larger group—brigade, commune, or nation—that was very different from that prescribed by traditional roles. As the Great Leap also showed, women's participation in organs of public decision making could have a significant impact on public policy priorities on the local level.

The Chinese experience during the Great Leap dramatically illustrated the depth of radical social change necessary to free women from traditional roles. More than any other historical event, inside or outside China, it showed that the mass mobilization of female labor for production outside the home was itself not just part of a solution but part of a whole new and complicated set of problems.

· 4 ·

Development Strategies in Conflict

FEMALE LABOR PARTICIPATION OUTSIDE THE HOME IS IMPLICIT IN MOST theories of development or modernization. Most often absent from these theories, however, is a concrete discussion of the process by which the contradictions between traditional family-oriented and modern participatory roles of women are resolved. During the Great Leap Forward, with its insistent demands for the mobilization of female labor power, these contradictions were fully exposed. Curiously enough, although Western liberal and Marxist theories of development differ in so many fundamental ways, the Great Leap had shown both to be lacking as each had evolved up to that time, for both seemed to view the transformation of female roles as a mechanistic by-product of the development process. Yet paradoxically, the experience of Chinese women, both under the First Five-Year Plan and in the Great Leap Forward, demonstrated an element of truth in a certain mechanistic view of the process. Increased production, the expansion of both agriculture and industry, and the increasing availability of some social services meant improvement in almost everybody's life, including that of women.

The very process of development from 1949 on, viewed from an incremental and accumulative perspective, created rising expectations on the part of women. The assimilation of women into the labor force and within the sociopolitical community gave them an objective stake in the process regardless of the partic-ular differences in policies adopted. First with the slow but definite increase in female workers under the First Five-Year Plan, and then the large-scale and rapid mobilization of women during the Great Leap Forward, a social context was created in which the active participation of Chinese women was both necessary and increasingly accepted by the Chinese people. However, the Great Leap had revealed clear limits to the mechanistic view of the relationship between devel-opment of the economy and the changing role of women in society. The mass mobilization of women during the Great Leap put sharp and intensified pressure on the traditional view which defined women uniquely within the nexus of familial-oriented activities, yet the Great Leap never challenged the priority of increased production. As new forms of participation and the values embodied

· 74 ·

within the new institutions came into conflict with the old, social and psychological transformation began to threaten the routines required for rapid production increases.

The small numbers of women assimilated into the work force prior to the Great Leap Forward meant that women entered a male-dominated and male-determined work situation in which their particular needs could easily be ignored and their participation considered marginal. However, the Great Leap Forward saw millions of women leave the home, thus increasing the social or public costs of services previously supplied by "private" female labor in the household. It was in this regard that the contradictions between the costs of female participation and the goals of production emerged most dramatically. Moreover, because women were the most oppressed and exploited under the traditional system (both their lack of skills and their low level of political consciousness illustrate this), they, in a real sense, embodied the major short-term contradictions in China between social justice and equality on the one hand and rapid production increases on the other. And this was true even when the two processes could be viewed as mutually reinforcing in the long-term perspective of socialist development.

By late 1960,[1] in the face of a mounting economic and political crisis, the importance of the woman question rapidly receded. Natural disasters (drought and flooding) and severe economic imbalances were important in shaping the outcome of the Leap.[2] Poor planning, unforeseen consequences of certain innovations, the precipitous walkout of Russian technicians (in the summer of 1960), and powerful opposition to the Leap within the Party and government, particularly in the planning apparatus, were also crucial factors.[3]

The policies of retrenchment and consolidation that remained operative in so many places until the Cultural Revolution placed limits on the ability of women to consolidate their gains and achieve new ones. Most notably, collective welfare services of all kinds contracted, especially in the rural areas. Retrenchment, in many cases, meant that production and distribution reverted to the control of the production team, or even the family. It was precisely at these levels that the conflict between new roles for women and the demands of production emerged so sharply. The immediate emphasis on grain production at least temporarily eliminated plans to expand the collective production of vegetables, fruit-tree cultivation, and animal husbandry. These were all areas in which female labor predominated. Thus, for many peasant women in many areas even the few opportunities for work outside the home which the Leap had created became untenable.

In urban areas the setbacks in the modern sector temporarily ended an expansion in which many women had begun to make important advances. The growing Sino-Soviet dispute and especially the withdrawal of Soviet technical advisers created severe problems in the industrial sector. Problems resulting from Leap experiments in management and planning resulted in more cutbacks and forced layoffs.[4] Women were probably more affected, since they had the least seniority, they were poorly skilled, and many had entered industry as a result of the "substitute women for men" policy of the Leap. Shortages of production materials seem to have led to the severe contraction of street industry projects which relied on larger factories for raw materials or whose production plans were linked to continued growth and expansion of the larger plants. Street enterprises organized for neighborhood production of consumer goods and services fared somewhat better.[5]

The period from 1961 to 1965 was one in which policies begun during the Leap continued, but were challenged by the pressures and necessities for change in the face of opposition and crisis. There were contradictions, both cultural and economic, between women's emancipation and the mass mobilization of female labor in a society still powerfully shaped by traditional, conservative attitudes. Ambiguities also resulted from the recession and consolidation of the post-Leap period which threatened to undermine the opportunities opened for and made visible to women during the Leap. The controversies over policies and principles regarding political and economic transformation that were so important in Chinese politics in the post-Leap period therefore had direct relevance to women even as the woman question faded rapidly from the attention of the mass media and the central political leadership. This at least was the case from 1960 to 1962. Beginning in 1962 with the socialist education campaign,[6] the media once again reflected a renewed concern with women's issues that could no longer be ignored.

First of all, the preceding years of readjustment and consolidation had revealed that in rural China there was a close relationship between the status and role of women and the health of the collective economy. During this period "feudal" practices and attitudes of treating women as a commodity to be sold in order to "marry well" and thereby arrange secure family relationships had never disappeared, but in the post-Leap period they emerged with renewed strength.[7] These practices were not only detrimental to women; they also supported the position of wealthier families and threatened to undermine the collective economy. Capital and resources went for brides, lavish weddings, and gifts, rather than for improving collective agriculture and technology. It was increasingly clear that the two revolutions—women's and the socialist—were indeed closely related in the Chinese countryside.

The close relationship between old-fashioned practices[8] regarding women and the future of collective production was brought to national attention during the socialist education campaign which began after the Tenth Plenum of the Eighth Central Committee in 1962. The campaign was part of a renewed emphasis on "class struggle" that grew out of this important meeting. Before the Great Leap Forward, these problems were viewed as part of the woman question, whose resolution was predicated, in large part, upon the struggles of women themselves. Now, in the socialist education campaign the Young Communist League[9] rather than the Women's Federation was seen to have a special responsibility. League writers usually portrayed the bridegroom as the advocate of "new-style" marriages, or as one who would insist that the young bride break with tradition and work after marriage, or as the upholder of women's rights. The women who were portrayed in this media were usually beset by problems resulting from early marriage and childbearing. By contrast, articles in *Women of China* portrayed the young woman as an independent decision maker willing to struggle against traditional parental interference in the matter of marriage. The projection of male authority in the media as the key to transforming the family, and the absence of female participation, reinforced the dependency role of married women.

The treatment of women about to be married or already married contrasted rather sharply with the projected image for single women. Young, unmarried girls were expected to pursue their studies, assume jobs in industry and agriculture, and work hard for the construction of socialism.[10] However, the tension between familial and other roles was faced by all Chinese women after marriage. In the post-Leap period, many young women in China who had been students or workers may have preferred to delay marriage because of the traumatic change in lifestyle it implied or until their careers were established enough so that traditional pressures could be withstood.

Women and Family Planning

The threat that uncontrolled population increase posed to economic growth in the post-Leap recession projected birth control as a national issue and not simply as a woman's issue. The role of females in birth control was emphasized, however, in contrast to the media-defined division of labor and responsibility in marriage. The appeal to practice birth control was, and still is, most often directed at women. Most articles are variations on a similar theme: a young woman undermined her ability to contribute to socialist construction when she married early, gave birth, left school or work, and was saddled with household drudgery.[11] The woman's key role in birth control was further reinforced by the lack of male participation in the problem. Traditional opposition to birth control and traditional images of male sexuality predominated until the changed economic and political context of the 1970s, despite the pressures brought to bear by the prestigious scientific community.

The seriousness of the need to control fertility had led to officially supported scientific participation in a campaign begun in 1962 promoting late marriages and birth control.[12] The dissemination of birth control information and techniques to the public was encouraged and funds and personnel were allocated to research new methods of limiting fertility. There were a few articles on vasectomy in 1963, a procedure favored by some doctors because it was simpler and involved less patient risk than operations on women and had no effect on sexual function.[13] The lack of more intensive media coverage of this form of birth control suggests there was male opposition.

The widespread use of birth control was, however, hampered by the lack of medical facilities, particularly in the countryside. The Chinese may have developed an oral contraceptive for women by 1960, but its distribution was very limited. Sufficient numbers of medical workers were not available and the young chemical and pharmaceutical industries could not yet produce large quantities of the pill. The Chinese appeared to be favoring intrauterine devices in this period as a practical means of birth control,[14] but the distribution network for IUDs was limited largely to urban areas. Nevertheless, the IUD held great potential for rural areas. Unlike the pill, daily consciousness of birth control was unnecessary, and this was important in a population still largely illiterate and unused to routines such as daily pill-taking.

While birth control ultimately lessened household burdens and increased the opportunity to work, the practice of birth control was clearly viewed as the responsibility of married women—a responsibility arising from their sexual roles as bearers of children. Marriage and a family were discussed in terms of contradictions posed for women, not for men. There was no discussion of male responsibilities in the family, and it was assumed that the woman's role in reproduction and household production took precedence over nonfamilial roles. As one woman described the problem:

> Well in a large family parents and the mother in particular get chained to tiring housework and demanding children. This drains their energy for production and study. They may find themselves gradually withdrawing into themselves and into the narrow confines of their family, thus falling behind in politics and their career. This contrasts with what the state expects of us.[15]

But did it? As long as family policy implicitly accepted the unique importance of the woman's role in the family, women would and did receive ambiguous and contradictory images of their roles in society. The justification for women's continued role in child care took ingenious forms. "It is far more difficult to take care of and teach a child than to look after a machine," noted one essay.[16] And the appeal for small families was frankly materialistic. For one rural woman with many children, it was noted that "all the children in the village wore new clothes during the Spring Festival except hers."[17] Given this context, women could not really be faulted for viewing "small family happiness" as their special province and as a valid goal.

Thus, instituting birth control was only a first step for women. Unless "small family happiness," with women as its provider, was discredited, the change from an extended family system would yield no substantive change in familial responsibilities or in the status of women. As more women went to work in the mid 1960s and as economic recovery got underway, contradictions between collective and individual familial production and orientation were bound to increase.

The ideas that emerged from the discussions of these issues that had begun with the socialist education campaign were part of a larger set of theoretical issues concerning the relationship between social revolution and economic development. There was no question that there was a relationship between the evolution of the family system and the success of social revolution.[18] But there was disagreement over the precise nature of the relationship and, by extension, over women's changing role within the family. To illustrate the difficulty of achieving rapid changes in older attitudes and practices regarding women, the debate in the mid 1960s began around a series of essays concerning implementation of the Marriage Law promulgated in 1950.

From one perspective, the attainment of female emancipation was seen as an evolutionary process in which technological development was the crucial variable in alleviating household drudgery. Emancipation and equality were inevitable with economic development, but technological and material impediments defined the limits of women's struggles. As one essay noted, "The implementation of the Marriage Law cannot exceed the development of the socio-economic system and the degree of social and cultural development *determined by the system* . . ."[19] (emphasis added). This technological determinism was maintained in contrast to another perspective which held that the "remnants of feudalism" in attitudes left "traces" which were "inevitably reflected in the position of women and in marital relations. . . ."[20] Thus, the resolution of the problem of the oppressed status of women became possible only through the development of the class struggle, not just through the development of the economy: "The struggle between the old and the new marital systems and new and old thoughts is a reflection of the class struggle of a transitional period in China."[21]

Viewing the oppression of women as part of the class struggle did not deny the validity of the relationship between underdevelopment and low status, but it did deny its primacy. For women the contradictions in this period of transition to socialism were not only economic but social and political as well. For one thing, women themselves had to participate in the technical revolution and this required overcoming old ideas about women's "proper" role.[22] The very process of revolutionary modernization would create new forms of human participation and break down the age-old barriers of inequality—including the sexual discrimination that characterized class societies. This participation must be reinforced by a high degree of political consciousness concerning class struggle at the point of production and in the home. Hence the patterns and process of the women's revolution and those of socialist revolution were very much related. As Mao understood the process,

> It's the same with women (the revolution is just beginning). Of course it is necessary to give them legal equality to begin with. But from there on everything still remains to be done. The thought, culture, and customs which brought China to where we find it must disappear, and the thought, culture, and customs of proletarian China, which does not yet exist, must appear. The Chinese woman doesn't yet exist either, among the masses; but she is beginning to want to exist. And then, to liberate women is not to manufacture washing machines.[23]

The existence of what was later to be called during the Cultural Revolution a "two-line struggle" with regard to the woman question at first appeared in the form of a very ambiguous and even contradictory affirmation of two kinds of life for women: the life of the traditional housewife-mother, and that of the revolutionary participant. However, while an uneasy coexistence of the two perspectives characterized the early 1960s, by 1965 there had appeared considerably more polarization as the general political-ideological climate heated up in anticipation of the Cultural Revolution. This ambiguous ideological context was made even more complex by very different levels of economic and technological transformation, both urban and rural, in Chinese society.

Urban Women

While many of the Leap's innovations in the industrial sector, especially those emphasizing cadre participation in labor and worker participation in management and technical innovation, became the substance of potential conflict in the post-Leap period,[24] it is unclear how many women were affected. Most industries still clearly employed a minority of women even though during the Leap the emphasis had been on getting women to work in urban industrial establishments. By 1962, women had indeed become an important segment of the urban work force. In industry, despite retrenchments, women numbered over eight million, and in educational institutions and science institutes they had become a significant part of the labor force. One-fifth of the Chinese Academy of Sciences was female, and five thousand women were teaching in Beijing's colleges.[25]

The period after 1962 in general was one of urban industrial expansion. As more and more women entered or reentered the industrial, cultural, and professional institutions of urban China, they brought with them some of the "problems special to women." Urban factories in the state-run sector, as they recovered from the 1960–62 recession, seemed able to provide necessary services for female workers by and large. As women were integrated with the male labor force, they were increasingly called upon to view themselves as workers, and it was in this capacity rather than as females, that they found themselves involved in many of the socioeconomic and political conflicts that were in process within the factories. By no means were all women in urban China factory workers, nor were even most in the active labor force. Even those who were were still operating in the ambiguous ideological context described above. The textile industry was one place, however, where a large number of women workers could be found. It is, therefore, an excellent place to view the conflicts and problems confronting women—both as females and as workers. And since as workers they were faced with the uncertainties of the experiments in management begun during the Leap, and as females they faced "feudal" attitudes toward women, this probably explains why the textile industry seemed to have had so much difficulty in sustaining the radical experiments of the Great Leap Forward in worker participation and management when compared to the urban heavy industry and machine tool sector.

Women workers in the urban sector were not viewed differently from other women in society—they too had to reconcile their "female" roles with their "productive" roles in the industrial work force. Even though many articles advocated job protection or the adjustment of work schedules, it was still primarily the woman's responsibility to integrate the two roles. Few if any articles suggested alteration or transformation of the traditional male-female division of labor to meet the demands of female participation in production. As one typical article put it:

> As a rule, women workers who have many children also have heavier burdens of household chores. At the change of seasons, they often have to apply for leaves of absence during which they can make and mend clothes for their children. Whenever household chores become heavy, the members of the committee of women workers and activists will pay extensive investigative visits to the houses of women workers who have many children, and in the spirit of class friendship, set young women workers to help them in making, mending, and washing clothes, cleaning houses, and repairing windows, so as to lighten their burdens of household chores.[26]

In spite of such help in "the spirit of class friendship," this meant, essentially, a double burden on women, with the costs of industrialization borne by Chinese working women greater than they were for Chinese men. As industry recovered in the mid-1960s and more childcare, nursery, and other facilities became available within factories, these questions receded somewhat—or at least media coverage of them did. However, it should be noted that even where factory facilities did exist, the burden for proper arrangement of home and children still remained totally a woman's responsibility.

Yang Guangzhi was a particularly good example of this. As a model for other women, Yang, a worker at the Chongjing Silk Factory, had successfully combined home and career. She had five children, worked hard and well with her co-workers, and had been promoted to secretary of the workshop's Party branch in 1955. In 1959 she was made manager of the factory and deputy secretary of the Party committee.[27]

Models like Yang, political activists, hard workers and leaders, existed for women to emulate. In other cases, like that of Liu Yinxiao, a worker in the Hong Xing Machine Plant, the double burden that women assumed was justified for more material reasons: to attain the "three items," a wristwatch, a bicycle, and a radio.[28] But whether a politically admirable model like Yang, or politically suspect like Liu, neither was reported as questioning women's double burden. And, as the socialist education campaign revealed, there was still an extremely low level of political consciousness among many workers in China and among women in particular. Many working-class women, victims of landlord and capitalist exploitation in pre-1949 China and now workers in regular industry, not surprisingly tended to view their work as a means to acquire family security and material possessions.

Many of these issues surfaced rather boldly in the wide-ranging 1963–64 discussions in *Women of China*. Under varous headings, such as "What Do Women Live For?" or "What is Happiness?" it was revealed that women who had participated in the pre-1949 revolution were now turning to small family life as a source of happiness; women who had been activists before marriage had succumbed to housekeeping burdens; educated young girls retired after giving birth; women still advocated finding a husband of high cadre status so they could live well; and many women simply saw a conflict (unresolvable at the time) between making revolution and doing household duties.

Though there were many themes in these discussions, two seemed to stand out. One was the theme of uncertainty about the primary responsibilities of women in the transition to socialism. Were they revolutionary activists, or were they dependents whose special province was proper arrangement of home and family matters so husbands and children could work? Many men seemed to reinforce the "dependent" role, praising women who helped their husbands become noted achievers.[29] The reemergence of this problem in the post-Mao period underscores the difficulties of resolving some of the contradictions. The two cases of Deng Yudang and Hua Fengdeng illustrate this theme. Deng joined the revolution in the 1940s, remained an activist, and was elected chairwoman of her county's Women's Federation. Yet, after marriage and two children, her work suffered. Given the seeming contradiction between work and family responsibilities, she asks confusedly, who should help her to do better work; is the responsibility only hers, or is it a male problem also? And what role should the Party play?[30] Hua, also a Women's Federation cadre, finds the seductive happiness of her family (two children) difficult to fight. She asks, "Is or isn't the warmth of the small family a woman cadre's greatest happiness?"[31]

The second theme discussed in the Women's Federation publications concerned a lack of political consciousness over the goals of socialism, goals which in many cases translated as simple material improvements on an individual basis. Why did women have such a lack of ideological consciousness? What in reality was the position of women in Chinese society? In what way was it a unique "female" position, and in what way was their consciousness a product of other, more general constraints and forces at work?

These problems were not the concern only of a tiny minority. By 1965–66 there is no doubt that women were highly "visible" in China's factories and government offices, both as workers and as administrators. In the 1965 National Peoples Congress nearly 18 percent of the deputies were women (compared to slightly over 12 percent in the pervious Congress).[32] Beijing had a female vice-mayor, Fan Jin, and 34 percent of the administrators in the city were women.[33] In Shanghai three hundred women served as factory directors or deputy directors and two-thirds of that city's medical workers, including doctors, were female.[34] In Beijing, 24 percent of college teachers, 44 percent of secondary teachers, and 62 percent of primary school teachers were women. In industry, in addition to dominating the textile industry, women could be found in significant numbers in other forms of light industry, chemicals, paper, and precision instruments. They were beginning to make inroads into the heavy industry sector as workers, technicians, and engineers.[35]

While female representation in leadership positions was still very poor, it was nevertheless clear that Chinese industrial, educational, and governmental institutions reflected a general social acceptance of female job participation, if not leadership ability. Traditional social attitudes notwithstanding, many women clearly viewed, and many men obviously accepted, female work outside the home as part of a legitimate female experience in revolutionary China. This does not preclude acceptance of traditional role definitions also, but it does suggest that many women, even while handling a "double burden," tended to view increased income or greater access to facilities that alleviated traditional chores as of central importance. This view tended to be reinforced by the educational and employment patterns of urban women.

The Chinese considered the educational system an important vehicle for the elimination of social inequalities based on status or remuneration, since the educational system was not only a training ground but also an integral part of the planned labor allocation system. Educational policy was therefore viewed as central in emerging debates about the nature of the transition to socialism. The pre–Cultural Revolution conflict over educational policy, whether to concentrate on a full-time formal system producing a small but highly trained technical elite or whether to promote an experimental system aimed at creating widespread educational opportunities for the broadest number of people and inculcating a socialist consciousness among the people, reflected the larger issue of how to build socialism in China.[36] The former approach is usually identified with the First Five-Year Plan and the latter with the Great Leap. The Great Leap type of educational policy did not die out completely in the post-Leap period. The continued implementation of these kinds of educational programs was taken over by production and service units. Work-study programs and in-plant technical courses for upgrading skills continued.[37] In some cases individual factories sponsored the advanced training of promising workers. Women, particularly in the textile industry, appeared to have been among the beneficiaries.[38]

Women formed a minority of those educated in formal, full-time schools. Yet this minority did make educational advances under the First Five-Year Plan, in the Great Leap period, and in the early 1960s that resulted in the increased numbers of women technicians, engineers, and designers that were staffing Chinese industry. As members of an educated elite, these women reflected the values and attitudes of their educational experience. Female senior middle-school graduates who were refused entry to the university and hence the opportunity to become specialists felt cheated. The ability to "receive more wages and endure less hardships"[39] should have been their reward as members of the intelligentsia. Obviously the eduational system created certain attitudes and values which female students shared with their male counterparts.

These educated women were only a minority of women workers, however. Most working-class women entered industry at the lowest levels. Lack of basic skills allowed them to do only the simplest jobs, and lack of skills was a primary factor in industry's refusal to employ female workers. A case in point was the Beijing Bus Company, whose refusal to hire women was partly because of the need to train them.[40] Low cultural and skill levels remained a problem for women workers. Given the fact that the majority of women workers tended to cluster at the less demanding jobs (in terms of skill) and hence the more poorly compensated ones, women probably formed a substantial portion of the workers designated temporary workers. Temporary workers lacked the job security and fringe benefits of regular workers, and there were significant wage differentials between the groups. Temporary workers contracted with individual enterprises when the permanent work force was too busy or too small. There can be little doubt that temporary/contract workers were not viewed or treated as the equals of regular industrial workers.[41]

Women therefore entered the industrial labor force as relatively high-level managerial and technical recruits and as relatively low-level ordinary workers. Both groups carried with them the values and attitudes assimilated through their particular backgrounds, educational and social, and these contrasting experiences and lifestyles became part of the political conflict that evolved within their organizations.

A closer look at the patterns of female employment in the urban work force on the eve of the Cultural Revolution reveals some interesting data. Although we lack information on individual factories and industrial enterprises, some tentative conclusions may be deduced from an examination of the data in Table 3.

Women workers were found in every enterprise listed in Table 3, but clearly female labor tends to cluster in certain sectors of the economy: textiles (60–90 percent of the work force); clothing (50–60 percent); shoes (33 percent); small instruments (50 percent); chemicals and drugs (20–50 percent); light durable goods (33–50 percent); and, in unique instances, in heavy industry also. What marks the 1960s as distinct from the pre-Leap period is that in addition to working in textiles and other light industries women made significant inroads both in the heavy industry sector and in the relatively new industries such as chemicals, drugs, and small instruments. Thus, without losing dominance in certain light industries, overall female representation in the modern industrial sector increased.

TABLE 3

Female Employment in Thirty-three Chinese Enterprises

Enterprise	Total employment	Percent of female employees	Number of female employees	Year established or reorganized
Wuhan Iron and Steel	35,000	10	3,500	1955
Shanghai Steel Mill No. 3	13,000	8	1,040	1914
Beijing Steel Wire	800	30	240	GLF

The Unfinished Liberation of Chinese Women

TABLE 3 (CONTINUED)

Female Employment in Thirty-three Chinese Enterprises

Enterprise	Total employment	Percent of female employees	Number of female employees	Year established or reorganized
Wuhan Heavy Machinery	7,000	21	1,470	1956
Shanghai Heavy Machine Tool	6,000	15	900	pre-1949
Beijing First Machine Tool	4,000	20	800	GLF
Hangzhou Machine Tool	1,000	12	120	pre-1949
Shanghai No. 3 Machine Tool	1,000	40	400	GLF
Shanghai No. 3 Forging and Pressing Machine Tool	405	15	61	1960
Wuxi Red Flag Machinery	300	22	66	GLF
Tianjin North Lake Instrument	165	50	83	GLF
Wuxi Diesel Engine	2,700	18	486	pre-1949
Wuhan Diesel Engine	992	40	397	GLF
Shanghai Truck	1,050	20	210	pre-1949
Suzhou Cement Products	680	12	82	1962
Wuhan Han Yang Paper	2,000	33	660	1956–57
Nanjing National Cement Fertilizer	10,000	25	2,500	GLF
Guangzhou Chemical Fertilizer	2,400	20	480	1963
Beijing Coke and Chemical	2,100	20	420	GLF
Beijing Pharmaceutical	3,000	50	1,500	1955
Shanghai Pharmaceutical No. 3	1,200	42	504	1953
Tianjin Watch	1,500	50	700	1957
Guangzhou Lan Yang Electrical Appliance	840	33	277	GLF
Shanghai Wei Ming Battery	563	45	253	1925
Shanghai No. 9 Song Xing Cotton Textile	6,000	70	4,200	pre-1949
Beijing Cotton Textile No. 3	5,000	70	3,500	1957
Shanghai Cotton Textile No. 19	4,800	70	3,360	pre-1949
Beijing Woolen Fabric	1,800	60	1,080	GLF
Tianjin Ren Yi Woolen Fabric	1,800	60	1,080	1950
Wuxi Silk Reeling No. 2	1,500	90	1,350	1949
Beijing Clothing	1,700	50	850	1952
Hangzhou Fu Chong Clothing	400	60	240	1954
Tianjin Shoe	1,000	33	330	pre-1949

Adapted from Barry Richmond, *Industrial Society in Communist China*, Table 9–1, "Employment and Personnel Data for Thirty-three Chinese Enterprises Surveyed," pp. 754–756. Richmond gives only the percentage of women workers. I have calculated the numbers involved and have added the last column noting the year production began or was reorganized. (GLF = Great Leap Forward.)

In the heavy industry sector women were hired in the older plants (Wuhan Iron and Steel, 10 percent, Shanghai Heavy Machine Tool, 15 percent; Wuxi Diesel Engine, 18 percent; and Shanghai Truck, 20 percent), but their numbers are markedly higher in those plants dating from the Great Leap Forward or later (Beijing Steel Wire, 30 percent; Shanghai No. 3 Machine Tool, 40 percent; Wuhan Diesel Engine, 40 percent). This suggests that management policies and traditions in some of the older heavy industry establishments might have discriminated against female labor. We know that the textile industry and other older plants had difficulty sustaining Great Leap reforms that contrasted sharply with pre-Leap management policies. However, the more egalitarian policies of the Great Leap and the general atmosphere of mass mobilization presented a greater likelihood that the newer plants would assimilate significant numbers of women. The influence of the Leap is also evidenced by Tianjin North Lake Instrument. Originally a housewives' street industry project dating from 1958, this successful undertaking, like others with similar origins, was incorporated into the regular state-operated industrial system.

Clearly important to the progress of women in industry was the general expansion of industrial production and the establishment of new industries. Particularly important were industries producing precision instruments, chemicals, and drugs. Many of the Leap experiments in small-scale industry were precisely in these areas, the women's participation in the pilot projects ensured their absorption into the larger projects that evolved. Thus economic development generally, geographical location, and development strategies associated with the Leap Forward appear as important variables in the growing and diverse nature of female labor in China.

The urban female labor force was, therefore, becoming fairly differentiated. Cleavages resulted from the nature of class formation as economic development proceeded and as different strategies were mixed together and left their impact on Chinese society. In the pre-Leap period the majority of working women were to be found in the traditional female-labor-oriented industries; the woman engineer, geologist, or factory director was a unique individual. By the 1960s, although female university graduates remained a significant minority, there were substantial numbers of women entering the labor force at several different levels. By the mid-1960s, women could be found in all industries, and several had risen to positions of authority. Both the educational background of these women and the social acceptability of female workers—a psychological climate created by the Great Leap—were responsible for these changes.

In addition to regular industry, women could be found working in neighborhood service centers and in street industry. Street industry, although suffering from material shortages in the early post-Leap period, did not die out. Although marginal projects were abandoned, many were from the beginning consolidated and reorganized with a view toward continuing operations.[42] Within those projects that continued operation, workers became more technically sophisticated as they experimented on their own.[43] Their production filled an important functional role. They tended to emphasize local consumer articles, allowing large-scale industry to concentrate on producer goods.[44] Thus, the municipal level in many areas emerged as an important administrative and decision-making level that could significantly alter employment opportunities for women.

While street industry afforded unskilled neighborhood women who were also burdened with home responsibilities the unique opportunity to work and in rare cases the opportunity to become skilled, these women in general had no status comparable to a regular member of the urban working class. They were working at a decided disadvantage, even when compared with those women who were temporary or contract workers. And the increasing numbers of a group of workers whose contributions to socialism, as important as it was, received scant attention during the mid-1960s, and whose remuneration was, in many instances, a fraction of the wage of regular industrial workers, pointed to a disturbing phenomenon. It was becoming increasingly clear that while overall production might be increasing, the particular kinds of jobs available to a large portion of the female population led to a more finely stratified female work force. Several patterns resulting from the evolution of policy and practices since 1949 were visible on the eve of the Cultural Revolution, whose rumblings could now be detected in all sectors of Chinese society.

The women who emerged as leaders—the highly trained specialists in industry, education, medicine, and the cultural media—were clearly a product of the educational system of the 1950s and early 1960s in which women were a significant and steady minority of the urban student population. Their emergence was a clear indication of the growing social acceptance of female professionals in society. This did not necessarily mean an end to discriminatory attitudes toward ordinary female workers, however. It simply meant that once women got into school, sex in and of itself seemed to be no major stumbling block to those women who were willing and fortunate enough to become part of the educated elite. It was also apparent, however, that in the educational system of both the First Five-Year Plan and the post-Leap period women remained a minority of students. In a system whose expansion was moderate this meant that the majority of women would, for the foreseeable future, have inferior chances to gain access to higher-level education (post–primary school) than would men. High-level professional and technical educational opportunities would remain very limited for both men and women, but on the whole, men were at an advantage. Outside of the technical elite, women would continue to fill primarily those jobs for which the mastery of skills was lowest. Many would remain housewives, a role reinforced by the confluence of family policy and a development strategy that largely precluded the extensive mobilization of female labor.

The increasingly diverse experiences of urban women suggest that the quest for equality (in the process of the creation of socialism) depended more on the particular strategies embodied in economic transformation, rather than on eliminating traditional discriminatory and superstitious attitudes. An ambiguous officially articulated family policy did imply the acceptance of certain traditional female roles and acted as a definite constraint. But it was becoming clearer that the specific employment and participatory opportunities made available by the overall development strategy, including educational policy, was in the longer run a potentially greater influence in creating real social and material equality. In China, the more radical mobilization-oriented policies aimed specifically at developing mass participation in all aspects of social life created an atmosphere and generated forces in which all kinds of inequality—including that of women— could be immediately and effectively challenged.

Rural Women

In the rural areas, the process of social transformation was quite uneven. Even while the entire economy, especially the agricultural sector, was in the grip of a severe economic crisis in 1961, which led to the abandonment of many of the Leap's policies and, with them, new roles for women, there was continued evidence of progress. As late as November 1961, the women of Jingxi Production Brigade, Jiu Bao Commune, Ruiyin Xian, demanded and received a more equitable system of allocating wagepoints. This was also true for the women of Zhujiao Chao Production Brigade of Wukan Commune, Lufeng Xian, in Guangdong.[45] In 1963, in Mazheng Xian, Hubei, eight thousand women—or one-third of the total—were rural functionaries.[46] While the overall trend may have been retrenchment, the legacy of the Leap in the post-1960 period was considerable and evident. Keeping in mind, however, the significant diversity that existed, certain overall trends with both positive and negative implications for rural women's struggle can nevertheless be discerned in this period.

With the slogan of "adjustment, consolidation, reinforcement, and improvement," the Chinese leadership began a period of restructuring the production and administrative units of the rural communes. In its most extreme forms, such restructuring became "contracting production to the household."[47] But the tendency to move away from collective production, evident in certain rural areas in 1960–61, was reversed after 1962 when greater emphasis was placed on the importance of a strong agricultural base in contributing to China's industrial and overall economic development. The socialist education campaign was the most central aspect of the mass movement launched to reinforce the collective economy and attitudes. But for women it was evident that old roles and attitudes were quite strong. The number of days that female agricultural laborers would be expected to work in the production teams or brigades per month in order to share in the unit's workpoint allocation was reduced because it was found that women who worked the required 27 days a month were unable to complete their household chores and tend to subsidiary production, both of which were crucial for rural life. Both of these tasks were regarded as female tasks. By 1962 full-time women workers were required to average 24 to 26 days a month, thus allowing more women time to complete their other tasks. The problem was defined as a conflict between a woman's individual interests and the larger collective's interests and not as a contradiction between the traditional and revolutionary roles of women. That the issue was viewed in this light indicated that the female role was still linked closely if not exclusively to the family in the minds of many. And the family still had an economically "rational" raison d'être.[48]

The contradictions that surfaced during the Great Leap Forward between traditional social practices and attitudes toward women on the one hand and the emergence of increasingly collectivized production on the other have already been described in chapter 3. These contradictions remained largely unresolved in the early 1960s. During the socialist education campaign the treatment of women as a commodity in exchange for personal profit was still embodied in institutions such as money marriages, dowries, and grand wedding feasts. These practices were strengthened by the resurgence of individual profiteering schemes and capitalist tendencies in agriculture. Women were used to cement relationships between potentially wealthy or politically powerful families and to accumulate large private plots and collections of animals. These practices and trends were criticized sharply for their negative impact on collective labor efforts, and it was on the collective economy that rural women depended if they were to get out of the home.

Female participation, limited as it was by burdensome domestic chores, nevertheless had begun to have an impact on rural production. In some places where women had become an important part of the labor force there was an attempt by the collective to meet some of their special needs. One brigade, for example, attempted to deal with the pregnancy of workers, who were clearly expected to return to the brigade after giving birth.

> Laying-in women were to be given days of leave with workpoints granted to them according to the average workpoints scored for the three months prior

to the expectancy date; these workpoints entitled them to the distribution of grain.[49]

The Chinese seemed aware of the significance that socialization of domestic labor would have for the liberation of women.[50] But there was also the memory of the opposition aroused by such expenditures of scarce resources during the Great Leap Forward. Thus, policies of the 1960s reflected not an attempt to collectivize the labor that women performed in the family, but an attempt to alleviate women's household burdens through increased production and the growth of family income. This would allow individual households to buy sewing machines or spinning wheels and other expensive labor-saving devices or products.

In reducing the burden of household chores, the development of sideline occupations and rural industry was important. Rural industry produced consumer goods which could relieve women of such burdensome duties as milling their own flour and processing their own oil. Increased income allowed peasants to buy certain ready-made products formerly produced by women at home. This policy had in fact begun during the latter stages of the Leap, and continued during the retrenchment period. It had the virtues of extending the collective benefits of development to the community at large while avoiding a direct assault on the traditional roles of women within family production that were still perceived as valuable and proper.

Rural industry also created a need for additional labor power without challenging traditional female roles or the relative positions of males and females in rural society. In fact, the local rural industries that began to develop were quite sensitive not to question frontally the traditional division of labor:

> Up to the present, as far as needlework and household work are concerned, women are still more capable than men. Rural young women should therefore take the initiative in developing this special skill. . . .[51]

But where female skills threatened to challenge the dominant role of male productive efforts, the issue quickly was transformed from an "economic" to a political concern:

> At first the workpoints from handicraft work was [*sic*] added to the workpoints from farm production for unified distribution. But some complained later because women workers were fast in handicraft work and they accumulated more workpoints from handicraft work than others from farming work.[52]

It would not be stretching things to imagine that the "some" who complained were most probably male peasants or families without daughters, although obviously not all male peasants were unhappy with increased family income that resulted from women's work in handicrafts.

While the Chinese avoided posing a conflict between progress for women and economic development, development policies in rural areas, especially in the socialist education campaign after 1963 when there was increased and increasingly collectivized production, kept the issue alive. Increased numbers of women had already joined the rural labor force and through handicrafts activity were making contributions to family income. Agricultural policy consistently emphasized the necessity to diversify crops, build water conservancy projects, develop the animal husbandry industry and, with it, the related food processing and fertilizer industries. All these policies demanded labor power, and the mobilization of female labor was one clear source.[53] By 1965 it was clear that in at least some areas large numbers of young girls were an integral segment of the rural labor force.[54]

While no hard statistics exist on the actual numbers of women who joined the rural labor force full-time, there are clear indications that women accounted for a significant portion of a general increase between 1961 and 1965.[55] As male workers were being assimilated by the slowly growing rural industrial sector, much of the new labor in agriculture was female. This female work force was engaged in the traditional low productive jobs and not in the prestigious modernizing sector. According to one report, women constituted 30 to 40 percent of the labor force of many production brigades by 1966.[56]

The work patterns of many women were such as to be compatible with their familial responsibilities. In addition, reduced requirements for labor days in field work reflected the importance placed on familial duties. Many of the other jobs performed by women—animal husbandry, the collection of manure, home-based handicraft production, afforestation, irrigation—allowed them to work out flexible work shifts and to remain near home. Even while working on collective plots, women maintained responsibility for home-centered activity:

> Women are hard workers: Do you see that the women down there have baskets beside them as they weed, but the men don't? That's because the women aren't only weeding, but are also collecting grass for the family's pig.[57]

The successful integration of familial and collective roles in this manner did not necessitate changing the prevailing social attitudes toward women, nor did it require treating women as economically equal to men. In other words, the experience of some rural women showed clearly that participation in certain kinds of recognized "social" production, while perhaps a first and absolutely necessary

contradict

step, was by itself not sufficient to challenge male dominance, no less establish female equality.

how

Thus, while the modified and reorganized commune system of the post-Leap may have contained the long-run potential for transforming female roles, in practice there were formidable restraints to female participation that it never challenged. The workpoint allocation system favored jobs men did; the definition of social production excluded services provided by women in the family, and there was a lack of collective services to alleviate these traditional female responsibilities. The absence of technological development made physical strength important, while reliance on individual home handicrafts to supplement the family income derived from collective production provided a reason to keep women close to if not in the home.

The reluctance of the Chinese leadership to oppose traditional social practices and attitudes affecting women (except where they threatened the collective economy or economic development) did not help matters. The inequalities embodied in the society were not effectively challenged or attacked in direct fashion, and thus the realities of inequality served to shape how women defined themselves. Poor or lower-middle peasant women, young, unmarried girls, and women who first began to work in the Great Leap Forward made up the backbone of the rural female labor force.[58] Their class backgrounds and over a decade of Communist rule should have predisposed them to favor increased collective production, and their very participation in production had set them apart from those who stayed at home. However, the inequalities embodied within the collective production system and the pervasive influence of traditional societal practices at times worked to reinforce apathy and selfishness.

Women were still victimized by a wage-point allocation system that remained substantially unchanged from the Great Leap. This was partly responsible for the lack of enthusiasm among women who did work, for no matter what their job in relation to men, they got a constant, and lower, number of wagepoints. "No matter whether the weeds are dense or thin," one woman noted, "workpoints are awarded just the same. You give me 7 1/2 points for weeding one mou, I just do work worth 7 1/2 workpoints."[59] And, as another woman stated without equivocation, "We're oppressed in workpoints—men each day record 10 points, 12 points; the most women get are 5 or 6. Thus, we aren't willing to come out to work."[60] Work was avoided where economically possible. "Why doesn't Chen Yingzu's wife go out to work?" one report asked. The answer: "Because she can rely on a 60% graded ration which together with part of the workpoints earned by her husband, enables her to get on without working."[61]

This inequality made many women reluctant to assume leadership posts in which they would be exposed to a community evaluation process that had already discriminated against them. As Yu Yuechui, a deputy team leader in Baoan, said, "If the work is well done, I gain nothing more personally; but if the work is not properly done, I have to take the blame."[62] There were similar cases from other areas.[63]

Women who did hold leadership positions were not immune from abusing power to escape from an often harsh life of manual labor, especially as political morale was lowered after the Great Leap. In one case the chief of the women's section of the Party in Baoan was criticized for always choosing the easiest jobs with the higher number of workpoints, and even claimed workpoints when she did not work.[64] Zhang Huiping, the chairwoman of the Women's Representatives, Shangshou Party Branch, seldom attended meetings and was careless in work.[65] Other women worked hard but did not like to work too close to the peasants. The Women's Federation realized that there was a need to develop women leaders, but without the adoption of a program that integrated the women's issue with development priorities and the commune organization and distribution prevailing in the countryside, there were poor results.

A more comprehensive approach began to emerge by 1964. The slogan "agriculture as the base" meant a concerted effort to mechanize agriculture through the development of rural industry. It also meant increased emphasis on developing the potential of the brigade and community levels in the administration and organization of production. At the same time the development of collective as well as family "sideline" occupations, especially animal husbandry, was encouraged as a means to raise production and peasant income.[66]

The tradeoffs envisioned by the three-pronged effort of mechanization, rural industry, and increased collectivization were substantial. Mechanization would free some of the labor force for rural industry and contribute to greater production. Rural industry, while mainly serving agriculture, would also produce consumer products for the rural areas, thus helping to close the gap between urban and rural areas in living standards. The use of the more advanced forms of collective organization would cultivate socialist attitudes and patterns of behavior in the process of increasing and diversifying production and guaranteeing adequate markets and supply sources for the evolving local industrial enterprises. Such, at any rate, was the announced goal, and when, during and after the Cultural Revolution, those policies began to be implemented on a more far-reaching and persistent basis, the overall impact on rural women would indeed be enormous.

But until then, the most immediate impact of the socialist education campaign was in the attempt to increase the proportion of production under collective organization. The 1961 policy of "*san zi yi bao*" (the extension of free markets, extension of private plots, promotion of small enterprises on a profitability basis, and fixing output quotas on an individual household basis) was soundly criticized for encouraging the growth of private vegetable plots and the raising of domestic animals under individual family production. All these things benefited those who had owned the better land before collectivization and who had enjoyed the benefits of managing their own relatively prosperous undertakings. There was, therefore, renewed emphasis on the importance of class struggle in the transition to socialism,[67] and simultaneously an attempt to diversify and increase subsidiary production and, most significantly for women, to add some animal husbandry enterprises to the collective economy, using female labor in this new collective subsidiary activity. This did not challenge the traditional division of labor or demand new skill acquisition, but it did contain at least the potential for female participation in the technical revolution. Workpoints were to be allocated for this job also, whereas before, this labor under individual households was not compensated. Moreover, acquisition of modern skills by women would also increase their productive contributions to the family.

The commune system made the transfer of technology to the countryside both efficient and rational.[68] The thrust of agricultural policies since the Tenth Plenum of the Eighth Central Committee (1962) had emphasized the technical transformation of the countryside because of the inability of simple additions of more labor to production to increase yields, as well as because of opposition to certain of the social experiments of the Great Leap Forward. The extension of the socialist education campaign into the countryside meant an uneasy coexistence of two kinds of policies: one emphasized the technical component as the key variable; the other, while recognizing the value of developing technology, insisted on the importance of political consciousness.

Women, significantly, profited from both kinds of policy in the short run. As animal husbandry became increasingly a matter of collective concern, efforts to increase production through the application of scientific techniques meant that more women would attend agricultural institutes. Women were, in fact, specifically designated to attend local technical institutes. In some cases it appears that the Party, at an early stage (1963), played a key role in encouraging the emergence of the female agricultural technician as a new role for women in the rural areas.[69] By 1965 the policy of recruiting women specifically for participation in the technical revolution had received support from national leaders.

> At present, women still have not caught up with men in the primary techniques of labor. In the future, intellectual effort must be made in the direction of getting women to study agricultural techniques, and in becoming

adept at all kinds of techniques. . . . Not so long ago, the Yinhe (Hua Xian, Guangdong) Brigade dispatched some of its members to enroll in pre-science courses at a college of agriculture. Half of the number sent there are young women, this is a good stand.[70]

This policy portended significant change for women in rural areas. Social attitudes based on the customs of exogamous marriage began to change as the community began to see the benefits of educating women who would contribute to collective material improvement. Yet there were still powerful traditions, such as the family's hesitation to "weed another man's garden" (invest in women who tended to move away after marriage). Since decisions to include women as students were made at the brigade or commune level, it is clear that collectivization weakened a powerful source of traditional authority, the family, and created alternatives for women that simply did not exist under familial production.

The impact of policies aimed at mechanization and developing rural industry was also potentially great. Mechanization tended to lessen the emphasis on physical strength as a means of labor productivity, thus challenging the traditional division of labor. Additionally, rural industry alleviated household burdens to some degree, hence freeing more women for social production. Flour mills, for example, a widespread early industrial project, relieved women of the onerous and time-consuming task of grinding and milling their own flour at home.

The absorption of women into rural industry presented more problems, however, than the mechanization of agriculture. The use of a female labor force was, and still is, closely related to the particular projects undertaken, the availability of literate or skilled women, and a psychological willingness to use female labor in that manner. The impact of this kind of participation goes byond the question of worker status, for it also offers young women the opportunity to effectively challenge traditional familial authority in marriage. Jobs that carry women beyond the perimeters of the village increase the chances for meeting members of the opposite sex and developing relationships that are beyond the control of the family. These kinds of contact are necessary to give young people an alternative to the traditional method of arranging marriage. All of these developments put long-term but powerful pressures on traditional oppressive social practices regarding women.

Two other policies which had a potential for increasing the participation of women in economic production and political and community affairs also emerged in this period: the absorption of women in growing numbers into the militia,[71] and the *"xia-xiang"* policy of sending educated youth to the countryside. Both policies were related to the Great Leap and emerged in the increased political and economic mobilization that marked the prelude to the Cultural Revolution.

Their significance is more clearly discernible in the post–Cultural Revolution period where they began to have an impact on rural women's participation.

Skill acquisition and hence the availability of educational facilities were and still are of great importance to rural women. As the socialist education campaign developed, it became obvious that there were inadequate educational opportunities in the rural areas, and that the system that did exist was not closely enough related to the priorities and practicalities of national development. While facilities in urban areas were not adequate either, this problem was perceived as an even more fundamental obstacle to rural development. Even in those facilities available in the countryside there were few women students. The necessity for peasant girls to help out in the home and care for siblings made full-time education during the day an impossibility.

The socialist education campaign's emphasis on educational experimentation led to the reassertion of part-time study, leisure-time classes, in-plant technical courses, neighborhood study groups, and other such activities characteristic of the Great Leap Forward. Female access to literacy and skill development was considered an important reason for this change in educational policy.[72] Basic literacy increased the chances for rural women to exploit new job opportunities opened by the increased and diversified production of the middle 1960s. The creation of new facilities flexibly organized not to interfere with ongoing traditional obligations which could not be immediately set aside increased the possibility that education would be available to many more women than had been the case under the kind of system that was characteristic of full-time village schools with a formal academic routine.

The Daqing and Dazhai Models in Industry and Agriculture

During the socialist education campaign the emergence of Daqing and Dazhai as national models for emulation indicated that the woman question was particularly relevant in what was now becoming a heated political and ideological climate. In the campaigns aimed at women these very different models of female participation exemplified the basically uneven levels of economic development and the different solutions arrived at in different geographical and productive sectors.

Daqing's self-reliance, the organization of its work force, and its high political consciousness channeled into solving production problems made it a model for industrial development. At the very beginning the work force at Daqing was overwhelmingly male, with workers' wives usually playing the traditional housewife roles. The desire to involve dependents of workers—mainly wives—was part of the larger national effort to mobilize female labor, develop locally self-sufficient communities, and reduce the pressures on male workers to "strive only for the family." A national campaign for raising the ideological consciousness of workers' dependents began to show success by 1965.[73] However, the integration of ideology and production meant different things to men than to women. Unlike the contributions of their vanguard proletarian husbands, the female contribution was to be in agriculture, in growing food and raising domestic animals.[74] The quest for local self-sufficiency and the desire to erase the differences between urban and rural life prompted the development of food production at Daqing. But this desire to integrate agriculture and industry did raise a question about a new division of labor. If sufficient numbers of women were also able to become part of Daqing's industrial labor force, and if men were involved in farm production, then the Daqing model would not be as ambiguous as it appeared for determining the future of male-female equality.

If the Daqing model remained somewhat ambiguous for women, the agricultural model, Dazhai, was less so. The Dazhai Brigade, in a poor, rural part of Shanxi Province, was particularly important for women because women assumed very nontraditional roles and became a significant part of the work force as Dazhai went about solving its development problems.[75] In the context of self-reliance, early in 1963 the Dazhai Iron Girls' Brigade was formed. These young female "shock workers" (of the twenty-three members the oldest was 20 and the youngest was 14), under the leadership of an experienced female activist, Song Liying, undertook some of the most difficult tasks in the brigade's program for expanding production.[76]

Dazhai was unique in other ways that benefited women. The Xiyang xian, Shanxi, area had a long tradition of Communist Party influence in the pre-1949 period, and many of Dazhai's members actively participated in the pre-49 struggles. Song Liying, a Party secretary, had in the early 1960s served as deputy Party secretary under Chen Yongguei and was head of the local women's federation. Song emerged as a model for women because of her participation in the pre-49 period, in the land reform movement, and as an active field worker and a protégée of the Party. Under her guidance the Women's Federation played an important role in mobilizing Dazhai women for labor participation. While many other areas in China were relying on young girls to form the backbone of the rural women's labor force, Dazhai managed to mobilize both older women and the young girls. The importance of women as a political and productive force in Dazhai was related to the "Dazhai workstyle," with its heavy reliance and participation in political and ideological study to enhance the women's own desire for change.[77] The Dazhai model has continued to play an important part in the political conflicts of the post–Cultural Revolution period, and the emergence of women in positions of political leadership in Dazhai might very well be part of the controversy surrounding the Dazhai model.

In contrast to the diverse nature of women's experience in urban areas during this period, the socialist education campaign in the rural areas created at least an ideological atmosphere in which the goals of women's emancipation and equality again assumed the prominence they had attained during the Leap. In this the socialist education campaign for rural women was clearly in the tradition of the 1943 and 1948 women's work directives and the Great Leap Forward. Women were to participate in production, but that participation also contained the potential for emancipation as well as being crucial to increasing rural productivity. Moreover, the growth of the rural female labor force and the willingness of the Party to allow the conflicts between women and traditional values and institutions to come to the surface were the basis for an even more direct confrontation with the woman question after the Cultural Revolution.

Conclusion

The period between the Great Leap Forward and the Cultural Revolution revealed more clearly than ever the possibilities and limitations that economic development would have on the traditional roles of women. It also revealed the close relationship between the women's revolution and socialist revolution. As the experience of Chinese women in the cities illustrated so clearly, progress resulting from economic development generally, whether from the First Five-Year Plan or Soviet model or from the Great Leap model, created opportunities in which some women could overcome both traditional prejudices and institutional impediments. Yet, it was also clear that unless policies were designed specifically to create participatory opportunities for the most backward, un-skilled, and oppressed segments of the population, a category to which the overwhelming majority of women belonged, then the appearance of individual women in political, economic, and social decision-making positions would only be tokenism.

In China, the more radical policies aimed specifically at developing mass participation and mobilization in all aspects of social life created a more favorable atmosphere and generated forces in which all kinds of inequality—including that of women—could be effectively challenged. Thus, those policies associated with both the Great Leap Forward and the socialist education campaign appeared potentially capable of integrating the masses of women into the labor force in the process of socialist construction.

The experience of Chinese women in this period also yielded some interesting theoretical insights. Whereas Marxist theory has always viewed sex oppression as separate from but clearly a result of class oppression, and thus socialism as the answer to the woman question, Marxists in general have never explored either the precise nature of the relationship between sex and class or had very much to say about priorities in the process by which sexual exploitation and oppression are eliminated at any given time. The dominant Marxist revolutionaries have usually seen women's liberation as a result of socialism, not as part of the process of building it. The particular experience of Chinese women under the contradictory policies and conflicting forces present in the 1960s sheds some light on this important question. As we saw, the urban female labor force became fairly differentiated, and the cleavages that appeared in the female population were clearly the result of class formation resulting from the economic development strategy. Some women became part of a technocratic elite and others, the vast majority, became part of the mass labor force or remained at home. This suggests that the struggle against sexual discrimination could not become a substitute for class struggle, but rather had to take place alongside it: for clearly those policies which benefited a sector of the urban female population did not have the same effects for rural women or for many urban working-class women. The Chinese experience shows that the relationship between sex and class was not always clear, nor were the interests of working-class men and women always synchronized at any given time. The struggle for female liberation, therefore, would have to pay very close attention to ideological factors as well as socioeconomic ones; but clearly the notion of sexual struggle when divorced from a clear conception of class interest did not necessarily imply liberation or equality for the overwhelming majority of women.

· 5 ·

Women in the Cultural Revolution

On August 8, 1966, the Eleventh Plenum of the Central Committee of the Chinese Communist Party adopted the "Decision of the Central Committee of the Chinese Communist Party Concerning the Great Proletarian Cultural Revolution," beginning one of the greatest political and social upheavals of modern history.[1] The close of the Ninth Party Congress on April 23, 1969, marked the end of the extraordinary activism of the movement. The Cultural Revolution, like the Great Leap, resulted in rapid social change and was accompanied by intense ideological debate. These debates ultimately concerned the relationship between the development of the forces of production and the consequent transformation of the social relations of production. As a political and social movement, the Cultural Revolution was based on Mao's perception that social change was more a result of class struggle than of impersonal industrial expansion and technological innovation.[2] This relationship is illustrated by the evolution of woman's place in Chinese society. The relative lack of sexual equality, particularly in the rural areas, stood in contrast to the increasing role of women in production generally, especially since the mobilization-for-labor campaigns that marked the Great Leap and, to a lesser degree, the Socialist Education Campaign.

The Cultural Revolution was an open, often chaotic and at times violent struggle over those values, attitudes, and patterns of behavior that had emerged from very different policies for socialist development, and which had become embodied as the contradictions of Chinese social life. Clarity of debate was often marred by the intensity of the power struggle which influenced and shaped the issues under discussion. For Mao and his followers, the Cultural Revolution was an attempt to create conditions favorable for the kind of social change they considered necessary. They did this by raising the crucial issues of politics and "modernization": what were the origins of inequality between town and countryside, between mental and manual labor, between worker and peasant; how did the general authority relationships between leaders and masses, the educational system, and the family perpetuate inequality and class oppression? Although the special problems of women remained peripheral to the debates of the Cultural Revolution, the more general issues raised did ultimately and logically lead to a consideration of the woman question in the early 1970s.

While discrimination, inequality, and tokenism in leading political and administrative positions continued to characterize the industrial system generally, many women had been assimilated and socialized as workers. The momentum of this process differed from factory to factory and office to office. A similar process was just beginning in the countryside. Rural mechanization and industrialization, the development of rural medical facilities, the increasing availability of educational opportunities, the growth of collective production in relation to family-centered production, and the sending of youth to the rural areas were of tremendous import to Chinese women in determining the context in which the struggle for emancipation and equality would be joined.

Specific feminist demands were notably absent from the Cultural Revolution. "Equal pay for equal work" or a call to have more women in leadership positions was not the substance of most of the struggles that dominated the period. Yet the Cultural Revolution's broad attack on all forms of inequality and privilege legitimized a more direct concern with the woman question. During the "criticize Lin Piao and Confucius"[3] campaign that followed the Cultural Revolution, unprecedented national attention focused on precisely this issue. In very clear ways the campaign both acknowledged the role of women in the Cultural Revolution and recognized the relationship between the woman question and certain economic development policies. It is therefore important to analyze how women participated in the Cultural Revolution, how traditional discrimination constrained their role, and how political alliances were formed that paved the way for further transformations in the position of women in Chinese society.

The Women's Federation in the Cultural Revolution

Cultural Revolution activism was most often focused on productive units (factories, offices, educational institutions) and, to a much lesser extent, on residential areas. Women participated in the political and ideological movements as workers, administrative cadres, teachers, students, or housewives, thus demonstrating the increasing integration and assimilation of women at all levels of Chinese society. Except in the small number of sex-segregated institutions, female activists emerged from the ranks of workers, students, and cadres. But there was no "women's movement" to speak of during the Cultural Revolution. The only mass organization that could speak for women as women was the Women's Federation, and it shared the fate of most mass organizations during the Cultural

Revolution. By early 1967 it was defunct,[4] a victim of a political struggle initiated to purge it of "revisionist elements." This was consistent with the goals of the larger political movement that was rapidly unfolding and gaining momentum. Dong Bian, editor of *Women of China,* the Federation's publication, was charged with abusing the power and authority entrusted to her and attempting to use the magazine to promote among women values and attitudes inimical to socialism. Thus, for most of 1966 *Women of China* printed scathing denunciations of the "Dong Bian faction" and laudatory accounts of Red Guard activities and Mao's works.[5] The lack of really substantive discussions of the "poisonous weeds of the Dong Bian faction," plus the rather quick though ultimately temporary demise of the Women's Federation in the Cultural Revolution, only underlines the Federation's essential irrelevance to the dynamic realities of politics during the Cultural Revolution.

The growing responsibility of workplaces and schools for mobilizing female participation had tended to lessen the viability of women's associations, especially in urban areas. The inability to represent adequately the increasingly differentiated needs of urban Chinese women and the organizational and political ties between the CCP and the Women's Federation had made the Federation essentially a faithful reflector of Party policy.[6] Thus it was the politics of intra-Party conflict that dominated the scene, and not the particular concerns of the Federation, when it came to the woman question. The theoretical position of both the Federation and the Party had been consistent in advocating women's emancipation through participation in socially productive labor. However, actual policies did not always support increased female participation in labor outside the traditional familial and household roles.

After an initial period of radical social change in the Chinese countryside in the 1950s, the Party retreated from its emphasis on social transformation and concentrated on economic construction within a new but yet far from totally transformed social order. The economic development strategy of the First Five-Year Plan combined with the conservative political tactics implied by the United Front created a situation in which the traditional housewife and mother roles were given renewed legitimacy in post-1949 China. Before the Great Leap dramatically reversed this situation, the Women's Federation found itself in the unenviable position of persuading women that work outside the home was not the only way in which to contribute to the construction of socialism. The priority given to women's domestic role in an overall economic context of high male unemployment was reflected by the women's media. Indeed, just prior to the Leap, women were encouraged to retire from the labor market when household burdens conflicted with holding a job.[7]

However, it was not only a question of bending ideological principles to conform to socioeconomic realities. Even in periods of accelerated social change like the Great Leap, when the participation of women was considered crucial to economic development strategy, the Women's Federation was not necessarily in the forefront of changes, at least in urban China. While articles in *Women of China* urged women to participate in the Leap, organizationally the urban federations did not appear very active. Even the development of street industry appeared less at the urging of federation chapters than because of the mobilization efforts of the Party and local neighborhood and residents' committees. The entry of women into regular industry was a result of the general economic expansion, the policy of "substituting women for men," and the educational advances of women that made them employable. The Federation's role in changing female participation in urban employment does not seem to have been terribly significant.

By contrast, local women's federations in rural areas were significant. They were responsible for mobilizing women to join production and for supporting women's rights. This institutional support, an important phenomenon noted earlier in the land reform and Marriage Law campaigns, was a significant element in rural women's progress in the Leap and remains so today. Rural women cadres act as liaison between the masses of women and local Party leaders at commune, brigade, and team levels. Deputy leaders are most often women responsible for mobilizing women for work and maintaining their enthusiasm by protecting their interests.

The economic needs of the countryside, where for most of the 1950s and 1960s a labor shortage was perceived, accounted for the rather consistent effort to involve women in production. And because mobilization for labor was, and still is, a functionally useful role in a still largely traditional countryside where many women have yet to join the labor force, women's associations have a relevancy that does not exist in the cities. Additionally, the organizational structure of local women's groups parallels the administrative organization of the commune, and the proximity of residence to place of work makes it easier to mobilize women who might be closely attached to the home. These factors take on greater significance in the allocation of labor in rural areas, a function fulfilled by the educational system in urban areas.

As important as the Women's Federation was in rural areas, its role too, like its less important urban counterpart, was shaped and limited by Party policy. The Federation did not take up theoretical issues on its own even when, as during the Leap, institutional developments provided a clear framework within which to question the traditional sexual division of labor. Thus, the issues that struck at the roots of sexual inequality—the role of domestic labor, familial roles, and the nature of the family—were not discussed in a direct theoretical way. Instead, the women's movement evolved and women's role in China was discussed as a result of issues raised in the course of China's overall development strategy and shaped by the political realities of Party power and not as a result of issues raised by an autonomous Women's Federation openly basing itself on an assumption that there were female generic interests. By the time the Cultural Revolution was well underway, *Women of China* had ceased publication and the Women's Federation was in limbo. Yet this did not mean that women or the woman question played no part in Cultural Revolution politics.

Female Worker Participation in the Cultural Revolution

It is perhaps indicative that the first rebel to emerge in the Cultural Revolution was Nie Yuanzi, a young female philosophy instructor at Beijing University and a Party leader.[8] Her actions and criticisms against the conservative elements within the university administration were representative of the thousands of young women students whose voices would join hers in the struggles and debates of the Cultural Revolution. That women did participate in the Red Guard movement in large numbers is clear both from newsreel pictures from China and from accounts of Westerners who were in China at the time.[9] It is, however, more difficult to ascertain what specific input the female Red Guards had and to what extent their input differed from that of their male counterparts. Most Red Guard publications appeared as collective efforts under group auspices, thus making it impossible to identify the individual authors. It is clear, though, that to be a rebel student or intellectual was a legitimate role for women within the urban educational system.

Significant developments regarding women occurred within the urban industrial system as well. In the textile industry the female component of the labor force was (and is) particularly large, and it had a long history of development in various parts of China. Textile production was, therefore, an industry where the female labor force was mixed along generational and geographical lines, and therefore seems a particularly useful place to examine the role of urban working-class women in the Cultural Revolution.

The central role of textile production and other forms of light industry in early Chinese industrialization created unprecedented opportunities for women and an important historical legacy. Factory production, beginning in the late nineteenth century, provided women with a rare opportunity to earn wages and achieve some degree of economic independence. The transformation of traditional skills under this new mode of production could modify the traditionally low social status of women.[10] Chinese industry, in fact, had a high proportion of women in the labor force until the post-1949 emphasis on heavy industry. Women continued to work in light industry, but the growth and diversification of the modern sector lessened the role of the traditional female-labor-oriented industries. Textiles and other light industry remained an important component of industrial production, however, and essentially the domain of female labor even though more males entered this sector also.

Women in the Chinese textile industry had a long history of collective action, both in large urban-based factories and in the rural base areas under Communist control. In the urban factories the exploitative and oppressive as well as sexually discriminatory circumstances under which women worked, combined with the convulsive and revolutionary situation in China's cities (circa 1920), led to the organization of a militant labor movement and numerous strikes in which women played a large role. In the rural bases, large numbers of women belonged to cooperatives engaged in textile production. Even those who worked at home were often part of a group effort organized at the village level.

But if a history of collective action characterized the female labor force in China's widely disparate textile production, other factors tended to create different experiences. For the textile industry and the women workers within it, as well as for the rest of the Chinese economy, the dual legacies of capitalist industrialization and the Yanan model of indigenous and foreign management transcended the political watermark of liberation in 1949. Since these approaches to industrial management and organization have been fundamental to the development debates in China, especially since the Great Leap Forward,[11] they naturally had an impact on women workers during the Cultural Revolution.

The initial phases of the Cultural Revolution were characterized by intense ideological debates in the press and by the famous Red Guard student movement.[12] The greater involvement of the industrial sector began with the publication of the "Sixteen Points Directive" in August 1966. The directive had the effect of moving the debate from strictly ideological issues to challenging the organization and authority of specific leadership organs, including the Communist Party itself. This led to the establishment of Cultural Revolution groups within individual factories and plants, creating an institutional vehicle through which the struggles and debates of the mass campaign could be conducted. These groups, in turn, led to the development of factions among the workers.[13] By December 1966, the *People's Daily* officially supported the Great Proletarian Cultural Revolution in the industrial sector.[14] An editorial acknowledged the widespread political and factional activism that pervaded many Chinese factories. From the struggles and debates of the textile industry, resulting in large part from worker grievances, certain issues came to the fore in factory after factory.

A Look at the Textile Industry

The following discussion, based on a careful reading of the Chinese press from August 1966 to the Ninth Party Congress in April 1969, is not meant to constitute a definitive study of the textile industry during the Great Proletarian Cultural Revolution, but it does provide some insights into female participation in the Cultural Revolution, and the influence of institutional innovations during this time on women's progress toward equality. By focusing on substantive issues in local conflicts, we may determine the degree to which women's issues regarding discriminatory attitudes and institutional impediments to equal treatment existed and how these issues were debated within this female-labor-dominted industry. [15]

The major issues in dispute appear to have been the wage system, including the use of material incentives and the piece-rate system; the cumbersome rules and regulations that controlled the workers; control over technical innovation; the participation of workers in decision making, and that of cadres in production; and the hierarchical, bureaucratic organization within the factory. Also important were problems associated with reorganizing production to increase output while at the same time creating a high level of political consciousness regarding the necessity to meet quality requirements. But not all of these issues were debated in every factory.

The volatile issue of material incentives, specifically the piece-rate system and bonuses, appeared in many mills but with greater frequency in those mills established before 1949. [16] This suggests that older workers who were in the mill before 1949 either were accustomed to individual material incentives and were opposed by younger more politically radical workers, or they opposed these incentives because they recognized bonuses and piece wages as management's way to increase work intensity and divide the labor force. Older workers were quick to equate the wage system with forms of exploitation associated with the old system. [17] The experience of Liu Xianglian, a spinner at Cotton Mill No. 12 is instructive. She was recruited from her village at the age of twelve and vividly recalled "the twelve hours of hard labor daily, the mouldy 'company meals,' the damp and filthy living quarters in the mill infested with bedbugs and mosquitoes," as well as the harsh discipline of the mill's management. [18]

It was this kind of association that seemed to lie at the heart of the violent denunciations of policies called "capitalist" and associated with Liu Shaoqi. [19] Workers who were quoted in the press clearly feared the manipulative and exploitative potential of these wage systems. [20] Even before the Cultural Revolution there was worker opposition to the resurgence of piece-rate systems, but it does not appear to have taken a collective form. For example, in the post-Leap period

Liu Hanying, a loom operator in Shanghai's No. 2 Cotton Mill, carried on a long-standing battle with the mill's management, refusing to use her bonuses for herself.[21] The situation in another mill was described as follows:

> In the past we thought of each other as class sisters. We used to be concerned about each other and help each other. Sometimes we'd get to work ahead of time just to help our sisters on the shift before us finish their job. We kept a close watch on quality, and anyone who put out a below-standard bolt of cloth felt worse than if she'd lost something she treasured. . . . But after the partial piece-rate system was introduced, we spent all day worrying that we might be fined. Many became concerned only about their own interests and our former relationship of intimate class kinship was ruined.[22]

The large number of mills in which bonuses and piece-wage incentives were issues and the intensity of the conflict suggest that there was no consensus of opposition to the prevailing wage system. Moreover, most female workers who spoke out against piece-rates and material incentives appeared to be older workers, like Liu Xianglian, who had vivid memories of pre-1949 conditions and who realized how piece wages and bonuses could be used to manipulate and to exploit workers. This suggests that at least some women workers were motivated by the possibility of greater short-term economic remuneration and less concerned with the political consequences of such a system. The successful elimination of individual incentives and the development of group-oriented incentive systems that emerged from the Cultural Revolution would clearly have to counter this form of opposition.[23]

Related to the wage system as a focus of worker grievance was the control of certain discretionary funds by management. The political utility of these funds was clearly demonstrated when management cadres in several mills used bonus payments to bribe workers to leave their production posts during the "January storm" (1967). It was during this period that political participation by factory workers, administrative personnel, and urban residents in the debates of the Cultural Revolution increased dramatically. It was common to fund travels by workers to "exchange experiences" and to support workers' spring holiday leaves, particularly in Shanghai where both production and exports were affected.[24] In one case management went so far as to organize workers' dependents to demand economic subsidies from the factory.[25] This form of bribery was frequent in the big city mills, such as those in Shanghai, but instances of management use of monetary bribes to buy off worker opposition appeared even in remote Tibet (Tibet Woolen Textile Mill).[26] Management's ability to manipulate the labor force through control over money was probably at least as successful among female workers as among their male counterparts, and might have been even more successful. For one thing, women were probably more likely to accede to the "suggestions" of those in authority than to challenge them. Those workers who refused subsidies seemed to be motivated by a high political consciousness and by a strong sense of security in personal capabilities, characteristics only beginning to emerge among the masses of Chinese women.

If some workers were concerned about the effects that piece wages had on interpersonal relations and resented managerial manipulation of the factory's wage fund, still others were concerned about the problem of contract labor. A large pool of irregularly employed labor which lacked the social benefits of permanent jobs constituted a wage and employment threat to the salaried worker. Clearly, part of the opposition to the piece-rate system lay in the possibility of reducing large numbers of workers on regular salary to substantially the same insecure wage situation as that experienced by contract workers.[27] And one goal of the Third Five-Year Plan was to restrict the numbers of new regular workers, thus severely affecting the new graduates of the 1960s, many of whom were women.

The contract labor system was justified essentially in economic terms, as it drastically reduced the social overhead costs of labor and gave management added flexibility in hiring. An undetermined segment of this group of workers were women whose household duties and lack of skills made them difficult to employ on a regular basis. But clearly, contract laborers acted not on the basis of sexual identification but largely on the basis of an economic interest group.

Because contract workers lacked an institutional base or any considerable support within the Party, the Cultural Revolution really did nothing to solve their plight.[28] Organized into rebel groups and stressing the inequities of the contract labor system, they pressed their case and were even received by the Cultural Revolution Group in Beijing. However, due to the inability of the Chinese leadership to resolve all the inequities of the past, and because the issue threatened to split the workers into warring groups, contract workers were treated rather harshly: they were one of the few mass organizations declared counterrevolutionary and outlawed.[29] Their short-lived, but vocal, efforts gave an added urgency to workers' insistence on secure wage systems, while dramatically illustrating the harsh economic inequalities borne by some groups in the process of economic development. Not until the early 1970s is there any indication of official efforts to ameliorate the situation of temporary and contract workers.[30]

The issue of political control in production was raised repeatedly by the workers. Common grievances concerned the detailed rules and regulations that prevailed in the mills, the reliance on technical experts divorced from the actual process of production, the lack of cadre participation in labor, the equally small role of workers in production decisions, and the negative effect of top-heavy administration on production.[31]

Resentment on these issues often ran high. In some mills, rule books exceeded one hundred pages and worker familiarity with their petty provisions was often tested verbally by management.[32] Failure to answer correctly often meant docked wages. Other mills kept watch on workers' productivity by means of daily production records.[33] The opposition to regulations in the textile industry was fairly widespread, but particularly so in the older, east coast urban factories where the related issues of technical control, labor-management relations, and the division of labor appear to have dominated internal factory debates.[34]

The debates that took place in the factories were often quite sophisticated. The system of rules was perceived as a means to uphold the "class" privileges of the technicians and the managers, whose political use of them effectively stifled worker initiative and blocked worker access to those skills that would threaten management's position. In the process the rules also denied the validity of worker expertise and experience. The frequent and obvious result on production was negative.

Control over technical innovation was another aspect of this issue. Commitment to an enlarged scope of worker participation in all aspects of production implied certain changes. Factories would have to institute their own technical education courses or assume the responsibility of sending workers to outside educational institutes. However, the role of experienced workers would assume greater importance.

For women, these kinds of reforms were particularly important. Veteran workers like Li Xiaomei and Liu Xianglian at Cotton Mill No. 12 in Shanghai,[35] whose socioeconomic backgrounds ruled out the possibility of schooling before 1949, had years of service in the cotton mill. They had attained a level of expertise and were now recognized for their contributions. They were consulted by new management-worker teams which valued their on-the-job experience. Moreover, as a result of worker participation in technical innovation, individual plants had a much larger pool of talent upon which to draw.

Because women had never achieved numerical parity with men in formal educational institutions, the creation of in-plant training courses had a significant impact on increasing opportunities for women to gain industrial skills. A number of the new revolutionary committees officially encouraged worker innovations (Yinchuan Woolen Textile Mill, Shenxi "Red Star" Textile Mill, Guangzhou Hemp Textile Mill), set up committees, or made other formal and informal arrangements to give workers a chance to participate in innovations (Beijing General Knitwear, Beijing State No. 2 Cotton Mill, Wuxi Printing and Dyeing Mill).

The reforms encouraging worker participation indicate the political and economic importance accorded worker grievances in the textile industry and reflects the growing political consciousness of women workers.

The increased level of worker participation in factory decision making implied a challenge to the technical experts and the bureaucratic staffs often divorced from any productive function. The national movement for "better troops and simpler administration" reinforced efforts within individual plants to reduce the numbers of personnel not involved in production by limiting the proliferation of administrative offices. The initial efforts in the Cultural Revolution in this regard were decidedly radical. Reductions in office staff and administrative cadres ranged as high as 70 percent in the Shanxi "Red Star" Textile Mill, 87 percent at the Beijing General Knitwear, and even 90 percent in the Zhejiang Hemp Textile Mill.[36] Most of these people were reassigned to production units. Their greater involvement in the process of organizational and managerial reform (criticism-struggle-transformation) appears to have been facilitated by this physical transfer to the production front.[37] This *"xia xiang"* of plant-level leadership was an important factor in mobilizing women workers, especially to criticize the leadership. Coming from a cultural context in which female passivity was encouraged, and given the prevalence of male leadership even in the traditional female industries, women hesitated before criticizing management.[38] However, once these officials began performing production duties and many began actively to seek out workers' opinions and suggestions, the opportunity for an exchange between women workers and a largely male leadership increased. Thus, the leadership workstyle of any one plant was significant in conditioning the participation of its women workers. Many textile workers felt distinctly uneasy with the worker-cadre relationship and hence were hesitant to speak until this relationship was challenged as part of a wider movement.

The achievement of national prominence by some women textile workers demonstrated the importance of the textile industry within the economy and the fact that women could use a base in industry as a stepping-stone to national political reputation and position. While most women who were politically active were involved in the factional strife that pervaded factory life from the "January storm" to the Ninth Party Congress, only a few women emerged as leaders beyond the walls of their factories. The most famous is Wu Gueixian, who became a vice-premier of the People's Republic of China, and was reelected to the Tenth Party Congress Central Committee and as vice-secretary of the Party committee of the First National Textile Mill of Xianyang, Shanxi.[39]

Wu Gueixian's political activism, both as a model worker in her factory and as a party cadre elected to national office, predates the Cultural Revolution. Significantly, so does that of Yang Fuzhen (Shanghai No. 1 Cotton Mill), who was a deputy to the 1964 National Peoples' Congress, attended the Ninth Party Congress, and was a member of the Shanghai Municipal Revolutionary Committee. So too does that of Hao Jianxu (Chingdao No. 8 Textile Mill), a prominent long-standing model worker and a member of the Shandong Provincial Revolutionary Committee. The only woman catapulted to national prominence from relative obscurity (according to admittedly very limited data) appears to be Wang Xiu-zhen of the Shanghai No. 3 Cotton Mill. She was elected to the Ninth Party Congress Central Committee and the Shanghai Municipal Revolutionary Committee, and presided as director of her mill's revolutionary committee.[40] These women differ from the men who came to prominence during the Cultural Revolution in that the women tended to be older and to have more extensive work or leadership experience. Thus, in spite of their Cultural Revolution activism, women did not make a major breakthrough into national political leadership positions during and immediately after the Cultural Revolution.

Generally speaking, even in the traditional female-labor-dominated textile industry male dominance of leadership positions prevailed. However, within the general framework of male control, the patterns of female activism that emerged from the Cultural Revolution were important. Even given the limitations of our data, certain trends appear evident. The impact of the Cultural Revolution appears to have been greater in those factories located in the larger metropolitan areas, most especially in Shanghai. And within the cities, activism peaked in the older textile factories. Shanghai appears to be a special case, for while factories elsewhere tended to have a high degree of rehabilitated cadres staffing their revolutionary committees, in Shanghai many new faces appeared.[41] By contrast, however, the female component of this new leadership tended to be workers with previous activist backgrounds. While Shanghai male activists deviated from the national pattern, all the women had been active since at least the early 1950s and some even earlier than that.

Most women activists, regardless of what factory they worked in, were members of the spinning, weaving, or, in a few cases, packaging departments. The men tended to be from the machine repair, designing, or bleaching and dyeing shops, or held previous administrative positions. The sexual division of labor within textile factories accounts for the high number of women activists, since women leaders came mainly from all-female departments. They fared less well at the factory level and beyond, where groups contained both males and females. The high degree of female activism in Shanghai was consistent with Shanghai's history.[42] It was also in these east coast factories that more women attained prominent positions on the revolutionary committees.

In factories further inland the pattern of activism is not so clear. For one thing, there are fewer women who received press coverage. From the few examples that we do have—Xie Yue, Zhang Ying, and Wu Gueixian—several alternative patterns of activism appear possible. Xie Yue[43] was a veteran worker and an activist from the 1950s, as was Wu Gueixian. Both were from poor peasant/poor worker backgrounds, both entered their mills at a young age, and both were from areas where the Chinese Communist Party had considerable influence during the Yanan period. Zhang Ying's case was very different. She was a spinner at the Gueiyang Cotton Textile Mill, which was built during the Great Leap Forward (1958) and where many of the Cultural Revolution debates focused on the same kinds of management reforms and worker participation that characterized the Leap period.

It appears that in the older mills it was the veteran female workers with a history of political activism who emerged prominently. In the mills built during the 1950s there is too little information and no consistency to determine whether the date of construction was influential in the emergence of female activists. Both Beijing General Knitwear and the Beijing No. 2 Cotton Mill were built in the 1950s, but the former's revolutionary committee contained only two women in a total of twenty-one members, while in the latter a woman (Liu Gueiying) was elected as vice-chairman of the revolutionary committee, another (Wu Aimei) emerged as a leading activist, and there was an unusually high number of women activists at the mill level. In yet a third mill built in the 1950s, the Northeast State No. 1 Cotton Mill (1952), we have no record of any activists, male or female. Thus, while geography and date of establishment may have been significant in some factories, the particular history and personnel of each factory appear to have been of considerable influence in determining the extent of female participation in the Cultural Revolution, the issues, and the kinds of activists who emerged.

For example, in the Northeast State No. 1 Cotton Mill in Shanxi, built in 1952, the repudiation of Soviet-style management methods was a crucial issue. In this particular mill the problem of a "two-line struggle" was of some significance. The workers associated Liu's industrial policies with Soviet revisionism.[44] In the struggles in the Gueiyang Cotton Textile Mill, several administrators were former Guomindang members, so it was this influence that was perceived as dangerous. The workers appeared especially resentful that many of the reforms of the Great Leap period had been abandoned.[45] In the Shijiazhuang Printing and Dyeing Textile Mill it was revealed that the chief engineer had been a major in the Guomindang army and a Guomindang Party member as well. His workstyle was criticized as embodying traditional attitudes. We can assume these attitudes extended to the proper roles of women.[46]

What we have seen from this discussion so far is that women workers were clearly involved in all the Cultural Revolution's debates and struggles, some playing very prominent roles. However, even in the textile industry it was not clear that female participation was equal to the proportion of female workers in the labor force, though there is no evidence to suggest it wasn't. There was, however, a greater propensity for males to be assigned to or to assume leadership positions within factions that developed.

Men were clearly in the majority on the revolutionary committees, the most important institutional development in factories that emerged from the Cultural Revolution. These committees replaced the discredited and complex administrative leadership organs that had dominated factory life. While it is probable that the committees were originally intended to be provisional and were established to maintain production,[47] their assumption of production, political, and ideological responsibilities and their acknowledged legitimacy in the eyes of the workers made them a formal feature of factory life.[48]

The alarming spread of violent factionalism in the fall of 1967 prompted efforts to unite the masses and create an institutional arrangement whereby grievances could be handled. At the same time, the proper treatment of cadres was considered of utmost importance, since only a small minority were considered beyond rehabilitation.[49] In the textile industry specifically, there was therefore a high percentage of retained personnel appearing in almost all revolutionary committees in textile mills. The revolutionary committees in Shanghai textile mills seemed to have relatively more workers, with the No. 17 Cotton Mill having a committee that was 80 percent workers.

The policy of rehabilitating former managerial and administrative personnel clearly had negative implications for women since almost all former cadres were men. The addition of army personnel on many factories' revolutionary committees did nothing to change the sexual composition of the new management organs. Thus, while the class composition of the highest management offices changed, the three-in-one formula (managers, technicians, workers) upon which the revolutionary committees were based had the practical effect of legitimizing male dominance. The only real category to which women belonged in any significant number was workers. And of course, there were many male workers who staffed the nonspinning and nonweaving departments and who were ready to share new positions with women.

Revolutionary committees were not necessarily based on proportional representation of workers and management. Conceived as a means to ensure greater worker participation and greater administrative responsiveness to mass demands and grievances on the part of leadership, the committees were usually dominated politically if not numerically by technicians and cadres. Thus, women workers benefited in the same way male workers did by gaining greater chances for assuming political power than had previously existed. But the lack of any provision aimed specifically at eliminating previous female disadvantages kept female visibility at the factory leadership level very limited.

Women in Residential Areas

If institutional and policy impediments as well as male dominance restricted the political participation of women workers in regular industry, this was not the case in residential areas where housewives and "former housewives" participated in the struggles of the Cultural Revolution. In the course of the debates and struggles of the period, residentially based female activism concentrated on issues women considered important.

Local neighborhood residential committees provided an organizational base for the political participation of women who did not work. In the pre–Cultural Revolution period, however, the work of these committees was hampered by the demands of family and the small number of outside activities women could support in the little spare time they had. However, the establishment of street industry and local social services was partly responsible for the rising expectations of women for extrafamilial roles. Indeed, it was the perceived failure of the residents' committees to provide adequate numbers of jobs, services, and other opportunities that led to the attack on them.

In the period after the "January storm" (1967), urban residents were increasingly involved in the debates and struggles of the Cultural Revolution. When the local Party committees in residential areas came under attack in the spring of 1967, millions of housewives participated in the struggle.[50] Although Party cadres were supposed to be the target, it appears that the cadres of the residents' committees bore the brunt of the attack.[51] As mass organizations elected by local residents and charged with responsibility for the establishment and supervision of social welfare services, they were extremely vulnerable. The cadres who staffed them were mostly housewives. Their proximity to the residents, combined with the general reluctance to criticize the Party, made them the targets of early criticisms. Though the media stressed the necessity to struggle against "those in power taking the capitalist road," the situation in the residential areas often got out of hand:

> The situation of the struggle against neighborhood cadres is grave. Quite a number of neighborhood cadres have been subjected to struggle by force or coercion and to corporal punishment and some have been confiscated of their properties. This can never be permitted and should firmly be checked.[52]

It appears that these residents' committee cadres were often blamed for the upset and confusion that the society-wide factional disputes of the Cultural Revolution had occasioned. They also were easy and visible targets for the release of tensions and frustrations that resulted from the political, economic, and social changes of nearly twenty years of at times rapid development. In a large number of China's urban communities disagreement with both official policies and the way in which they were implemented at the local level led to mass criticism meetings in which neighborhood cadres were attacked for policies which they had had no part in determining.

Under pressure from the municipal leadership (especially in Shanghai) and in the general unfolding of the debates of the Cultural Revolution, the broadside attacks on local cadres gave way to more substantive policy criticism.[53] The criticisms articulated by the urban residents raised issues central to the developmental process: the *xia-xiang* policy, the lack of employment opportunities for women, and the changing role of the family and, hence, women's role within it. Although the criticisms lacked a general theoretical consistency and, in certain cases, were clearly personal grievances, for women they often represented increased political participation and consciousness of the radical social changes occurring in Chinese society. But these criticisms also revealed that many women were still strongly family-oriented and that the family itself was a powerful conservative institution, at least in regard to specific development strategies associated with the Chinese approach up to this time.

In Shanghai particularly, the *xia-xiang* policy of sending educated youth to the countryside came under strong attack. The criticism revealed discontent both with the ideological justifications of the policy and with the economic realities of life in the rural areas. It was clear that many parents of these youth considered it a personal hardship for their children to become pioneers in China's frontiers. Many Shanghai students had been sent to Xinjiang during the 1960s. Some parents considered the economic costs they were made to bear in the reduction of the "three great inequalities" (between town and country, mental and manual labor, worker and peasant) too high.[54]

In considering the *xia-xiang* policy a waste of human resources, these parents revealed one of the dilemmas resulting from prior development. The success of the educational system up to the Cultural Revolution led to a large pool of literate and skilled young people, many with high school backgrounds. However, the industrial sector was unable to generate enough jobs to absorb them. While many would accept the validity of a policy aimed at reducing the unemployment and congestion problems of cities like Shanghai and meeting the needs of the vast countryside for development, parents were not always happy when their own children had to "*xia-xiang.*"

In the weakening of administrative control that accompanied the high tide of the Cultural Revolution, many students returned home. But it was clear that their prospects for urban employment were rather slim. Under ideological pressure, parents were urged to facilitate the students' return to their rural assignments.[55] The *xia-xiang* issue remained important well into 1968. There were even rumors that residents' committees in Shanghai were being paid for each youth they persuaded to return to Xinjiang.[56]

Youth were not the only segment of the population affected by the lack of urban employment opportunities. The Great Leap had indicated that housewives could be an important source of additional and cheap labor in creating useful undertakings in urban street industry. In the period between the Leap and the Cultural Revolution it appears that this form of production was neglected, and, at times, discouraged.[57] As an alternative source of employment and income it was less central to industrialization strategy after the Leap than during it. This was a particular hardship for women who were mindful of the ideological premise of women's emancipation being conditional upon labor participation and who therefore viewed street industry as a viable alternative to a regular full-time job. The necessary social services that alleviated women's household burden and freed them to work were, however, insufficiently developed, and this added to the criticisms of local street cadres in the early campaigns. Women perceived that these facilities were the responsibility of the local cadres. Yet, the lack of official support for this marginal sector of production was the real culprit.

Widescale development of street industry began during the Great Leap Forward. But in all the years since, there had never been an analysis of the role of street industry in a socialized economy or of the implications for those who participated in this form of labor production. Moreover, in the years between the Leap and the Cultural Revolution, the role of street industry lessened considerably, and in some places enterprises were closed down. Thus, the renewed interest in this form of production that resulted from the Cultural Revolution was important to women.[58]

The existence of community medical services was also important to women, not only because of medical needs related to reproduction and birth, but because women were most often the ones who staffed these facilities. Although the Cultural Revolution was primarily concerned with the lack of peasant access to adequate medical care, the new medical policies emerging from the Cultural Revolution had important implications for urban medical care as well.

The urban counterpart of the rural "barefoot doctor" was the Red Guard doctor who operated the local lane or street health station. Since one of the foremost duties of the local health station was the implementation of birth control programs, women ordinarily staffed this station. Usually a local housewife familiar with the neighborhood took on the task.[59] Insofar as young, unmarried females served in this capacity, the Cultural Revolution broadened opportunities for women in medicine since new admission policies stressed recruitment from among local health workers.[60] The extension of medical services in urban areas meant greater involvement of women in community affairs. The decentralization of production and services to residential areas not only increased residents', and most especially women's, participation in local affairs but also tended to break down the isolation of women in families, integrating them into the community. It eased tensions within a rapid development process that in so many other ways had created strains on the family, and as the criticism of the *xia-xiang* policy had shown, many Chinese women were still strong defenders of the family's interest when these were challenged.

Thus, while considerable integration into the larger society was reflected in employment demands, issues relating to families remained central. Women were concerned that the political labels attached to their families were not unfavorable.[61] Often, the factional splits in the factories were transferred to neighborhoods and streets via the family. Arguments developed with such intensity that the People's Liberation Army often had to be called in. By mid-1968 political study groups and revolutionary alliances were established in neighborhoods and residential areas.[62]

The establishment of the Guling Road Revolutionary Committee in Shanghai, the first neighborhood revolutionary committee, marked a shift toward concern with administrative reorganization.[63] The new committees also used a "three-in-one" formula for representation, including representatives from local street organizations, public security substations, and local residents.[64] Unlike factories where female participation on revolutionary committees was rarely if ever a majority, the new street organizations often contained a majority of neighborhood women who had time to serve on the committees. This accounts for the greater visibility of women on these revolutionary committees. But, as in factories, presence did not always mean political power.

Many women were concerned that their "cultural level" was so low that they would be unable to do a good job in the neighborhood revolutionary committee; some complained they lacked leadership experience and they therefore were willing to defer to more experienced cadres, particularly to Party members. They were reluctant to assume responsibilities. The political-administrative status of these neighborhood committees remained unclear, although they fulfilled important functions. Whether these committees and the women on them played a prominent role in local politics and society depended, it seems, upon the particular area and the individuals involved.

The Cultural Revolution's emphasis on simplified administration resulted in a decentralization of urban social services and greater emphasis on some of the experiments most clearly associated with the Great Leap Forward. Urban communes had been abandoned in the post-Leap retrenchment, but many of the experiments associated with them began to reappear in the last phases of the Cultural Revolution after the establishment of revolutionary committees at all levels of administration had been largely completed. The emphasis was different, however. The urban communes had emphasized all-around economic and social self-sufficiency, but the trend immediately after the Cultural Revolution appeared to be toward development of interurban economic relationships while at the same time developing local production and self-reliance in other matters.[65] Thus, the post–Cultural Revolution period encouraged the integration of urban areas with their neighboring suburban and rural areas. This effort to restructure the urban community emphasized neighborhood influence and responsibility in education—mostly at the preschool and primary levels—availability of social services, and the promotion of local production.

In comparing the different forms of urban female participation in the Cultural Revolution it is clear that overt sexual politics and radical feminist consciousness played no conscious part in determining the substantive issues with which women dealt. This was no less true in residential areas than in factories. In the factories, both because large industrial organizations were the cutting edge of China's industrial effort and because men were present in large numbers playing key roles, the efforts of women in the Cultural Revolution reflected their assimilation into the urban labor force. Factional involvement suggested an increasing differentiation of the female labor force with no evidence at all of factions forming around feminist issues.

However, for women in residential areas the family seemed to remain central, and women seemed anxious to defend its interests, and, by extension, their roles within it. Yet, the lack of social services and job opportunities meant that women would be trapped or limited by their traditional roles, and the criticisms aimed at the residential committees showed clearly that many women were quite willing and able to challenge these limitations even while defending the family that created them.

Rural Women in the Cultural Revolution

Although the debates of the Cultural Revolution reached into many communes, in general the countryside's involvement, particularly in factional disputes, did not approach that of the urban areas. In many places the socialist education campaign was still in progress during the early stages of the Cultural

Revolution. Moreover, in spite of the relevancy of the issues of the Cultural Revolution and the extensive travels of the many Red Guard groups, there was no great effort to involve the rural areas deeply in the Cultural Revolution. Nevertheless, the issues and the resulting policy changes contained important implications for the countryside. Reorganization of the health care system was one area in which rural women had a very definite interest.

The Great Leap had dramatically revealed the relationship between adequate rural medical care and women's participation in production, as well as the reluctance on the part of a male-dominated leadership to invest in facilities that threatened immediate production goals. Thus, even the rudimentary health care systems that appeared in rural areas during the Great Leap were severely criticized after the poor harvests of 1959, 1960, and 1961. Even the paramedical training of barefoot doctors and other personnel was limited in the post-Leap period.[66] This trend was reversed by the Cultural Revolution's renewed emphasis on rural areas, not only in the training of medical personnel, but in establishing mobile medical teams and in requiring all major urban medical facilities to put their personnel on rotating rural duty tours.[67] The increasing harvest resulting from the "green revolution" in China from about 1963 somewhat ameliorated the reluctance to invest in social services.[68] Thus, from the perspective of economics and politics, health care was a timely issue.

For women, in addition to the general increase in medical facilities, the special attention paid to training midwives was very important. Not only did this help increase the care available; it also involved more women in the medical system and provided women with new role models. In addition to assisting women with deliveries, midwives provided pre- and postnatal care, were responsible for birth control, and acted as a support for the proper use of female labor in production.

Education and the availability of birth control devices could not, however, immediately overcome the ideas of male dominance and other traditional attitudes toward women in the countryside. A report from one commune recounts the following conversation:

> "She is going to ask the doctor at the commune hospital for an abortion. They'll do it if she wants and her husband agrees."
> "But why don't she and her husband learn about family planning? That's much better."
> "They think about it but then they know that the mother-in-law doesn't hold with it and they are scared of a family row."[69]

Contraception and family planning remained an embarrassing topic for many Chinese peasants, something only a busybody would talk about.[70] This attitude was only beginning to disappear in the late 1970s.[71]

Yet, in spite of traditional resistance to outside interference in matters that related to family decisions and welfare, the extension of general health facilities was welcome by the peasants. In 1968 and 1969, counties, communes, and even brigades reported the successful establishment of some level of health care.[72]

Many of the *xia-xiang* students were apparently recruited for medical service, and about half of the barefoot doctors were female students.[73] Women would be especially suitable because performing this service was compatible with the historical role of women in medicine and because even the practice of modern medicine can be viewed by conservatives as a legitimate extension of women's traditional role in caring for others. Working women in this field would be less apt to arouse opposition. At the same time, since barefoot doctors' salaries are usually derived, in part, from agricultural work, these women tended to reinforce the more extensive and rational use of female labor in production. The impact of women barefoot doctors could be seen as a positive influence for change in rural society.

Traditional customs which frowned upon social participation by women were blamed for the low level of activism by young rural women in the Cultural Revolution.[74] Women still had to contend with the parents' desire for early marriage and their desire to choose their children's spouses.[75] The question of dowries caused considerable concern. However, a slight difference can be discerned in the pre- and post–Cultural Revolution periods regarding this particular question. Up to and including the early phase of the Cultural Revolution, it was usually the young people who were portrayed as taking the initiative in opposing dowries. But in the latter part of the Cultural Revolution, parents who opposed the custom were given publicity. As one parent reportedly said indignantly to a proposed husband's offer, "If I will not give you my daughter until you give me money, then it becomes a sale."[76]

Although one might prefer women to be more prominent in these kinds of decisions, and not rely on family arrangements at all, there is the clear implication that the community, not just an individual woman, has to struggle against traditional forms of female oppression. Furthermore, the rejection of these kinds of traditional marriage customs represents the integration of the woman question into the larger social revolution, for the buying and selling of women was morally and politically equated with bourgeois society and incompatible with the values of a socialist society.

The growth of political study groups in rural areas after the socialist education campaign increased the legitimacy of female activity outside the home. Many study groups were all-female, but some contained both men and women. This sexual integration was not accomplished without a struggle, for young girls who participated were often a target of rumors and gossip.[77] Study groups were often opposed by conservative elders and even by women themselves who accepted the traditional attitude that "women can't study."[78] In some places a key role was played by a young local female production leader, by a female militia member, or simply by an activist representing and pushing new ideas.

Women militia members were often important in the struggle to create new female roles. Growing numbers of women in local militias were noted approvingly by 1966.[79] Since these women were not full-time army, they also participated in production. Their militia training led them to play leading roles in supporting women's roles in production, in scientific experimentation, in study, reclaiming new lands, and in being good leaders.[80] Their physical training gave them the skills and the strength to perform even the most arduous agricultural tasks. Most of these women were young, implying that it was easier for them to refuse the traditional family-centered roles than it was for those already caught up within these roles.

In some cases, rural women emerged at the instigation of men who were taken with political ideals of female equality. In one commune,

> It was really the men who got the new ideas about women. They attended meetings where the Communist Party's policy was explained. When the activists came home from these meetings, they urged their wives to "stand up." And gradually more women began going to the meetings. . . . First the women began to attend our own women's meetings to hear the revolutionary policy explained. Then soon we began attending the general meetings along with the men.[81]

Clearly the supportive atmosphere in this village accounted for the high degree of female participation. While this particular kind of situation does not appear to have been terribly widespread, in some of the poorer areas of rural China where the degree of collectivization was fairly well advanced, greater participation by women was evident.[82] A comparison of the situations at Liu Ling and Yangdan communes[83] illustrates this.

Liu Ling, a poorer-than-average Chinese village but one in which women played important economic roles, gave women two mu of land on which to grow crops. The money earned from this land was used to buy sewing machines in order to establish a local industry aimed specifically at relieving the village women of the onerous task of individually making family clothes. The project was initiated by the women and considered a legitimate undertaking.

In contrast, at the more prosperous Yangdan Commune women tended to work sporadically and in all-women teams. Their chief responsibility was the cotton crop, from which they averaged 5.6 workpoints per mu. Many of the women worked to earn money to buy, individually, sewing machines to help make the family clothing. At a cost of 140 yuan per machine, this involved a substantial investment sum not made available to the commune.

Thus, the situation in rural areas was dependent on local conditions, in which the economic elements were modified by both the history of the area and the nature of the political-ideological work carried out. But local communities all over China were influenced by national policies, including the *xia-xiang* movement, attention given to rural medical facilities, and the renewed stress on local rural industry.[84] The pressures and momentum created by the Cultural Revolution for social change clearly supported those begun with the Great Leap Forward.

Conclusion

The debates and struggles of the Cultural Revolution focused on the issues of development strategy and the nature of the social transformation of Chinese society. Feminist issues remained largely marginal. However, both wide-scale involvement of women and the success of a more radical and innovative approach to development were important in defining the context in post–Cultural Revolution politics for women. The nature of these more radical approaches, many of which recalled policies of the Great Leap Forward and many of which were comparatively innovative, did not become clear until after the dust of the Cultural Revolution had settled. Still, while the general ideological context was favorable there were signs of certain institutional and organizational impediments to progress toward female equality.

The revolutionary committees in industrial enterprises did not as a rule recruit women members unless specific attention was paid to this problem. The shift from mass organizations to production units as a prominent theater of political activity meant that large numbers of women who did not work would have to enter politics through residents' committees, whose independence and relationship to the municipal bureaucracy remained ambiguous. And, since employment opportunities and non-family-provided services remained limited, the still largely familial-centered activities of many women raised very difficult dilemmas for women. However, this situation could be turned to advantage under conditions of decentralization and community control wherein local communities sought to expand the availability of local services and production which could absorb female labor and encourage political participation. Thus, the Cultural Revolution created ideological and institutional opportunities for a potentially more favorable context for women's progress, but a context in which women found change difficult and in which past influences remained powerful.

·6·

Theoretical and Political Developments from the Post–Cultural Revolution to 1976

THE INTENSITY OF THE DEBATES AND THE FACTIONAL STRUGGLES THAT so strongly characterized the period from 1966 to 1969 could not continue forever. With the Ninth Party Congress (March–April 1969) they gave way to efforts to rebuild the Party and almost all other social and economic institutions. However, many of the issues, economic, political, ideological, and organizational, that had triggered and fueled the Cultural Revolution were not resolved. All of them now were treated as part of a "two-line struggle" between "revolution" on the one hand and "revisionism" on the other. While "revisionism" stressed only increases in production and economic growth, the revolutionary political groups, led by Mao, emphasized the dialectic between increased production and transformation of social relations and ideology. For women, this revolutionary approach was crucial.

What characterized revisionism most markedly was the lack of concern with the development and institutionalization of old and new inequalities flowing from the industrialization process itself. Thus, revolutionary policies which emerged from the Cultural Revolution had to aim specifically at the gradual elimination of historical inequalities as well as those which would result from the way in which history interacted with present conditions during the transition to socialism.

Increased political participation in the revolutionary committees was intended to reinforce the new institutional and policy changes that characterized the early 1970s. As important as the domestic political context remained in post–Cultural Revolution China, the new policies were inevitably shaped by an international political reality as well, and over this the Chinese had little control. Though the strategic and military issues of the period are beyond the scope of this study, it is important to note that external factors restricted the possibilities for internal revolutionary experiments. Throughout the first half of the 1970s, the increasing fear of a Russian attack reinforced the desirability of a détente with the United

States, and increasing economic and political ties with other nations became more important. Yet, in spite of these foreign policy concerns, there was continued stress on ideological transformation, and this provided a domestic context in which the woman question received intense and sustained attention.

Theoretical Developments

Traditional Marxist theory perceived the problems of women's emancipation within the broader framework of class struggle. The primary interests of women were, therefore, class interests, and it was clearly implied that undue emphasis on strictly feminist goals was a sign of bourgeois ideology. As we have seen in our discussion of the Great Leap, under conditions of severe poverty feminist demands were in fact both narrower than those of class and in conflict with class interests. But with the development of collective social and economic institutions in the Chinese countryside and with the further development of the economy this rather static view of the relationship between sex and class, in which feminist interests were always subordinate to class interests, was increasingly questioned in post–Cultural Revolution China.

The "criticize Lin Biao and Confucius" campaign that began in 1973 and lasted until the coup that ousted the "Gang of Four"[1] marked the beginnings of change in ideological thinking about the woman question. In a larger sense, the campaign continued the serious debates over the problems of the transition to socialism that had begun before the Cultural Revolution, and it heightened both ideological and political conflict in these years. For women, this campaign was characterized by intense efforts to analyze the origins and development of an ideological system in which oppression of women was a fundamental, necessary premise. Simultaneously, there was new research into women's participation in movements and rebellions that challenged this system. All this was a significant departure from previous general and superficial critiques of Confucianism.[2] Female goals and equality were not placed in opposition to class goals and equality, but it was noted clearly that more attention should be paid specifically to the woman question, not just to class struggle.

> Comrades of revolutionary committees at all levels must pay greater attention to bring the role of women into full play. This is an important aspect in carrying out Chairman Mao's proletarian revolutionary line. In organs of political power at all levels and in mass organizations, there should be a certain number of women representatives and in actual work their opinions should be listened to seriously and with respect, so as to give full play to their role.[3]

The new emphasis on women that emerged in the early 1970s and the national attention to the woman question during the "criticize Lin Biao and Confucius" campaign were the results of several different but congruent developments. The rapidly increasing numbers of working women in the 1950s and 1960s had made the growing female component of the labor force significant. Institutional and ideological developments as well as significant economic growth reinforced this trend while weakening and in some cases eliminating some of the structural obstacles for women's participation in social and economic life outside the home. The Great Leap had concretely demonstrated that sexual equality and development of collective socialist institutions were closely related. Moreover, the considerable numbers of women activists that had emerged during the Cultural Revolution from Chinese factories, neighborhoods, schools, and communes heightened the demands for reexamination of women's role in revolutionary China.

The new focus on women had begun even before the "criticize Lin Biao and Confucius" campaign with the admission that even after the Cultural Revolution there was "severe class struggle on the question of women."[4] Liu Shaoqi, the disgraced victim of the Cultural Revolution, and, after 1972, Lin Biao, were identified as advocating the continued oppression of women.[5] Both were supposed to have advocated the primacy of family ties and the importance of the familial responsibilities that kept women tied to the household. Independent achievements by women were denigrated by the attitude that "a woman's future is determined by her husband."[6]

Liu and Lin, it was charged, were merely the most recent proponents of old traditional ideas still strongly present in China, with Confucianism the summation of these attitudes. Because the Confucian tradition was perceived as responsible for attitudes, values, and behavior inimical to socialist development, the critique of Confucianism naturally led to a critique of one of its main principles: male supremacy. It was this, combined with the changing role of women in China's recent economic and social history, which largely accounts for the focus on the woman question in the early 1970s. In the course of the campaign even the most sensitive issues concerning women's biological function and familial roles were subjected to public discussion and analysis.

The new campaign differed significantly from previous attempts to raise the status of women. Both ideologically and institutionally the Cultural Revolution paved the way. The ideological context favored the wholesale criticism of inequalities. Institutionally, the small study groups created during the latter phases of the Cultural Revolution for the process of "criticism-struggle-transformation" were ideally suited to eliciting maximum female participation. Small, and consisting of persons well known to one another, these study groups afforded women the opportunity to learn how to express themselves and gain confidence. This was an important step in confronting a major subjective obstacle to sexual equality: women's own self-deprecating attitudes. The small all-women groups now provided a psychologically supportive atmosphere previously unavailable to women.

It was highly unlikely that most women, especially relatively uneducated rural women, had any degree of familiarity with traditional feudal codes which defined proper female behavior. However, the pervasive influence of these codes in daily folklore was clearly evident. Popular sayings embodying these attitudes included: "If women go into the fields, things won't grow"; "If women go out of the house, chaos will ensue"; or "If women waddle off barefoot to the fields then everyone will laugh."[7] The small groups, mindful that the old attitudes locked women into their traditional familial-centered roles, undertook historical analyses of the institutional and ideological conditions that underpinned Confucianism. The results of their efforts were quite impressive and were clearly similar to the work of many Western women who had begun studying Western history from a feminist perspective.

The criticism of Confucianism which dominated the media from 1974 to 1976 gave women access to many historical documents found only in libraries. Many women's groups learned how the Confucian legacy was responsible, in large part, for the continued subordination of women in post–1949 China. The unresolved problems impeding women's liberation—lack of equal political representation, unequal wages, familial roles—already a significant part of the national debates concerning development policies, were perceived as originating in the Confucian system of male supremacy. Indeed, a concept new to the Chinese women's movement began to receive a good deal of attention.

> The Confucian ethics, including the concept of "male superiority and female inferiority," played an extremely reactionary role in the course of the change from the slave system to the feudal system in Chinese society. But when the former had been completely destroyed and the latter firmly established, the landlord class inherited the whole of Confucian ethics out of its need to consolidate feudal autocratic rule. So feudal society remained a society with a patriarchal hierarchy. Promoted with might and main by successive feudal dynasties and energetically trumpeted by the followers of Confucius, the reactionary Confucian viewpoint advocating the oppression of women became more concrete and more systematized than ever.[8]

The persistence of patriarchy throughout history, a phenomenon Western feminists were also examining,[9] was an important discovery for Chinese women. No longer could the Chinese accept a mechanistic theory concerning the transformation of women's roles. Patriarchy, a persistent feature of class society, but not identical to or a simple function of class, was clearly in conflict with the egalitarian relationships associated with socialism. As we will see later on, there were policy implications that flowed from this theoretical discovery.

Both in China and in the West, an important development of the women's movement has been the creation of women's history. The research work by some Chinese women's groups has been able to document the active and important participation by women in all major resistance movements throughout Chinese history.[10] For Chinese women, knowledge of women's participation in the historical struggles against oppression was an important development, for it directly refuted the Confucian notions of women as powerless and dependent beings. They began to understand how issues of a class nature shaped and influenced issues of sex, for history was written by the ruling class. Those groups which focused on women's participation in the long struggle for liberation in the twentieth century were aided by the existence of factory histories, by the work done since 1949 on the women's movement in China and on such important women as Xiang Jingyu and Yang Kaihui,[11] and by the numbers of women still alive who could relate their own personal histories of struggle.[12]

The confidence and understanding women gained through their study and critique of Confucianism were used to tackle the inequalities still prevailing in Chinese society. The household roles of women and the division of labor that resulted from their continuance were questioned. Even the biological roles of women did not escape scrutiny. Confucianism was attacked for its distortion and manipulation of the biological differences between men and women.[13]

All of this theoretical development and historical "study" was directly relevant to wider social policy concerning collectivization. Whereas Confucianism implied that the family would be endangered from increased collectivization, the post–Cultural Revolution campaigns emphasized collectivization as important in restructuring and democratizing the family by diminishing its ability to exploit some of its members (women). The Chinese had come quite a distance since 1956, when official policy was described in these terms:

> Participation in agricultural production is the inherent right and duty of rural women. Giving birth to children and raising them as well as preoccupation with household chores are also the obligation of rural women. These things set women apart from men.[14]

Emerging from the anti-Confucian campaign was a significantly different attitude:

> Women after marriage, it is said, "must not withdraw to the confines of family. After marriage a woman must spend much of her time and energy on household chores," but *no longer is this what "sets women apart from men."*[15] (Emphasis added)

In case people did not understand the implications, this important article went on:

> "A revolutionary woman certainly does not allow such chores to cut into her social responsibilities; and men comrades should offer to share a portion of the household chores from the standpoint of equality, to enable women comrades to participate properly in social revolution and social construction."

While the extent of female responsibility for household chores was, and is still, greatly dependent on male willingness to help out in the home, the implications of national support for the idea of male participation in traditional "female" work marked an important step toward the destruction of traditional attitudes toward the division of labor.[16] Often the media, in articles written by men, stressed male assistance in traditional "female" work:

> Men and women helped each other, and when the women were engaged in study, the children were looked after and household work was attended to by the men commune members.[17]

However, practical realities in Chinese society did not allow this approach which questioned the traditional division of labor to develop. Instead, as will be seen later, the Chinese reverted to an older, and more practical solution: the socialization of female work in the home.

The "criticize Lin Biao and Confucius" campaign continued until 1976 and the ouster of the Gang of Four. In a fairly radical way, there emerged a general set of principles that directly challenged traditional values and attitudes held by and toward women. These included:

1. Destroy the notion that women are useless. Replace it with the idea that women "hold up half the sky" and must fearlessly struggle to play their role.

2. Destroy the feudal mentality that justified female oppression and defined them as "good mothers." It was necessary to create new women "revolutionary proletarians."

3. Destroy the mentality of dependence and subordination to men. Create the determination to be free.

4. Smash thoroughly the bourgeois concepts of the good life. Develop proletarian ideals.

5. Smash the concept of narrow family self-interest. Cultivate the proletarian attitude of the nation as the family.[18]

The small study groups, both at production sites and in the home, were the vehicle through which these instructions were publicized. Popular slogans emerging in this period bluntly and openly stressed sexual equality. "Whatever men comrades can do, women comrades can do." "Women hold up half the sky." And, "In comparing women to men, do women lack anything? Definitely not!"

Ideological campaigns, as important and necessary as they are to change attitudes and traditional patterns of behavior, need to be reinforced politically and in social and economic institutions.

Post–Cultural Revolution Political Integration of Women in the Party at the National Level

Emerging guidelines for the rebuilding of Party organizations during the early 1970s favored the advancement of women. Spontaneous development of political institutions outside the Party during the Cultural Revolution created new avenues of political mobility and led to the rapid rise of many younger activists to positions of authority. The Party, which had been previously weakened by the Cultural Revolution, began to rebuild with the calling of the Ninth Party Congress in March–April 1969. Party organizations began to recruit from the ranks of poor peasants and workers and women in an effort to make the Party more representative of and more responsive to the population.

The campaign to recruit women into the Party reflected some of the long-standing obstacles to female political participation, but it also reflected the breakthroughs brought on by the Cultural Revolution and its aftermath. Clearly, it was the Party's efforts before the "criticize Lin Biao and Confucius" campaign that laid the groundwork of support and reinforcement for women's participation in the years 1973–1976. The growth in representation at the national level was one indicator of the seriousness of the Party effort during this period. At the Ninth Party Congress in 1969, two women (Jiang Qing and Ye Qun), were elected to the all-powerful Politburo, eleven to the Central Committee (including at least three textile workers, Wang Xuijin, Yang Fuzhen, and Wu Gueixian), and ten to the Central Committee as alternates.[19]

The Tenth Party Congress, operating under a new Party constitution, elected twenty women (10 percent of the total) to the Central Committee and twenty-one (17 percent of total) as alternates. In the Central Committee, therefore, women increased their participation from 8 percent to 13 percent.[20] This increase from 1965 to 1973 was important in creating a political base for the anti-Confucius campaign. The Party's active leadership in the campaign to foster female leadership reflected a growing recognition of women's contributions to socialist development.

> It is necessary to comply with Chairman Mao's great teaching to educate women so as to strengthen revolutionary unity and to understand that the women of new China are a force which *determines* the victory or failure of the revolution.[21] (Emphasis added)

This theme was reiterated by Mao himself:

> Women comprise one-half the population. The economic status of working women and the fact of their being specifically oppressed prove not only that women urgently need revolution but also that they are a *decisive* force in the success or failure of the revolution.[22] (Emphasis added)

By 1971 the reasons for the previously poor record of female representation were subjected to analysis. At first the political formula left over from the Cultural Revolution was used, and its influence was blamed.[23] Party committees, especially in the rural areas, appeared hesitant to upset the social organization of rural society by supporting new roles for women. They complained, "It does not pay to foster female Party members because they cannot play much of a role anymore after they get married,"[24] or, "After receiving training a woman Party member cannot play any significant role; it is a loss to train women Party members."[25] Or doubt was expressed at their ability to handle the job, and it was said that "even if [good women] Party members are trained, they will go away sooner or later."[26] But the legitimacy of these complaints was now challenged and during the nationwide anti-Confucius campaign they were rejected as no longer valid. By 1974, at least some men were beginning to understand how a social system that confined women to household chores and deprived them of opportunities to gain skills and participate in social and political affairs created the impression of female lack of capabilities.[27] In short, women appeared to lack skills precisely because they had been denied access to them, rather than the other way around.

Efforts to recruit women for leadership training, which put additional demands on women's time, could not be successful, however, unless the household burdens of women were ameliorated. Some Party committees began to acknowledge this: "Some rural women comrades indeed play a smaller role after they get married because of household work, but this situation *can be* changed."[28] Others began actively to organize collective child care facilities to create conditions for women's participation in labor. Most solutions concentrated on collectivizing the most burdensome household chores (child care, grain milling, processing of food) rather than on restructuring the traditional division of labor (though there was discussion of solving the problem by having men take on tasks traditionally viewed as women's work).

Party and revolutionary committees concentrated on establishing new local "women's committees" and congresses throughout the countryside as training organizations from which women Party members could be recruited.[29] Aimed at developing leadership elements from among the masses of women, these training and recruitment efforts were maintained throughout the early 1970s and through the "criticize Lin Biao and Confucius" campaign.[30] Women were also organized into study groups, many of which had their origins in the Cultural Revolution. The campaign, especially after 1973, was aimed not only at articulating and destroying attitudes resulting from previous socialization (the Confucian influence), but also at the creation of new socialist values and perspectives. The methods used were based on the theoretical study of basic Marxist texts and the practical leadership experiences of women as they assumed their new posts.

By 1975 the emphasis appeared to be on studying the basic texts of Marxism-Leninism. The model in this respect was the much publicized Wang Yuying, deputy secretary of Zhaolu People's Commune, Anhui. In her intensive study, Wang had mastered "The Communist Manifesto," "Anti-Duhring," and "A Critique of the Gotha Programme."[31] And in Junshu neighborhood, Beijing, it was reported that over 60,000 women were engaged in the study of Marxist theory.[32] Of course not all these women sought entry or were accepted into the Party, but many of the new female cadres were assigned to leading positions at the work site. Even those who were not given leadership posts acted as activists when they returned to their production posts.

The new opportunities opened to women did not substantially change the picture of male dominance in the countryside at once, but they paved the way for future inroads. Certain patterns began to emerge that go far toward explaining the mechanics of female mobility in a countryside still dominated by traditional modes of production and in which traditional attitudes toward women's proper role receive a degree of reinforcement from material conditions. The individual women who emerged as local activists and the women who increasingly participated in labor outside the home represented activists of very different backgrounds. Old-time activists from pre-Liberation days continued to play important roles, with many of them becoming Party secretaries or commune officials.[33] They continued to be the core of female leadership, "backbone elements" in the countryside. Coming from poor peasant backgrounds, they played consistent roles over the years and were most often noted for their leadership style, which put them hard at work with the peasants in the fields regardless of their political duties. But new female leaders began to emerge also, women like Wang Zuizui, Party branch secretary of a production brigade in Jinzheng County, Shanxi, who was elected to her post in 1970,[34] or Liu Fengying, leader of the Dong Taiping women's team, Chenji Brigade, Henan, who emerged as an activist in the Cultural Revolution and was trained by her commune's leadership.[35] These women were either young or middle-aged, and most often came from poor or lower-middle peasant backgrounds. Unlike the *xia-xiang* students who emerged as leaders in some places due to their skills and educational backgrounds, the new female leaders appeared to be local women who simply decided to forego more traditional roles. For many the decision to work and assume leadership posts involved personal struggles to overcome feelings of inferiority, lack of ability, and family opposition. For these women to succeed, Party support was crucial.

In rural areas, county-level support for women's new roles appeared to be a factor. In periods of decentralization, such as during the Great Leap and after the Cultural Revolution, when the commune and county levels emerged as politically significant, women's demands seemed to receive greater attention. At the commune and county levels the pressure on scarce resources generated by women's demands and the influence of familial opposition is ameliorated. Moreover, investment in facilities that benefit women and support of policies that create greater opportunities for them have both occurred when the county has played an important role in development planning and political mobilization. Many county-level Party committees throughout the 1970s established women's work committees or "women's work offices" whose tasks focused on holding "line-education" and political study classes for women.[36] Most of these women were already working when they were recruited for leadership training. They were then assigned to leadership posts at the district, commune, brigade, and team levels. The results of these efforts in at least some places were truly impressive. In Danqing County, Henan, 30 percent of the leading cadres were women.[37] In Xinxing County, women were members of the standing committees of the Party in eleven of fourteen communes; 7 women were vice-chairmen of commune revolutionary committees; 448 participated in brigade-level leading groups; 32 were secretaries or deputy secretaries of the brigade-level Party committees and chairmen or vice-chairmen of brigade-level revolutionary committees; and 1,286 were leaders or deputy leaders of production teams.[38] In Lanshan County, Hunan, Party committees in twenty-five communes had a total of 52 female members and the county had trained 2,390 women for leadership.[39] In Yunxi County, Hubei, there were three times as many women at all leadership levels than there had been in the period prior to the Cultural Revolution,[40] while in Daoyuan County, Hunan, the Party trained 1,200 women for leadership posts at county, district, commune, and brigade levels.[41] Yunnan's Luxin County boasted 374 female cadres at or above the production team level.[42] The Danjin Region of Gueizhou recruited 6,670 women for Party and Young Communist League membership, while an additional 583 women were assigned to leadership posts at or above the commune level. These are but a few examples of an increasingly widespread development.[43]

Clearly there were advances for rural women in many places, but the significance and effects of the changes on female progress generally were somewhat mitigated by certain factors. For one thing, it is not clear how widespread were the patterns described above. The process of female cadre training was very uneven nationally. This was due, in part, to the decision in Beijing to allow local areas a great deal of control over their own affairs. Secondly, the general lack of leadership experience meant that the immediate impact of women cadres would be somewhat limited. This is not to minimize the symbolic importance of the physical presence of women in nontraditional roles, but it does suggest that in the short run there was an element of tokenism which resulted not from manipulation so much as from practical reality. Perhaps most important was the fact that recruitment was based on production participation, and many rural women were still in fact tied to the home. The nonworking woman's lot was very different from that of the working woman.

Women and Production in Urban China

The results of nationwide Party recruitment efforts was markedly different in the urban centers than in the countryside. The history of political involvement of urban women was greater, with women participating in residential areas as well as at production sites. Women in residential areas were still mainly concerned with mobilization for production. Those who already held regular jobs, however, became part of a concerted campaign to develop female leadership within their work units. Although other industries were involved,[44] the textile industry was clearly in the vanguard of training women for leadership positions. Many women had participated in the debates and struggles of the Cultural Revolution in the mills, but few had emerged immediately afterward in leading positions in the revolutionary or reorganized Party committees. This was because of the low number of women originally in those groups from which leaders were recruited. Moreover, in the interests of stability, many former cadres, most of whom were male, were reinstated in positions of leadership.

Thus, it was significant that after a few years the leadership attempted to place women in leadership positions that involved technical expertise as well as supervisory skills. Several women emerged in charge of workshops.[45] Other women, with years of work experience and participation in post-Cultural Revolution study groups, became new Party members or members of revolutionary and Party standing committees in factories, and attained municipal revolutionary commit-tee posts.[46] And although women rarely held even half the supervisory, adminis-trative, and political leadership positions, there were impressive gains in the short period from the Cultural Revolution through 1973.

The joint efforts of the Chinese Communist Party and the Beijing Municipal Bureau of Textile Industry led to women assuming 37 percent of the on-the-job leadership positions in that city's textile mills. Some women were appointed directors, for example, at the Beijing Silk and Satin Factory.[47] At the Beijing Woolen Textile Mill, women accounted for almost 37 percent of the total number of cadres in the mill, but only 30 percent in the middle-level of higher posi-tions.[48] Beijing's achievements in this area were surpassed elsewhere in the coun-try. At the Chengdu Textile Mill, for instance, 42 percent of the mill-level leading cadres and 62 percent of cadres at the workshop level were women.[49] At the Fujian Mill in Fuzhou, 40 percent of the cadres on the Party committee and the revolutionary committee were women.[50] At a mill in Xian, women were 70 percent of the factory's leadership.[51]

What emerged most clearly was the increase of women activists, particularly at the workshop levels or in the intermediate levels of management. This in-creased representation was precisely in those groups from which middle- and plant-level leadership was recruited and which the Cultural Revolution had re-vealed as so important for political mobility. Thus, the textile industry emerged as a model in developing female leadership.

All these attempts at recruiting females for leadership positions in industry had a ripple effect in the wider urban society. The patterns of female employment which had formed in the post-Leap period did not change drastically although the context in which women worked and the numbers of women involved did. Younger, educated, and unmarried urban women who were not involved in the *xia-xiang* movement tended to find employment within the ranks of regular industry. Because extensive in-plant child care and welfare services were available, these women remained at their jobs even after they married and had children. Uneducated married women with several children, and older women, tended to be employed in street industries near or in their residential areas. Some of these street industries had evolved into regular industrial enterprises included within the state plan,[52] but their beginnings were dependent on the existence of local welfare and child care services to facilitate female work outside the home in the first place. The relationship between work outside the home and the provision of such services was perceived by urban women, whose Cultural Revolution de-mands, it will be recalled, included significant expansion of both street industries and welfare and child care services.

For those women in regular industry, the number and kinds of jobs had increased since the pre-Leap period. The expansion and diversification of industrial production that accelerated in the 1960s had a positive impact on female employment. Before the Great Leap Forward, industries that were the main absorbers of female labor were also those which were the largest employers in the economy. Heavy industry, while expanding under the priorities of the First Five-Year Plan, represented a relatively small portion of total employment.[53] Furthermore, throughout the 1950s, heavy industry absorbed only token numbers of female workers. By 1966, however, the continued growth of the heavy industry sector saw women entering into a broader range of production, from iron and steel to machine tools. Indeed, in some individual plants women became a significant percentage of the work force: for example, 40 percent at the Shanghai No. 3 Machine Tool Plant; 30 percent at the Beijing Steel Wire Plant; and 50 percent at the Tianjin North Lake Instrument Factory.[54] By 1974, women represented 33 percent of the labor force at the East Is Red Auto Factory, 33 percent at the Foreign Language Printing House, 26 percent at the Loyang Tractor Works, 25 percent at Tianjin No. 1 Machinery Factory, and 50 percent at the Dong Feng Watch Factory.[55]

Some industries had considerable levels of female employment in several plants. The chemical industry was notable in this respect, because many street industries begun by housewives during the Great Leap Forward grew into integral parts of the rapidly growing chemical industry.[56] By the post-Cultural Revolution period the success of many earlier street enterprises resulted in their incorporation as regular state industry and afforded women a different but significant vehicle to worker status. Thus, entry into the labor force for women was closely related to both increased production and the role of local industry and street industry in China's development strategy.

The increasing numbers of women working in the post–Cultural Revolution period, particularly in the regular state-owned sector, suggest that the campaign to develop female leadership reflected not simply a desire to utilize cheap female labor, although this was clearly present. It also reflected a political commitment. Female labor also had extra cost factors built in (the provision of maternity leave and pay, in-plant facilities for women) that should not be ignored. Furthermore, in the wake of the wage-scale adjustments made in industry after the Cultural Revolution, the gap between the most highly paid workers—notably those in heavy industry—and workers in other sectors had been narrowed. Salaries in industries where female labor traditionally predominated closely approximated those where male workers predominated, although variations continued. Women were an increasing portion of the labor force in urban China, and were recruited as workers in industries which put them on an economic footing more nearly equal to that of men.[57]

Training women workers for leadership positions complemented and reinforced trends toward growing economic equality. However, conservative male attitudes concerning the proper use of female labor still prevailed. These attitudes were not left at home, but were carried to the workplace and operated to limit female opportunities in finding work, acquiring skills, and getting advanced training. With the workplace viewed as the arena for social change through the process of study groups and struggle meetings, the still male-dominated authority structure that prevailed in most factories represented an obstacle to female equality. Thus, limited access to in-plant technical training courses and plant-supported college education remained an important obstacle to sexual equality since it tended to reduce mobility for women workers.[58] During the "criticize Lin Biao and Confucius" campaign, the close relationship between the woman question and the dynamics of socialist development was widely discussed in the media. Publicity was given to women in individual factories who had successfully proven their job capabilities and technical competence.[59] Women were cited working in what had been predominantly male lines of work.[60] And women in industries such as chemicals[61] and more especially textiles emerged as technical innovators where men had always dominated the technical aspects of production. Typical was the case of Sun Yufang, a woman technician at the Shanghai No. 1 Textile Machinery Plant who was responsible for organizing a worker-technician-cadre ("triple combination") group for redesigning a piece of machinery. She and the other women participants were credited with its success.[62]

Women spinners at a Beijing mill took on the project of developing a mobile chair that would ease the job of loom tending and lessen worker stress. The significance of their success in regard to women's liberation was made explicit:

> Seven months after the operation began, we spinners were using the chairs. In making them we not only liberated ourselves from a lot of strain, but more important we had freed ourselves from the old idea that there are things women can't do.[63]

There is no doubt that the old prejudices still had a strong hold on people. The educational experience and socialization of the younger generation had reinforced more egalitarian ideas, but undoubtedly the lingering prejudices against women were part of the generational differences regarding the pace and substance of change that were increasingly recognized as an aspect of political conflict in China. Many of the older cadres were slow to assimilate new ideas, particularly when they appeared to threaten production quotas. And, while regular industry represented the vanguard in the struggle for female equality, it did not account for the majority of urban women who worked, many part time, many on split shifts and in home-based activity. In these sectors, the hold of tradition could be even stronger.

The renewed emphasis on street industry as a significant component of China's industrialization strategy was important to the growing number of women employed in these workshops, factories, and service centers. In most cities these street industries rapidly became a significant part of total production. In Shanghai the production of street factories in 1970 was 3.4 times that of 1965 and came from 380 neighborhood factories and 4,000 teams. The output consisted of 10,000 products ranging from rivets, toys, and clothes to motors, instruments, and computers. And in Fuzhou, 570 street factories and groups produced over 400 products, 61 of which were included in the state plan.[64] The striking difference between the street industries of the Great Leap Forward and those in the post–Cultural Revolution period was the increasing sophistication in the level of technology and in the product produced. For example, a Changchun factory which in 1960 produced simple grinding wheels by hand in mat-covered sheds was mass producing the wheels by machine in 1973.[65] Another workshop produced cotton cloth in 1958 and by 1971 was manufacturing synthetic polyester fiber.[66] Still another began production of door and window handles and suitcase buckles in the Great Leap Forward; by 1966 it was manufacturing small electronic computers, and by 1972 it had a wide range of contracts and relationships with factories and with scientific research departments of educational institutions.[67]

The utility of street industry prompted changes in official policy. In the difficult period of the Great Leap Forward when resources were scarce, street industries were cautioned to be self-reliant and not depend on the state for technical guidance or material assistance. Now, with the collectivization of production and greater resources available, street industry projects were coordinated and supported by municipal authorities and received local party support.[68] Street factories often received help from regular factories in the form of technical cadres "borrowed" from regular industry. Some sent their own workers to a technical course in a local regular factory or attached institute. These women then came back and taught the others what they had learned, thus transmitting technical knowledge and combining formal learning with practical experience.[69]

In 1971–72, there was a national effort to increase the role of street industry by encouraging the development of new workshops and the expansion and sophistication of existing production facilities.[70] These production sites served two basically different needs. A great many of these projects serviced the local inhabitants by producing articles for daily neighborhood consumption. Often, neighborhood enterprises supplied certain welfare services such as repair or child care. However, street industry production was also closely integrated into the total urban production network, providing essential linkages and flexibility in planning. Moreover, street industry allowed urban areas to integrate production needs with nearby rural or suburban areas. Female labor was significant in the decentralization efforts aimed at fostering regional self-sufficiency and reduction of the urban-rural gap. Just as city medical facilities were sent to service the countryside, certain kinds of urban street industry were geared specifically to service the countryside. The development of small cotton textile mills in cities located in cotton producing areas was singled out for commendation.[71]

After the Cultural Revolution, local textile industries were established to take advantage of the local cotton crop. Other light industries suited to processing local agricultural or industrial wastes also created new employment opportunities for local women. Thus, while state investment still recognized the crucial importance of heavy industry, overall state plans gave priority to the development of light industry and the relationship between light industry production and agricultural production.[72]

> The development of light industry depends, to a great degree, on the supply of raw materials. Fully aware of this point, the broad masses of light industrial departments in Beijing have actively cooperated with agriculture, heavy industry and scientific research departments in developing the production of raw materials for light industry. They have helped rural communes in the Beijing suburbs to popularize five-strain seeds, develop a diversified economy and build bases for growing vegetables, grapes, juicy peaches, apricots, strawberries, peppermints, mushrooms, and roses. Many light industrial plants have utilized waste gas, and liquid residues to make important products such as hydrogen, medicines, and silicone single crystals. Factories under the Second Light Industry Bureau have used waste or inferior steel products to produce daily necessities, saving more than 12,000 tons of quality steel produced annually for the state.[73]

In this manner, street industry became an important link between town and countryside and supported efforts at rural industrialization. In the post–Cultural Revolution period the purpose and perspective of women involved in street industry were broadened and the political principle of reducing urban-rural inequality assumed practical application, as street industries became involved in processing agricultural products and in producing agricultural materials such as chemical fertilizer.

The administrative unit responsible for overseeing street industry was the street committee. Detailed information concerning the street committee's relationship to the municipal administration is scant. However, in some areas the committees appeared to be directly responsible for operation of collective street industries. In Beijing's Fengsheng district, the street committee had six "street factories" and one service center, employing approximately 40 percent of the housewives in the street committee area who did not have full-time jobs at regular factories.[74] Moreover, the street committees acted as the liaison when individual factories subcontracted with larger state-owned and -operated plants. Wages in some of these factories were almost comparable to wages in regular industry, and neighborhood child care facilities were available.

One model example in Shanghai's Gongjiang district was described as follows:

> Those housewives who leave their infant children at the child-care centers and work in the "cottage industry" workshops subcontracted to the "regular" factories, earn a respectable wage. In Gong Jiang New Village, the house-wife-workers make on the average 32 yuan, which is the equivalent to the lowest monthly wage for a worker in a "regular" factory.[75]

While Gongjiang was probably a leader both in its successful mobilization of female labor and for its workers receiving near parity wages with the regular industrial sector, the increasing significance of street industry created powerful pressures to accord women proper compensation and status commensurate with their growing role. The street committees, made up mostly of local women activists, many of whom also worked in local street industry or service centers, provided an organizational vehicle through which their demands could be communicated.

In addition to directly administering industrial projects, street committee activists in study groups reached out also to the older women, often grandmothers, who were placed in charge of young children.

> Every woman in Gong Jiang (Shanghai) under the age of fifty works; there is not a single one who doesn't. But after age fifty the women stay at home to look after their grandchildren and do embroidery and knitting for the neighborhood.[76]

Many of the local collective child-care facilities were run by "grannies," who were educated in their duties and socialized in terms of attitudes by participation in the study groups run by the street committees.

Street committees also helped mobilize urban residents to go to nearby rural areas to help with the harvest. The efforts appeared to be an integral part of the national effort to decrease urban dependency on the rural sector for food by mobilizing the urban unemployed to engage in agriculture.[77] These efforts were not new, but they illustrated the continuous attempt to get women away from traditional roles so they could "hold up half the sky." In addition to urban residents, the targets of these efforts were often women who had moved with their husbands to new industrial projects in newly developing areas like Daqing and other oil and mining communities. Often these wives did not work until mobilized, as in Daqing, to take part in agricultural production. As a result of their participation in agricultural production, they became more active politically.[78] Workers' wives were not, however, employed only in agriculture, where peasant-worker inequalities could be reinforced or complemented by sex. Machinery plants and mines used dependents to develop subsidiary production using old or scrap materials or to remodel equipment and simplify technological processes, using whatever skills or talent could be mobilized.

Under the direction of the Pingxiang Mining Bureau, for example, women set up sixty "satellite" factories, producing cement, chemicals, machines, tools, and machine-repair shops. They also gathered medicinal herbs and raised hops.[79] Dependents of urban cadres in Beijing set up a factory for making ropes and later a colliery, sewing group, and cobblers' group.[80] In Shenyang, wives of workers built a tile factory, making their own bricks, while others opened a small coal pit.[81] Whether in agricultural production or in industrial production, women's employment outside the home was emphasized as necessary to transform their consciousness and not simply to make use of their labor power. The campaign to involve workers' wives in these activities was really part of a general emphasis on small-scale production, which, like street industry, aimed to promote both production and political transformation. The inequality that existed for workers in street industry prevailed in small-scale production as well. But, as in street industry, these efforts also represented an opportunity for women to work and participate in the larger community.

Rural Women and Labor Participation

Peasant women faced a situation different from that faced by women in urban China. In rural China the progress of women toward greater equality, in which participation in production was regarded as a necessary first step, was much more immediately interpreted in relationship to the primary goal of economic development. As the Great Leap Forward showed, progress for women was impeded by the persistence of poverty in rural areas and the traditional organization of labor for agricultural production. Moreover, the nexus of familial relationships that structured female roles shaped, and in turn was shaped by, the relationships between culture, technology, and women's progress in a very dialectical manner. And although these relationships were by no means the only impediments confronting women in rural China, the resolution of short-run contradictions between the costs of using female labor and the investment needs of economic development, a problem that had emerged over the past two decades, was crucial.

Post–Cultural Revolution policies aimed at rural transformation contained the potential for changing both the ideological and the material conditions of women's struggles for emancipation and equality. The support for increased integration of women economically and politically that emerged from the Cultural Revolution came both from the ideology of the "criticize Lin Biao and Confucius" campaign and from official policies. Increased collectivization, equal pay for equal work, rural mechanization and industrialization, the *xia-xiang* movement of sending educated youth to the countryside, the expansion of educational opportunities, and the renewed emphasis in support for free-choice marriage, family planning, and the creation of health facilities all were official policy during the early to mid-1970s. Clearly, these policies, aimed at extensive social and economic restructuring of rural society, would require years to mature, but even by 1976 there were reports of some important trends and developments.[82]

The issue of equality, so central to the debates of the Cultural Revolution, became the basis for the early 1970s campaign to raise the status and increase the participation of rural women. The continuing persistence of this issue from the early days of cooperativization in the 1950s suggested it was a stubborn problem. The principle of labor compensation used (from each according to his/her ability, to each according to his/her labor), combined with the lack of mechanization in agriculture, tended to create in the 1970s a workpoint system that favored physically stronger males. But for the first time, this period also saw a concerted effort by the mass media to address a major area of sexual inequality: equal pay for equal work.

Certain justifications for a more egalitarian wage policy were put forth in the post–Cultural Revolution years. The media first of all created the impression that as a result of the Cultural Revolution (or Socialist Education Campaign) and the favorable political climate of this period, many more women were willing to demand equal compensation for equal work. The Party was, moreover, a strong supporter of the women, not only in backing up their demands but in using the opportunity to explore the implications of the old policy. At first opposition to equal pay for women was simply called revisionism, but by the mid-1970s the influence of the anti-Confucius campaign led to more thorough historical and ideological analysis.[83] The seriousness with which the women's struggle for equal wages was regarded was illustrated by the numerous articles in the Party journal, *Red Flag*, and in the *People's Daily*.[84]

It was reported that when men were told that women's lack of enthusiasm was due to unequal pay they replied, "A woman is a woman. How can women be given as many workpoints as we are given?" This male supremacist attitude, which was admitted openly, was quickly answered by the women, who cited the reality of obviously unjust discrimination in daily work:

> The ridges of wheat seedlings we have pulled up is [*sic*] no narrower than those of the wheat seedlings pulled up by you. The speed of our work is no slower than the speed of your work. The quality of our work is not inferior to the quality of your work. Why shouldn't we be given ten wage points?[85]

Sometimes, it was reported, men even got more workpoints for doing *less* work. In Kengxi Brigade, Zhejiang, for example, the men picked fewer catties of beans than the women but the men received ten workpoints and the women five. When the women protested, the men answered, "We have stronger labor power." To which the women retorted, "Why did you who have stronger labor power pick fewer beans than we did? He who picks fewer beans is given more wage-points— this is a policy of remuneration according to individual and not a policy of remuneration according to work done."[86] In the end, the women were accorded equal wagepoints when equal work was done.

In cases like this, Party secretaries used the opportunity to get at the roots of traditional prejudices against female equality by organizing study groups to discuss and criticize traditional Confucian maxims and the ways in which these attitudes influenced policy. To understand its importance, the issue was defined as a major political principle and not simply a question of "work method."[87] Indeed, by 1973, the question of women receiving equal pay for equal work had been defined as a problem of class struggle. This was accomplished by an analysis of women's interests in society which stressed "affirmative action" type of policies; because the particular oppressions women had suffered under the traditional system made them special victims within the peasant class, special provisions would have to be made to resolve the resulting inequities.[88]

> When we began the evaluation, some men had said, "All a man has to do is stick out his fist and he does as much as a woman does in six months. If women want the same base rate, they have to do just as we do in plowing, planting, digging, and carrying sacks of grain." We pointed out that women had never had the chance to learn some of these jobs. If you make strength and skill the basis of your comparison you'll be pitting men's strong points, physiologically and historically, against women's weak points. First and foremost the comparison should be on attitude toward work, on patriotic and collectivist thinking and contributing to the collective.[89]

In some areas, *xia-xiang* students were instrumental in questioning old and discriminatory wage systems. Some communes were pressured by their presence to implement the equal pay policy "among intellectuals who have settled in the countryside and for male and female commune members."[90] From groups of young urban women "sent to mountainous and rural areas (from cities), there have emerged a number of activists doggedly following the socialist road."[91]

Women also appeared to fare better where the brigade was the unit of accounting and the percentage of women working was high.[92]

The post–Cultural Revolution push for large-scale mechanization of the agricultural sector and the expansion of production supported women's progress toward equality in wages. In those units where production expanded and collective wealth increased, the collectivization of women's work did not appear in such direct conflict with the need to accumulate savings to reinvest in production. Moreover, in the reallocation of labor that was perceived, as the level of collectivization increased and plans for mechanization and the establishment of rural industries were formulated, women's participation was considered necessary. As one article in *Red Flag* noted, "after collectivization, many collectives will be insufficient in labor power and will find that they must develop the labor of the broad mass of women who are not participating in field labor to go to the labor front."[93] Labor shortages resulted both from expanding production and from the use of male labor in engineering projects, the building of irrigation systems, capital construction, and the establishment of livestock breeding operations. The mobilization of women peasants to replace the men was not unlike the effort to "substitute women for men" by recruiting urban women to work in industrial and commercial establishments during the Great Leap Forward.

The Dazhai Brigade had raised the living standards of its members through increased collective undertakings at the brigade level. Women were an active presence at Dazhai, and women peasants were exhorted to follow the Dazhai model, to actively engage in field work and in projects to diversify agricultural production and increase commune wealth. Indeed, Dazhai remained a model under the leadership of its female Party secretary, Guo Fenglian, as the percentage of Dazhai's collective income from economic diversification and local industrialization rose from 27 percent in 1967 to 53 percent in 1973.[94] Animal husbandry, fresh and dried fruit processing, fishing, and small local factories had all been developed. Women's labor tended to be most heavily utilized in the production of raw materials—crops, animals, fruits, and the like.

For some women peasants, work meant more than an increase of income. Recruited for political study during work breaks, women had the opportunity to increase their community participation, and some emerged as local activists who, as new role models, mitigated the influence and dominance of traditional roles to some extent.[95]

Education for Rural Women

The large-scale and intensive efforts at rural mechanization and rural industrialization that emerged so prominently in the mid-1970s underscored the importance of education. If women were to be able to contribute, the lack of educational opportunities for them had to be overcome. As the Leap so vividly demonstrated, lack of skills, even basic literacy, was a considerable obstacle to the rational and efficient use of female labor, even under traditional farming methods. In the ideological campaigns of the post–Cultural Revolution period, traditional attitudes flowing from the centrality of the family's role in production and consumption were scrutinized and critiqued.

Surviving even the debates of the Cultural Revolution was the widespread feeling that education was a form of property to be used for individual or family upward mobility, the hopes for which rested traditionally on boys, not girls. Such attitudes concerning female educational payoffs severely limited access to an education for many peasant girls.[96] The early stages of the post–Cultural Revolution campaign against traditional ideas concentrated on simply making education available to young women. Attitudes according men greater importance persisted, however, so that special efforts were now made to "pay attention to selecting girls" to attend school.[97] Yet the family-defined traditional role for women was still a powerful one, and was not made any weaker where poverty still made the family look like a logical solution to problems of material security.

The educational reforms of the Cultural Revolution, like those of the Great Leap Forward, tried to accommodate the family by experimentation with full-time education, part-time education, literacy classes, and the integration of education with labor. While the resultant increase in educational opportunities was favorable for women,[98] the persistence of traditional marriage patterns, wherein women leave their natal family, remained an important obstacle.

The development of the urban nuclear family (with the addition usually of one parent) had reinforced the idea of education as a means to serve the wider society, even though urban educated youth could still think of it as a way to promote their own fortunes. Rural areas, by contrast, were much more interested in the immediate acquisition of technical information and methodology that would be applicable to the narrower, but no less important, production problems faced in local villages. Individual rural production units which sent young students to schools were interested in the student's service to their own collectives after graduation. Girls were looked upon as a risky investment, for if educated and then married, they were likely to move away to their husband's village rather than remain in their own. This attitude was reflected by the low numbers of women in leadership positions in rural educational institutions.[99]

Party efforts to increase the numbers of women in schools at all levels were numerous. In many villages girls and young women still comprised as much as 85 percent of the children who were not in school. In some brigades, all of the children unable to attend school were girls. To rectify this situation, two realistic alternatives existed: one was to develop educational programs that would enable young girls to meet familial demands for helping out at home, or to allow young women (including those already married) who were engaged in collective labor to attend school part time on flexible schedules; the second possibility was to collectivize those tasks which prevented women from attending school, or to suggest a sharing of household tasks among all siblings.

The Party usually opted for the first alternative, because it was the least disruptive and it minimized the possibility of direct ideological conflict over the principle of female equality. Educational facilities were planned to meet the problems of families where the girl's help was needed. Many communes set up half-day classes, noon-hour classes, and evening classes to accommodate the young women.[100] These arrangements were not, however, the equivalent of full-time daily attendance at school, and while they represented progress in breaking down opposition to education for females, they could not train women for the more skilled and better paying jobs. In some instances the women fared better when the brigades took over the responsibility for primary education from the production teams.[101] For many rural women, support from the Party or production units above the team was an important factor. In spite of the obstacles to education for female peasants, there was in the 1970s a vast expansion of schools in the countryside. Many young girls received not only primary but secondary education as well.

Xia-xiang Youth

Young girls born in the rural areas were not the only new source of educated females in China's peasant population. Another was the educated youth sent from urban centers to the countryside to become workers and peasants in the communes and on state farms on a more or less permanent basis. The precedent for the *xia-xiang* movement was the transfer of cadres to integrate with the masses in the aftermath of the *Zhengfeng* movement in 1942. In the decentralization efforts of the Great Leap Forward and the early 1960s, this policy reemerged but the numbers of people involved did not match those sent down from 1968 until Mao's death. Since then, the policy, which has virtually been eliminated, appears to have lost its political significance as a major component of rural policy.[102] The *xia-xiang* movement has been analyzed as a way to deal with the employment problem, as an attempt to narrow urban-rural inequalities, and as a source of political conflict resulting from this radical transfer of urban population.[103] The *xia-xiang* movement has also had significant impact on both urban and rural women.

The national press did not publish a statistical breakdown of the male-female ratio among *xia-xiang* youth, but it was clear that young women formed a large part of these groups. Sometimes they amounted to half the total. [104] The movement, therefore, had an impact both on the women who participated and on those in the rural communities to which they were sent. From the beginning the situation was exceedingly complex and uncertain. Rural assignments were and, even more so now, are viewed rather negatively by some students. Many students had sought an education as a means of upward mobility, and an industrial job remained the preferred goal even for female students. But a rural assignment could have some advantages for women. Since there were still social barriers and greater competition in urban areas, especially in higher education and in the most skilled job categories, the existence of alternative areas of work offering possibly greater career mobility was important. It helped prevent large-scale disaffection by women whose training qualified them for better positions but who were denied access to them. Viewed in collective terms rather than in terms of individual upward mobility, the degree to which women students overcame both their own own preferences for urban jobs and the peasant hostility they met both as women and as "outsiders" made them effective agents in the transformation of the countryside.

Community acceptance of these educated young women was reinforced by diversification of production and expansion of productive capacity through mechanization and the development of rural industry. Young urban women possessed those skills needed by the modernization policies. As a result, some young women were given positions of great responsibility and status rather quickly. Others were entrusted with important construction or industrial development projects, while still others rose to local agricultural leadership positions, emerged as activists in Party work, became leaders in developing health care services, or became respected school teachers or agricultural technicians. [105] Their command of scarce skills, combined with the urgent demands of production and services, at times overcame the rural prejudice against women, especially when the woman in question was a stranger and hence more readily seen as different.

Aside from their participation in production, the impact of these young women on other aspects of life in rural communities was also potentially significant, although their presence was fraught with ambiguity. Sophisticated and educated urban girls posed a threat to their rural sisters in the competition for the most eligible local males, but they also served as models for the local girls to emulate. They destroyed female stereotypes and demonstrated that women were capable in fields far removed from bearing children and managing the household. Widening the horizons of village women and reinforcing the idea that women "hold up half the sky" were crucial in this period when the old institutions and women's roles within them were increasingly coming under attack and new roles were struggling for growth and survival.

In an attempt to harness the potential of these urban-educated young women, the rural women's associations assumed the task of helping them get settled in the countryside and provided an institutional shelter against local opposition. [106] The antipathy toward the educated youth that surfaced in many areas and the lingering disappointment at not having received a factory or other urban assignment were important problems to be worked out by the youth and by the local communities in which they settled. There was great pressure on the young people to accept their rural assignments as permanent, and thus marriage to local commune men became an important indicator of their commitment.

The lifestyle of urban women, especially those who came to the countryside and then married local men, would also affect those familial roles that most Chinese women assumed at some point in their lives. The success of the rusticated female youth in adjusting to life in the countryside, their marriage to local men, and the success of the attempts to promote late marriage and birth control were closely related and fundamental to rural women's progress. The role of educated youth in delaying marriage and using contraception was considered an important factor in reducing the growth of population in the Chinese countryside. Moreover, urban experience had shown that educated women tend to continue working after marriage, becoming a permanent part of the labor force as opposed to a marginal or temporary part. Insofar as the rusticated women would live their own lives in this way, they represented to local women the possibility of integrating familial and socially productive roles.

Young women who married local commune members were given great publicity, particularly during the campaign to criticize Confucius. They were praised for defying the traditional prohibition against marrying "lower" than one's class, and also for insisting on freedom of choice in marriage. [107] The case of Wan Ninglin is instructive.

> People told her: "If you marry a common peasant in the countryside, you will never be able to enter a college for advanced study or an industrial plant for work. How foolish you are. . . . Conditions in the countryside can never be as good as the cities. What do you see in the countryside that has won your heart? And her parents told her: "Ninglin, you should know that a person who has shown such progressiveness as you do is very likely to be nominated for receiving a college education in one or two more years. Do not be so shortsighted as to ruin your good fortune." (father). "By all means, try to be transferred back to the city. Don't marry a mere peasant." (mother). [108]

Wan Ninglin married a production team leader and made the decision to live in the countryside permanently. Wan's decision was portrayed as a conscious blow against traditional behavior patterns and norms regarding career mobility and the role of parental interference in marital affairs. As more youth went into the countryside, the pressure to change old customs and habits regarding women increased. No doubt it was partly this pressure that led to the near-abandonment of the *xia-xiang* movement by 1979, but while it was in effect, its impact on women and relationships between the sexes and within the family was enormous.

Conclusion

For women, the post–Cultural Revolution years represented significant progress as the Chinese leadership displayed an increasing understanding of the dialectical relationship between the politics of women's progress and the process of socioeconomic development. In the "criticize Lin Biao and Confucius" campaign the Chinese attacked directly not only the ideological roots of women's oppression but also confronted some specific issues such as equal pay. Moreover, national policies of the period, like the *xia-xiang* movement, also raised many women's issues in a rather direct way, especially those concerning female roles in rural Chinese society. The progress made in defining and articulating the problems facing Chinese women and integrating them into the larger issues of development policy was not equalled in the analysis that would resolve some of these cultural and structural problems.

In paying attention only to ideological issues, the Chinese did not analyze the important structural impediments with which women still had to cope. Nobody attempted to analyze the work women did in the household and family—how it was determined by history, social structure, and development policies, and, in turn, how it determined women's role in Chinese society. Nor was there any social analysis of the increasing stratification of the female labor force and the conflict between class interests and sex interests. The inability to resolve the problems raised by the radical economic, political, and social policies of the post– Cultural Revolution years made the continuity of these policies extremely problematic in the post-Mao period.

but she has not discussed this.

Post-Mao Policies and the Campaign to Limit Population Growth

MAO ZEDONG'S DEATH IN SEPTEMBER 1976 AND THE SUBSEQUENT AR-
rest of the so-called Gang of Four abruptly changed the configuration of political
forces and policy priorities that had characterized post–Cultural Revolution China.
The anti-Confucian campaign, which had shown strong sensitivity to the problems of women, rapidly drew to a close. News of women's achievements and
growing participation in production at all levels receded, but women figured
prominently in supporting the new leadership's vociferous denunciation of the
Gang,[1] and this continued for the remainder of 1976 and well into 1978. The
Hua Guofeng–Deng Xiaoping coalition seemed preoccupied with consolidating
control and eliminating opposition, and not until November 1978 did a more or
less comprehensive explanation of and theoretical justification for the new development approach called the "four modernizations" (in industry, agriculture, science and technology, and the military) appear in an official publication.[2]

The publication of certain political documents and the announcement of new
policies indicate a clear departure from previous official policies toward women,
and also mark a change in the Party's understanding of the woman question.
Since official policy and theoretical understanding shape the context within which
real problems are resolved, it is to these matters that we turn first.

Political and Ideological Developments

A new approach to the woman question in China was signaled by the Fourth
National Women's Federation Congress in September 1978. The National Federation had been disbanded in the early years of the Cultural Revolution and had
been politically moribund ever since, at least on the national level. However,
local women's organizations appear to have been rebuilt and were quite active in
the early 1970s. This was often the result of efforts to mobilize women for
production and study when local development plans had required female labor.
The convening of the reestablished Women's Federation reinforced a shift in Party

policy that had already been signaled by the publication of an article in *People's Daily* in September 1977 by the veteran female cadre Kang Keqing.[3]

The reemergence of Kang as spokeswoman for the women's movement was in itself a harbinger of change. Although her revolutionary credentials dated back to the pre-1949 period when she led a detachment of female soldiers, in post–1949 China she had been most closely associated with the Children's Department of the Women's Federation.[4] Now in her eighties, she was part of the grand old guard of the women's movement, which also included Cai Chang, Deng Ying-zhao, and Song Qingling. All of these older women were leaders in the newly reestablished National Woman's Federation.

Kang's *People's Daily* article was a clear statement of reorientation for the officially supported women's movement in the post-Mao period. Although the rhetoric of the Cultural Revolution was used, greater emphasis was placed on the pre–Cultural Revolution struggles in the pre–1949 liberated areas and in the early 1950s. The analysis focused on the supportive tasks undertaken by women in those periods and on the importance of the Marriage Law as a guarantor of female rights. The past was presented as a model for the present and the future. Kang concluded by exhorting women to do their part in the "four moderniza-tions." What that part was became clearer as March 8, International Women's Day, approached in 1978.

Articles which appeared in the press on that day clarified the extent to which women's roles were being reevaluated in light of the new strategy for Chinese development. The themes were clear. Even though women held up "the other half of the sky," with important contributions to socialist construction, their release from "backbreaking manual labor and tedious housework" was to be *gradual*. In the meantime, a double burden was clearly stated. "Women workers, commune members and women scientists and technicians need to work hard and study, but they have to spend a considerable portion of their time tending to housework and children."[5] The clear identification of women with familial re-sponsibilities, the lack of discussion concerning male participation in these mat-ters, and a redefinition of the sexual division of labor contrasted sharply with publicity given to precisely these kinds of innovations a scant two years before.[6] Images of the 1960s continued to appear. By the time the Women's Congress opened in September 1978, any lingering doubts about the shift in policy toward women were dispelled.

Although twenty years, encompassing the Great Leap Forward and the Cul-tural Revolution, had passed since the last Congress, the leadership of the rees-tablished women's organization in no way reflected the vast changes that had occurred in China. Cai Chang presided over the opening of the Fourth National Women's Federation Conference as she had over the Third. Members of the

Praesidium included Song Qingling, Deng Yingzhao, Kang Keqing, Dong Bian, and Lo Qiong, names which could also be found on the Federation's leading organs in the 1950s. Many of these women, prominent in the 1950s, represented the urban-based intelligentsia and national bourgeoisie. Female workers and peasants constituted only 20.4 percent of the delegates in attendance[7] at the national convention, although they made up a much larger percentage of local federation organizations.

Wang Dong, representing the Central Committee of the Party, set the tone for the Congress in his general remarks to the plenary session. As the Party always had, Wang viewed the Women's Federation as a transmission belt between the Party and the female masses. He identified the major task for the Federation in this period as the mobilization of women in support of the new development policies. In the national effort to raise the scientific and cultural level of the Chinese people, he remarked: "We should consider women and *train a certain percentage of them*"[8] (emphasis added). Following Wang Dong's remarks, Kang's work report, clearly the most important document of the Congress, elaborated on these and other issues.[9]

The major thrust of Kang's speech suggested attitudes and policies that in recent years had been perceived as major obstacles to women's progress. Since the Federation is the key national organization in any matter dealing with female rights and opportunities, its analysis of women's tasks under the "four modernizations" in post-Mao China is not to be ignored. Four main themes predominated in Kang's report:[10] (1) women as rear service workers; (2) female responsibilities to home and family; (3) a united front policy emphasizing unity with women of the national bourgeoisie; and (4) the need for family planning.

In contrast to the post–Cultural Revolution attitude that "whatever men comrades can do, women comrades can do," Kang now clearly envisioned a secondary and supportive role:

> "Women form the main force in logistics. Among them are women childcare and education workers, salesclerks, cooks, street sweepers, nurses, barefoot doctors and other service personnel who are making extraordinary contributions in their ordinary posts.[11]

Instead of emphasizing the acquisition of new technical skills necessary for jobs in the modern sector, the report suggested harnessing the traditional skills of women in a developing network of child care institutions, public canteens, sewing, laundry, and other services primarily located in the collective sector. Reinforcing this service role were female responsibilities for household chores and child care in general, whether in or out of the public or collective sector. Although men were urged to help in these matters, and it was even argued that "men and women should be equal in the home with housework rationally proportioned between husband and wife,"[12] there was no doubt that the ultimate responsibility for these matters fell upon women.

> The problems that usually concern women comrades are the burdens of children and household chores. Should we blame them because of their burdens? When you blame them for having children and therefore, being cumbersome, you should listen to your conscience and ask yourselves whether you have helped them solve their problems. . . . We should understand that manning kindergartens and nurseries well and doing a good job in support work are by no means unrelated to production but are beneficial to promoting production.[13]

It was difficult to see how "equality" in the home could be reconciled with the policy that put only women there or in a "supporting" role while the main responsibility for production outside the home remained male. Even employing the majority of women as service personnel in the collective sector outside the home put women in an unequal position. Wages, fringe benefits, and social status in this sector were not comparable to that received in the state sector. Moreover, the policies of the post–Cultural Revolution period were that women should be recruited in all sectors of the economy, and indeed women workers had made substantial gains in other than service-oriented industries.

When women's productive and personal responsibilities both centered around household management and parenting, it was not surprising that Kang Keqing identified the interests of women in China as the resolution of those problems relating to marriage and family. Thus, it appeared that a major focus of the Women's Federation's efforts would be directed against individuals who threaten "harmonious" and "democratic" family development.[14] Strikingly absent from Kang Keqing's report and other conference documents was discussion of the need for women to struggle against wider historical, social, and economic forces that perpetuated female inequality in Chinese society.

From the beginning of the Cultural Revolution until the ouster of the Gang of Four, the themes of class struggle in a socialist country dominated political discussion. The leadership after 1976 instead stressed the united front policy, emphasizing unity for the purpose of promoting economic production. The Women's Federation reflected the new policy in two ways. First, female workers and peasant delegates to the National Women's Federation Congress made up only one-fifth of the total number of delegates. Second, the congress stressed the unity of women of all classes, most especially including the national bourgeoisie.

> Working women and women revolutionary intellectuals should be relied on to unite all women patriots, including those from Taiwan, Hong Kong

and Macao and the women and all their family members of Overseas Chinese. . . . The principle of "unity, education and remoulding" should be followed among the women of the national bourgeoisie.[15]

In the anti-Confucius campaign of the earlier 1970s women's interests were clearly identified as class interests even while sexual oppression was acknowledged. Peasant and worker class unity was stressed. In 1978, the new calls for national unity stressed the generic interests of all women and neglected the question of class.

The last major theme in Kang's report was the importance of family planning in the new period. This theme quickly began to dominate most of the literature about women. The gravity of the issue and the measures adopted by the Chinese to limit population growth demand that we return to this theme later. For now, let it suffice to say that both population control and women in the labor force were recognized as significant variables in the relationship between capital accumulation and investment. Lower numbers of children meant less expenditures necessary on schools, child care, medical care, and other services. Kang's report discussed both the pressing economic reasons for birth control and the necessity to protect the health of women and children.

The documents of the Fourth National Women's Federation Congress bear striking similarities to those of the previous congress, held in 1957. The continuity of leadership was seen in the membership in the new Praesidium, and both congresses stressed the united front, household responsibilities, marriage, and family planning. Yet China was not the same as it was twenty years before. Complex and rapid economic development had occurred. Collectivization and the ideological campaigns of the Great Leap Forward and the Cultural Revolution substantially changed the economic and political landscape. Women had been educated, trained, and recruited for jobs in the agricultural, industrial, and collective sectors of the economy. The superficial likeness of the pre–Cultural Revolution period and the late 1970s should not be allowed to obscure the vast changes that had occurred. The contradiction between the new attitudes and past progress was reflected by the Eleventh Party Congress, where women's representation in the central Party organization, although somewhat diminished, was clearly evident.[16] Moreover, the prominent female Party members of the 1970s were still around: Wu Gueixian, Lu Yulan, Hao Jianxiu, Guo Fenglian, and others.

Birth Control Policy and Women's Roles

The demand for birth control has always been associated with the women's movement in that family planning would decrease the centrality of the traditional housewife-mother role, thereby creating the opportunity for work and study. In the post-Mao period, there was in fact a tremendous national effort to support birth control and to control population growth. The goal has been to reduce population growth to less than 1 percent a year by the early 1980s. State support for family planning is officially recognized in the 1978 Constitution[17] and has been backed by extensive press coverage of the issue,[18] and rather severe reward and punishment systems have developed throughout China. The widespread development of local programs and the enormous publicity given them have created the idea that birth control is a new policy under the "four moderniza-tions." Indeed, the Hua-Deng leadership has charged that the deposed Gang of Four, and by implication official policy during and after the Cultural Revolution, opposed both birth control and late marriage, severely impeded implementation of birth control programs, and compromised public health efforts generally.[19] Although the intensity and scope of the present effort, combined with a new system of financial and material rewards and punishments, are a departure from previous policy, family planning was an integral part of the development policies emerging from the Cultural Revolution, and significant though perhaps scattered progress was being made.

A mass campaign against early marriage and unplanned births was unfolded in rural areas in the early 1970s, and was reinforced by a developing network of health services using many *xia-xiang* students in the countryside. The develop-ment of collective sideline production and rural industry which used female labor also had an impact on the birth rate.[20] It is this larger context, which provided a set of integrated policies to support birth control, that is presently being restruc-tured by the "four modernizations." Thus, while the approach to family planning has assumed a new prominence, and birth control is more a direct and single object of policy, the context of the effort is changing dramatically.

The general expansion of health care services, especially in rural areas in the post–Cultural Revolution period, benefited women in several ways.[21] Increased participation by women in the health care delivery system in the early 1970s substantially increased the level of health care available to women. More impor-tant in the long run, it fostered the increasing integration of women into the labor force and helped raise the status of women as they occupied respected professional jobs. The number of women in medical schools rapidly increased.[22] Many of these graduates staffed the gynecological and obstetrics departments of urban hospitals and participated in the *xia-xiang* of medical personnel and facili-ties to the Chinese countryside, where they helped rural women in such matters as childbirth and birth control.

As purveyors of a badly needed service, women doctors, nurses, and paramed-ics encountered less opposition than the younger and less experienced *xia-xiang* female students. Their acceptance by local rural communities helped these students as well as local women by reinforcing new public roles for women. At the same time, these urban women participated in the national effort to reduce the inequalities between urban and rural areas by reorienting the national network of medical facilities to service those most in need.

In Chinese cities, the network of health care did not end with the hospitals, which organizationally were administered by the state. Most cities are divided into neighborhoods and lanes, and the growth of health stations at these levels, staffed by neighborhood health workers or Red Guard doctors, was an increasingly common phenomenon.[23] These local health facilities were run by the residents' committees and, though separate from the local hospitals, apparently worked in close cooperation with them. Medical policy set by municipal authorities was implemented by local health workers. The Red Guard doctors became involved in a significant birth control program, illustrating a definite attempt to reduce population growth in the post–Cultural Revolution period.

The birth control or family planning campaign was part of a wider campaign against the "feudal practice" of early marriage. Contraception, planned births, and late marriage were all identified as contributions to building a socialist society as well as factors in women's liberation. The Red Guard doctor, most often a former housewife who had been given one to three months training, was responsible for the distribution of contraceptive devices, which had been free since 1970.[24]

The success of efforts to limit births appears to have been quite significant in the urban areas, although data is fragmentary. Individual factory achievements reflected the success of a municipal campaign to control population growth in Suzhou. At the Suzhou Dungfanghong Silk Mill, the birth rate dropped 11.4 percent from 1971 to 1972, and at the Xiadong Machine Tools and Electric Appliance Factory 91 percent of the women workers were practicing birth control.[25] At a Nanjing Textile Mill prior to the Cultural Revolution births numbered in the hundreds but in 1970 there were only 65 and in 1972, 42.[26] This particular factory experienced a rather intensive birth control campaign, reaching women workers through their study groups. The goal of a 2 percent or less population growth rate per annum was considered desirable, and there were claims that by 1974 Beijing's rate had dropped to 1.17 percent and Shanghai's to 0.6 percent.[27] The political pressures maintained by the institutionalization of birth control work by residents' committees and reinforced by increasing opportunities for female employment were important variables in the program to limit population growth.

The progress made in Chinese cities was not, however, matched in the vast countryside, where even in the 1970s decisions to allocate scarce investment resources to health facilities still came into conflict with the more immediate demands of production, especially at the team and brigade levels. As one brigade in 1973 complained: "We are already fully occupied in production and yet we have to grasp the work in women's disease."[28] The large-scale establishment of cooperative medical systems at the commune level after the Cultural Revolution was, however, important.

The communes assumed the burden of more expensive health care, while the brigade established less costly clinics and teams concentrated on training barefoot doctors.[29] The national effort to develop rural health services went beyond commune hospitals and training paramedics. Capital construction budgets at the county level contributed to building medical schools where they could be most responsive to local needs. Maternity and gynecological care was often considered an important aspect of the new facilities. Individual provinces, communes, and brigades differed markedly in the quality and extent of medical care offered to the rural population. The overall development of rural medical facilities was related to the progress of economic development generally. But nevertheless, in post–Cultural Revolution China, medical care in general was a politically important issue.[30] So too was the question of family planning.

The demand for family planning, long associated with the women's movement, acquired new support and legitimacy with the expansion of general health services in the countryside. The idea that unbridled population growth endangered socialist construction was increasingly publicized. Birth control work, while still largely the responsibility of a woman cadre (most often the head of the local women's association), was increasingly portrayed as something that demanded male cooperation. Commune committees on planned birth work usually included male and female members who shared the responsibility for supervising and coordinating the work on planned births. Here, as in other matters, the Dazhai Brigade was portrayed as a model, because at Dazhai the campaign for planned births had succeeded in spite of considerable opposition. It can be assumed that similar forms of opposition were operative in the myriad other teams and brigades of rural China.

> At the beginning of the family planning propaganda program, there was little positive response because of the misgivings clouding the minds of the women. But Comrade Song Liying, member of the Party branch and Chairman of the Women's Congress, broke the ice by taking the contraceptive measure first herself, saying, "this is not merely for reducing the number of children and my family burden, but also for enabling one to study, work and labor more successfully, thus making great contributions to the revolution." By now, 98% of the men and women of our brigade who are able to produce offspring have joined the family planning program. This has enabled more and more women to participate in collective productive labor.[31]

The Dazhai approach suggested that a successful program of family planning had to have the active support of men, had to be reinforced by the participation of women in collective production and by active female leadership, and had to be motivated by the desire to contribute to a national effort at socialist production and revolution. Here was the crux of the matter, for by 1974 the ability and willingness to participate in family planning was not a matter of availability of contraceptives. Even remote villages could be supplied with any one or a combination of the methods of contraception: pills, IUD, male condoms, diaphragms, and injections. Sterilization and abortions were also widely used.[32]

Thus, Dazhai's experience suggested that the educational and motivational work done by women cadres in rural areas was as significant in the gradual but steady acceptance of birth control as was the availability of particular contraceptive devices. The organization of study groups, a development of the "criticize Lin Biao and Confucius" campaign, especially among those women who did not work and were probably most in need of contraception, was considered crucial to carrying out the tasks of women's work.[33] These groups attempted to deal with the underlying fears of economic insecurity in old age, a major reason why peasants traditionally had large families and favored males over females as potential laborers. The study groups were made up of men and women. It was stressed that the collectives' ability to guarantee minimal security in old age meant that women no longer had to bear several male children to avoid parental poverty in old age. A major cause of female subordination could thus be eliminated, and female infants would be equally cherished. Moreover, health advances increased infant survival rates and thus made irrational the need to produce many children so that one would survive. Finally, the groups stressed the importance of allowing women the opportunity to study and work and contribute to building socialism. These face-to-face meetings with political cadres, as well as the "home delivery" of contraceptives, were the main ways that the policy for birth control was implemented. Linking the birth control issue to the socialist revolution increased if not legitimized public discussion of what had heretofore been considered too personal.

Efforts to promote family planning were reinforced by a simultaneous campaign against early marriages and the promotion of free-choice marriages, neither of which had become universal even though the Marriage Law had been in effect for twenty years. It was argued that if young women did not marry early, they were more likely to acquire education and skills that allowed them to play more prominent roles in "political and class struggle." The assumption was that once they had been active, they would be more likely to continue to work after marriage and childbirth, just as their urban counterparts did.[34]

All of these campaigns during this period appeared to rely greatly on political organization and exhortation. One of the more popular tactics of the Party was to use theatrical productions like "Late Marriage is Good" to propagandize the effort against early marriage.[35] Also important were efforts to publicize examples set by the young people themselves, especially the educated youth sent to the countryside.

> We propose that the vast majority of educated youth must take the lead in changing outdated habits and customs and insist on getting married late for the revolutionary cause. We also hope that rural cadres actively support the educated youth in this revolutionary practice.[36]

Rural women who emerged as active decision makers in rejecting feudal marriage customs were given great publicity. Whereas in the pre–Cultural Revolution period it was the men who were so often credited with revolutionary consciousness, now the women came to the fore. In some places progress was noted by the increasing numbers of women who had made free-choice marriages.[37]

Yet, the economic realities of rural China remained. The fact was that rural economic development had not progressed, on a macro level, to the point where enough women had been pulled into the kinds of work or education that would have reinforced fewer births and later marriages. Nevertheless, post–Cultural Revolution development strategy did have a positive impact on women's economic position in rural China, and economic developments did reinforce the political and organizational emphasis of the period's policies.

Free-choice marriage meant that women more frequently remained in their natal areas. As the family's institutional role in the arrangement of marriage ended, women became free to assume productive roles in the collective economy shaped by the commune or brigade rather than the family. This helped to break down the fear that educating and training a daughter was "weeding someone else's garden." The growth of commune and brigade-level economic activity reinforced these possibilities by providing job opportunities for women who could then become part of collective efforts to increase services and income to the teams and families. Thus, women's real and potential contribution to the local collective becomes more important. Young women who remained in their natal areas could now take advantage of kinship ties in this transitional context to become leading activists, while those who left to work at the commune or brigade level could still make contributions to their original families or teams. Either way, new roles reinforced new economic possibilities, and new economic possibilities reinforced new roles.

What emerges strikingly from analyzing the situation for women in rural areas is that social change was dialectically shaped by a conflict between fiercely resistant traditional customs, attitudes, and behavior patterns and new ones emerging from the changes in material conditions in the countryside. Post–Cultural Revolution policies attempted to deal with both aspects of the woman question.

However, material conditions did not always correspond to ideological principle or political rhetoric. The tensions generated in some areas as the realities of a still poor countryside clashed with the political demands of the leadership must have been enormous. Yet the successful beginnings made in curbing population growth suggest an inherent rationality in a policy that was based on a recognition that there were ideological roots as well as socioeconomic conditions that oppressed and exploited women in Chinese society. And in combating these, the *xia-xiang* youth and the promotion of both collective sideline production and rural industrialization played an important role.

Post-Mao Policy on Birth Control and Women's Roles

The post-Mao leadership has set a target of achieving a population growth rate of less than 1 percent per year by the early 1980s. Building on the legacy of the pre-1976 period, in which Party committees and municipal and provincial political organs began assuming more active roles in the implementation of family planning programs, a new national policy on family planning emerged fairly quickly. Throughout 1977 and 1978, provincial conferences on planned parenthood were held,[38] and a national conference was called in January 1979.[39]

Chen Muhua, a vice-premier of the State Council and leader of the National Group on Planned Parenthood, used the example of eleven provinces and municipalities which had already reduced their population growth rate to less than 1 percent (Beijing, Shanghai, Tianjin, Sichuan, Hebei, Jiangsu, Shandong, Shanxi, Shenxi, Zhejiang, Hupei) to stress the importance of having only one child, or two at the most, and of spacing them at least three years apart. Population control policies were to be integrated with other policies, and indeed they reflected the radical changes that were occurring elsewhere.

Whereas previously there had been a reliance on collective economic development combined with political persuasion and peer group pressure to limit population growth, now a system of material rewards and punishments aimed at individuals and families would be used to ensure compliance with a family planning policy that was considered basic to the success of the "four modernizations." Although Chen did not elaborate on the nature of the new system, other than to suggest that it would involve increasing or decreasing welfare benefits, the message to individual provinces, counties, and cities was clear. The national press reported on early experiments with the new policy.[40] By the summer of 1979 several localities had experimented with reward and punishment systems and, while the individual localities differed somewhat, the major outlines of a coherent system of family planning began to emerge. The following discussion is based on the experience of Shulu Xian, Hebei Province, in the summer of 1979.[41]

Shulu Xian, the easternmost county in Shijiazhuang Prefecture, lies less than one hundred miles southwest of Beijing on the North China Plain. The high ratio of population to arable land—about two mou per person—has led to a widespread rural industrialization effort that is more intensive than in most other Chinese counties. As part of a liberated base area in the pre-1949 period, Shulu has strong Party and mass organizations and a relatively high degree of collective production. Shulu's previous success in family planning is evidenced by the decline in the birth rate from 20.2 per thousand in 1972 to 14.7 by 1978. Thus, for Shulu Xian, family planning was an already established program. Local book shops in Shulu carry a variety of publications discussing the methods of contraception and explaining the importance of family planning. Most of these materials were published before 1976 and had been available for several years.[42]

Song Jiure, deputy director of Shulu Xian's planning office, outlined the county's efforts to comply with the national effort to reduce the rate of population growth. The Family Planning Office was responsible for implementing policy formulated by a county-level committee of twelve "responsible persons," headed by the chairman of the Revolutionary Committee of Shulu Xian. The family planning committee included only three women, all of whom were involved in women's work. By contrast, the Family Planning Office and the local women's federation were responsible for actual policy implementation on a daily basis, and were staffed entirely by women. These women worked in cooperation with office, factory, commune, brigade, and team personnel specifically charged with the task of implementing family planning policy in their units. Thus, women were an integral part of the organizational network involved in population limitation programs that rewarded compliance and punished violation.

The system of rewards for familial acceptance of the new birth control effort focused on the creation of single-child families. The individual work unit could give single-child families material rewards in the form of "honorable passes" (entitling the holder to purchase special goods not generally available), a wage increase of five yuan per month to factory workers (until the child reached age fourteen), or, in the case of peasant families, an additional two or three days' workpoints per month and an adult grain ration once the child was three. But rewards went beyond immediate subsidies to the family or to the child. The single child was also given special consideration in educational opportunities and medical treatment, and the family would be eligible for room space in new housing. All of these privileges were revoked with the birth of a second child.

The system of punishments became operative when families had more than two children or children born less than four years apart. For the latter, the severity and duration of the fine depended upon the time elapsed between births. Just as rewards sought to increase the standard of living, penalties were calculated to make the costs of raising an additional child outweigh the benefits. For factory and office workers a third child meant a 4 percent reduction in pay for four years. Commune members lost three to five workdays per month for four years, a stiffer fine which probably reflected the urgency of achieving control over population growth in the land-poor countryside. Additional children resulted in further income reductions, but were never to allow the family to fall below the subsistence level. Nonmonetary penalties included loss of maternity benefits to women, parental assumption of educational and medical costs, no promotion for four years, and, for peasants, buying grain for these children at higher prices. Communes had the right to deny families access to additional land for private plots and rights to collective grain, the latter important in times of flood and drought.

To meet the manpower needs of the county over the long run and to accommodate the individual desires of families to have children, each productive unit was responsible for developing its own plan to limit population growth, and each woman was given a year in which she could have a baby. For those who persisted and did not practice birth control, or if a woman became pregnant out of turn, maternity benefits were denied and deprivation of wages or workpoints resulted. In addition to monetary and other penalties all violators were subject to public pressure and criticism.

Shulu Xian's quick response to the national effort to decrease the rate of population growth was far from typical among China's 2,200 counties. For many counties, particularly where the pressure of population density per unit of arable land was mitigated by fertility of the soil, mandatory countywide programs did not yet exist as of the end of 1979. Typical of these was Wuxi County in Suzhou Prefecture, Jiangsu Province. Wuxi,[43] a relatively rich, fertile area, with several "one-ton rice fields,"[44] and a political history markedly different from Shulu, preferred leaving the initiative for birth control programs in the hands of individual communes, although even here a reward system was mentioned. As the pressure to conform to basic goals of the new development policy increases, many counties will probably develop programs similar to that of Shulu.[45] Thus, assuming even minimal acceptance throughout China, the new policy and the development strategy of which it is an integral part have important implications for structuring the ideological and material context for Chinese women in the 1980s.

Family planning committees generally are under the control of Party committees, revolutionary committees, and the leadership of various production units. Most of these organizations tend to have a predominantly male leadership. This perpetuates women's lack of access to decision-making bodies which formulate policies that shape women's roles in Chinese society. This problem, unresolved even by the Cultural Revolution's innovative efforts at creating institutions for mass participation, many of which have since disappeared, remains as a formidable barrier to women's equality. Women are responsible for implementing fertility control policy as cadres of women's organizations, barefoot doctors, and clinic personnel, but they have little input into the policy-making process. Insofar as the new policies reinforce the role of the family as an economic unit and undermine the importance of collective production outside the family, traditional female roles have received new reinforcement. In this manner, the present policy is consistent with previous efforts.

The new policy, unlike pre-1976 efforts to control population growth, apparently separates the birth control issue from the larger one of expanding health services in general. In the post–Cultural Revolution period birth control was emphasized within the context of developing gynecological and obstetrical services for rural women. Reports concerning efforts to solve the special problems of individual pregnant women or women whose reproductive function was threatened by disease appeared frequently in the press.[46] *Xia-xiang* youth were actively involved in the effort to bring gynecological and obstetric care to rural areas as part of the decentralization and dismantling of urban medical facilities.[47] Since 1978, however, reports emphasize the development of preventive medicine in rural areas and the adoption of modern Western medical technology in urban-based hospitals.[48] The use of educated youth to provide minimal medical services in rural areas has also been sharply reduced as the numbers of educated urban youth being assigned to the countryside recedes and the *xia-xiang* policy is criticized. Rural areas, in short, are being asked to assume the burden of local health care efforts by themselves.

Previous success in the effort against early marriage and for family planning was due, in large part, to the larger context of economic and political change within which the woman question was viewed and evolved. Policies supportive of the gradual acceptance of birth control included use of *xia-xiang* youth, especially young women, in the development of productive and welfare services in rural areas, the emphasis on rural industrialization under the decentralized policies of the post–Cultural Revolution period, and the increase in educational opportunities. The policies associated with the "four modernizations," however, may substantially change what was beginning to appear as a supportive context for the decline of the traditional familial roles of women and the development of alternative ones.

The *xia-xiang* of educated youth to the Chinese countryside, where their skills and education could help to eliminate the inequalities between urban and rural life, was clearly one of the most controversial but innovative aspects of development strategy in the Maoist period. Whatever the problems raised by this policy, it was clear that the introduction of urban-educated women into the countryside challenged traditional attitudes about female capabilities and showed that women's productive and social contributions could be made outside the nexus of familial relationships still so prevalent in rural areas. Whether or not this policy will be totally eliminated remains, as yet, unclear. Conflicting reports in the press suggest that no final decision has been made, but several areas, especially those like Shanghai, where Cultural Revolution criticism of the policy was strongest, favor its end.[49] Other areas, mindful of the needs of economic construction and the lack of urban employment, favor its continuance but on a reduced scale.[50]

Whatever the economic benefits or costs of ending this policy of *xia-xiang,* there is no doubt that the education and social welfare services, not to mention the social ferment, that had in some measure been provided by the *xia-xiang* youth will now dissipate if not disappear altogether. Slower development of these services will hinder women's ability to develop nonfamilial productive and social roles, and traditional forces have eliminated an important source of challenge. Insofar as the policy will continue, those sent to the countryside will largely be disappointed candidates for university or college entrance or the urban unemployed.[51]

If the elimination or severe cutback of the *xia-xiang* policy raises potential problems for rural women, the effect of this change in policy on urban women will be more immediate. Middle-school graduates who do not attend college need jobs, but a relatively slow expansion of employment opportunities continues to characterize the modern industrial sector in most Chinese cities.[52] To avoid sending these unemployed youth to the countryside, the present leadership intends to promote collective services and light manufactures to provide jobs for the increasing numbers of young men and women graduates. With the collective sector absorbing as much as 80 percent of the people assigned jobs,[53] the original composition of this labor force—predominantly "former housewives"—is bound to change dramatically.

> In arranging jobs for educated youth, the various departments concerned in Shanghai have put into full play the effective role of neighborhood processing groups and service groups. Since this year service groups in Shanghai Municipality have recruited some 45,000 persons.[54]

An accelerated expansion of production and services by street industry will depend upon the willingness of national and local authorities to invest in this heretofore neglected sector of the economy. While the press has been silent regarding the nature of investment and growth planned in this sector, it is clear that many of its products are slated for export in the Chinese attempt to create a competitive position in world markets. The need to earn foreign exchange to pay for the greatly increased imports of foreign technology[55] necessitated by the "four modernizations" strategy may place increased pressures on the collective sector to develop in ways that will limit "former housewives' " participation but provide employment for young men and women.

Standardization and specialization of production to ensure sales abroad require skills and a full-time labor force, therefore it may be likely that women, once married, will return to the home to be replaced by eager young people seeking urban jobs. Once out of the labor force, these women may find reentry difficult. Thus, urban women might easily become an important, though temporary, part of the urban labor force,[56] and some women—for clearly many of the educated youth will be females—may find their opportunities to participate in social production limited to a secondary, temporary role. For other women, employment opportunities may increase because of the central role played by textiles and light industry in the export market.[57] Although the new policies of the Deng leadership appear to threaten the patterns of female employment created by post-Cultural Revolution policies, the extent of their impact remains unclear.

As the collective sector develops and more youth are recruited to work in it, pressures to adjust wages and benefits may increase. Already it is evident that some youth are less than happy with assignments to work in collective undertakings, where the pay, benefits, and status are not commensurate with those of the state sector. The continuation of women's labor within this sector, problematic though it may be, reflects a major transformation in China: the growing acceptance of women's labor outside the home, at least in Chinese cities. For rural women the new development policies pose further questions.

Central to the agricultural development policies of the pre-1976 period was the emphasis on increasing the levels of collective production as embodied in the Dazhai model, including the move from team to brigade-level accounting. This emphasis on collective production was maintained in the early post-Mao period where family sideline production remained subordinate to the collective's role: the policy was summed up in the slogan, "In developing rural sideline production, first it is essential to develop the collective sideline production."[58] As the post-Mao leaders solidified control and the "four modernizations" unfolded, the stress on rural collective production gave way to efforts aimed at expanding the rural free markets, private plots, and family centers of subsidiary production aimed at increasing family income.[59] Women, traditionally responsible for sideline production, may come under increasing pressure to spend larger portions of their labor time in support of family production, thereby restricting their ability to participate in collective production. And, as we have seen, it was under collectivized production, especially above the team level, that women appear to have made significant progress in gaining wage parity and educational opportunities and in developing political leadership. Collective production at the team and brigade levels, and especially rural industrialization, freed women from the conservative power of the family and the natal village by mobilizing increasing numbers of women for work in new and less constricting jobs.

Rural industrialization, initiated under the Great Leap Forward and continued unevenly during the early and mid-1960s, was a major aspect of rural development policy in the post–Cultural Revolution years. Under the decentralization policies of the early 1970s, the county became a major initiator, organizer, planner, and coordinator of rural industries, whose function was to spur development of the local economy, especially in the quest to mechanize agricultural production.[60]

Diversification and expansion of the agricultural sector in the early 1970s, aided by the favorable ideological climate for women, led to increased mobilization of female labor and the beginnings of a small but significant female labor force in brigade and commune industry. Although more women were recruited for field work and related subsidiary production, educated young women were increasingly absorbed in the rural industrialization projects that mushroomed across the Chinese countryside. Female employment in industry was significant in several ways.

Wages in brigade and commune industry were paid in workpoints, a large portion of which reverted back to the collective unit (team) from which the worker came. A small cash stipend for living expenses was given to the worker. This meant that women workers now could make a direct and larger contribution to collective income, and that the status of women would therefore rise in the community. Women tended to get the same workpoints as men when there was a shift from physical to technical expertise based on the use of machinery. In many cases women gained access to the most skilled jobs, such as lathe operation, while men often did the heavier, dirtier, and less skilled jobs.[61] Female acquisition of skills was an important basis for rural wage equality, a phenomenon that has wide repercussions as more peasants become aware of the ability of women to add significantly to family or collective income. For the large industrial projects in towns or county seats, some services, on a small scale, such as housing and child care, were available.[62] But, the necessity to run local industry on the principles of self-reliance, diligence, and thrift necessarily restricted the availability of such welfare services and accounted for the predominance of young, most often unmarried girls as workers. It also explained the larger number of *xia-xiang* female students among the workers, since their educational backgrounds made them ideally suited.

In addition to the impact on female employment, rural industry was significant in other ways. The generation of additional income from rural industry also increased collective wealth at a level above individual production teams, where women's demands for increased facilities generated so much opposition during the Great Leap. The establishment of some basic industries, such as cement, chemical fertilizer, machine repair stations, grain milling, and the development of agrotechnical institutes and educational facilities, created conditions for further growth of the agricultural sector by increasing irrigation and mechanization and the cultivation of larger areas with increased yields. The increased use of machinery tended to lessen the male advantage of physical strength in the fields as it did in the factory. And even women who have had no education may benefit. Here again, the Dazhai model was operative. Women in Xiyang County (where Dazhai Brigade is located), for example, operated one-third of all the agricultural machinery in the county.[63]

The establishment of industries which alleviated household burdens and provided special opportunities for female employment was also significant. Flour mills appeared to be a consistent feature of most industrialization programs, and they freed women from a most onerous and time-consuming chore. Food-processing industries, cotton textile manufacturing, the use of sewing machines, all tended to reduce the household burdens of rural women thus freeing them for other work. The organization of cotton or textile factories in areas growing the raw material was important because females were the main source of labor even in those mills established at the county level.[64] Insofar as rural industry facilitated the establishment of social welfare services like health and child care, the effect was to lessen the individual's reliance on the family.

Although the labor force in rural industry is still predominantly male, the proportion of females is growing. By 1975, women appeared to average 20 to 30 percent of the workers in rural industry. There were exceptions, such as Lin County, Henan, whose 65 enterprises contained some with up to 40 percent female workers, largely because of the experience of this county in the Great Leap Forward. The future of women in rural China is, therefore, closely tied to the role of rural industry in the development strategy. Recent changes regarding centralized planning and specialization may have a significant impact on the role of brigade and commune industry, on the extent of support that local industry will get from the center, and on the ability of localities to carry out or initiate their own industry projects.[65] Insofar as the new policies stress a "go it alone" strategy for brigade and commune industry, economic support for new rural industrial projects will, apparently, have to be generated by brigade and commune income. This means richer communes will advance more rapidly, and hence women on these communes may leap ahead of their less fortunate sisters in the poor areas.

Local industry is still considered important in raising the standard of living and income in rural areas. It will increasingly provide exports for the growing volume of foreign trade, and other local plants will become part of specialized production networks making machinery. The growth of handicrafts, processed foods, and machine parts factories therefore seems to be the main avenue of development for local industry under the new strategy. Whether women will be assimilated into all sectors of rural industry or whether their increased importance in family-based sideline occupations will keep them tied to the home remains an open question.

Accompanying the new post-Mao policies is a greater emphasis on formal education and experts.[66] The inability of rural areas to provide even elementary education for all children, combined with the cutbacks in aid from urban areas, the decline of the *xia-xiang* movement, and the decreasing opportunities for rural youth to receive college educations in light of the reinstitution of the examination system, will make it more difficult for women to gain those skills needed for industrial work.[67] This will be true, at least in the short run, until rural development can support increased educational facilities.

Conclusion

It is still too early to evaluate the impact on Chinese Women of the "four modernizations" policy. Yet certain observations regarding the implications of the departure from policies associated with the pre–1976 period can be made. It is clear that the present Deng leadership perceives socialist development more as technologically solvable issues of economic growth than its predecessor, which viewed the social revolution as an integral part of the process of economic modernization. In this, the present approach to development is more closely identified with that of the period of the First Five-Year Plan and the early 1960s. And the roles most women play in China under this development strategy are analogous to those identified under the First Five-Year Plan and the early 1960s. Thus, in political-ideological terms, the resolution of the woman question in China is to be dependent upon the future success of economic modernization.[68]

The attempt to defuse the politics of women's liberation, however, may prove difficult as the need for population control mandates the development of the small nuclear family, thus undercutting the importance of familial roles for women. And, the acknowledgment of the legitimacy of female participation in the labor force, especially as the quest for foreign exchange is met by exports of light industry, a sector in which female labor is both traditional and a present target for mobilization and recruitment under the "four modernizations" strategy, further suggests increasing contradictions regarding the proper roles of women in Chinese society. The ambiguities regarding women reflect both the ideological and the material constraints of the new policies. In an economy unable to generate sufficient numbers of jobs for all those able to work, the political decision to curtail and/or channel female labor force participation reflects the influence of traditional attitudes regarding women. Moreover, the tensions between ideology and reality are great.

As we have seen throughout our discussion of post–1949 China, the increasing levels of female labor force participation and sociopolitical involvement especially in the Great Leap Forward and the period after the Cultural Revolution have created powerful pressures within Chinese society to support the demands of women's liberation. The present attempts to identify women with home and family and certain kinds of jobs, in what must be considered a retreat from the goals of female emancipation, are likely to create new tensions within Chinese society.

Epilogue

We began with a critique both of Western modernization or development theory and of traditional Marxist theory as being inadequate for our understanding of the woman question. Neither could adequately explain the reasons for female inequality and oppression, and hence neither could adequately point the way toward liberation and equality. Where modernization theory did deal with women, the analysis often took female roles in contemporary Western bourgeois society as the implicit standard by which to analyze changes and trends in other societies. The significant contribution that Marxist theory made to understanding the role of women was in identifying the family as part of a wider social division of labor and hence as a source of female inequality, a barrier to wider participation in social labor. But Marxist theory lacked a coherent analysis of how female roles would be transformed in a society where women's social and political position would not be defined by her identification with the family or by a predetermined "female" role within it.

Both traditional Marxism and Western development theory shared a rather optimistic and mechanistic view regarding the inevitability of change in women's place in society as a result of industrialization and technological development. Unlike Western modernization theory, however, Marxism was much more direct in postulating the desirability and possibility of male-female equality as the division of labor was transformed by social revolution. The Chinese, as Marxists, were therefore ideologically committed to the principle of female equality but heir to a mechanistic theoretical version of Marxism which, like Western modernization theory, put the woman question in a clearly dependent and subordinate position in relationship to economic change and development. What then does the study of China suggest about the relationship between women and economic development?

In some ways, ironically, the Chinese case reinforces a certain mechanistic perspective. Women's roles did change, and women did play important and increasingly more frequent roles outside of home and family simply as a result of economic development. Moreover, the Chinese experience highlights what is often only tacitly confirmed and often overlooked altogether in modernization theories. Like their Western counterparts and those in the Soviet Union, Chinese women were the *mainstay* of the light industrial labor force at the early stage of industrialization in pre–1949 China. In post–1949 China, Chinese women in increasing numbers were working outside the home in a wide variety of industries and services and in agricultural production. Insofar as modernization theory or Marxist development theory has ignored or underplayed this vital role of female labor in industrialization, both have missed a crucial aspect of the dynamics of economic development.

In other ways, however, the Chinese experience clearly shows that a commitment to female equality *cannot be simply the outcome of economic development but that it can and must shape the patterns and processes of development itself*. The major hypothesis emerging from this study is that the role of women in society generally is a function not of female sexuality but rather of the mode of production or, in cases where "modes of production" are conscious choices, of "development strategy." Further, there is a short-range or even intermediate tradeoff between the goals of development and women's equality even while the two are ultimately dependent upon each other, and this is especially true in a poor country like China where development is an immediate or pressing priority. There is no clearer indication of this than to note how the different development strategies adopted since 1949 have affected women.

Those policies implemented during the First Five-Year Plan, with its emphasis on heavy industry, the development of urban-based welfare facilities, a formal education system, and centralization, meant that relatively few women would begin to transcend traditional roles. Industrial policy and investment priorities created limited employment opportunities, for which women had to compete with men. Relatively high degrees of labor surplus even in the favored urban centers led to a reemphasis on the traditional roles of women as housewives and mothers. Thus, while not insignificant numbers of women were being assimilated into the labor force in this period, women as a group were considered marginal to the process of socialist construction. The result was that even though the First Five-Year Plan saw significant economic development, as a whole the position of most women even in urban areas, and especially in rural areas, remained essentially unchanged.

By contrast, the policies of economic development and social change associated with the Great Leap Forward, the Cultural Revolution, and the post–Cultural Revolution period,—decentralization, mass mobilization of all labor, the development of all forms of production, the creation of services, and a political emphasis on the elimination of all kinds of inequality—created both material conditions and an ideological climate far more conducive to the rapid transformation of female roles throughout society. This transformation did not only affect a relatively small group of women, but implied a radical transformation of female roles in general. The result was as increasing recognition of the relationship between female participation and the creation of a more egalitarian socialist society. At the same time, however, the Great Leap revealed that the issue of female equality was not the same as other issues of equality in Chinese society.

The Great Leap created widespread opposition precisely because of the social and political implications of the mass mobilization of female labor. It was crucial in revealing the economic and social utility of female oppression and in demonstrating the tradeoffs between increased production and women's progress in the short run. Politically and economically the Great Leap dramatically revealed that the systems of health and education and the role of the family needed to be transformed in order for women to play major economic and political roles, and, ultimately, in order to utilize the abilities and talents of one-half the population of the country to speed up development. After the Cultural Revolution all of these problems and relationships concerning equality, the speed of development, and the choice of development strategy finally found a focus in the Maoist definition of socialism as a period of uninterrupted, simultaneous social revolution and economic development. In this context, the solution of the woman question became an integral aspect of, rather than a mechanical result of, the socialist transition to Communist society. The greater and more direct involvement of the Chinese Communist Party was illustrative of this very basic and important change in theoretical perspective.

The Chinese experience has suggested that the relationship between class interests and female interests is a subtle one. In a poverty-stricken agrarian society where labor-intensive modes of production prevail, women share with other workers an objective economic interest in economic development and technological change, and an objective political interest in egalitarian modes of organization and democratic decision making. Yet, the Chinese experience has suggested that there is also a genuine female interest that cuts across class lines and is embodied in a strategy of development that emphasizes egalitarian and participatory values that speak to the historic inequalities, oppression, and needs of females in general. Moreover, this female generic interest does not contradict and in fact supports the objective long-term interests of poor and working-class men and women. Yet, as the Chinese experience has clearly shown, in the short run class and female generic interests can *appear* to be in conflict because of perceptions shaped by poverty and values shaped by a history of institutionalized female inequality.

Comparisons between urban and rural China and the analysis of each sector have indicated that after a certain amount of development, the generic interests of females can be modified significantly and even overshadowed by emerging class formations. As industrialization proceeded, a fairly differentiated female labor force emerged in urban China. Rural peasant women found the going more difficult than urban working-class women. These essentially class cleavages would clearly compromise the notion of generic unity of interests among women.

The realities of Chinese society remain extremely complex and uneven. In comparison with the position of women in pre–1949 China, there have been tremendous and positive changes. From a traditional agrarian society in which women were commodities and where the predominant female roles were those of housewife and mother, Chinese women have emerged to play important roles in an increasingly diverse and sophisticated economy. Female social and political participation in neighborhood street committees, women's associations, the Party, study groups, and publicly elected bodies has steadily grown since 1949.

While there is little quantative data on actual labor force participation, it is clear that many Chinese women remain tied to traditional roles. Even with the enormous amount of development since 1949, China, especially the rural areas, remains poor. Economic and technological impediments still limit and shape the creation of employment opportunities for women. Inadequate health facilities, lack of educational experience, and labor-intensive modes of production severely restrict the use of female labor in the vast countryside. Moreover, the still important role of the family in economic production and the provision of services means that when women do work outside the home they often bear a "double burden." Male participation in traditional female work, an extremely important and unprecedented reality in China today, clearly remains the exception rather than the rule.

We have also seen that the relationship between economic and political power is conditioned by the influence of traditional attitudes toward the "proper" roles of women. A close examination of the textile industry during the Cultural Revolution, so quintessentially a female labor industry, revealed that even where women's labor predominated, political power did not necessarily result. Positions on the revolutionary committees, the locus of political and economic decision making in factories until 1978, remained largely in male hands. Although women made significant progress even in the short period between the end of the Cultural Revolution and 1973, there was no absolute correlation between their positions on these bodies and their numbers in the factory's labor force.

Economic development strategy remains the context for the dialectical struggle between revolutionary roles for women that demand a high degree of participation in public life, and a traditional culture that emphasized passivity, subordination, and domestic confinement. Insofar as the recent changes in development strategy stress the modern sector and the role of technological change, and deemphasize the politics of social revolution and social transformation, women's progress will be more difficult. In fact, the recent policy changes that stress the importance of the family unit and women's role within it may lead to a temporary detour from the road to liberation and equality. In any case, it is clear that the woman question remains part of the ongoing dialectic between theory and practice in China, where the transformation of female roles will continue to depend on economic development. As Mao Zedong pointed out, the process of liberation is a long and difficult one. At this historical moment the process of female liberation in China remains unfinished.

BIBLIOGRAPHIC NOTE

In this study I have used both Chinese and Western source materials. The latter are widely available and need no further explanation. Chinese newspapers, books, journals, magazines, speeches, and radio broadcasts were among my most important sources of information. These materials were either in the Chinese language or were translations into English. The translations used were done by the American Consulate in Hong Kong. All broadcasts were translated by the Foreign Broadcast Information Service. Not all important materials are translated. However, whether in English or in Chinese, most of these materials are available only at a few universities or in libraries and offices in Washington, D.C., making accessibility very limited.

A more complete bibliography of Chinese sources, both in Chinese and in English, from 1949 to the post–Cultural Revolution period (about 1975) can be found in my dissertation, "Sexual Politics and Socio-Economic Change: China from the Great Leap Forward Through the Cultural Revolution," Columbia University, 1978.

I have used the Hanyu Pinyin system of romanization. It is used by the Chinese, and more and more institutions in the United States are adopting it.

LIST OF ABBREVIATIONS

Below is a list of Chinese/English equivalents and abbreviations used in the notes.

ACDWF	All China Democratic Women's Federation, usually referred to simply as the Women's Federation
CB	*Current Background**
CCD	*Communist China Digest*
CCP	Chinese Communist Party
ECMM	*Extracts from Chinese Mainland Magazines**
FBIS	Foreign Broadcast Information Service (the date of the broadcast is cited)*
GMRB	*Guangming Ribao (Illumination Daily)*
GRRB	*Gongren Ribao (Worker's Daily)*
HQ	*Hong Qi (Red Flag)*
JJYJ	*Jingji Yanjiu (Economic Research)*
JPRS	*Joint Publications Research Service**
NCNA	*New China News Agency,* and known as *Xinhua*
RMRB	*Renmin Ribao (Peoples Daily)*
SCMM	*Survey of China Mainland Magazines**
SCMP	*Survey of the China Mainland Press**
XZGFN	*Xin Zhongguo Funü (New Women of China)*
ZGFN	*Zhongguo Funü (Women of China)*
ZGQN	*Zhongguo Qingnian (Chinese Youth)*

---

* United States Government Translation Service Collections

NOTES

Introduction

1. Helen Foster Snow [Nym Wales], *The Chinese Labor Movement* (New York: John Day Co., 1945), p. 16. See also Jean Chesneaux, *The Chinese Labor Movement, 1919–1927,* translated by A. M. Wright (Stanford: Stanford University Press, 1968), pp. 75–76.

2. John Halliday, *A Political History of Japanese Capitalism* (New York: Pantheon, 1975), p. 62.

3. Harriet H. Robinson, "Early Factory Labor in New England," in Miriam Schneir, ed., *Feminism: The Essential Historical Writings* (New York: Vintage, 1972), p. 52.

4. Sheila Rowbotham, *Hidden from History* (New York: Pantheon, 1974), p. 29.

5. See, for example, Cyril Black, *The Dynamics of Modernization* (New York: Harper and Row, 1966); Henry F. Dobyns, Paul L. Doughty, and Harold D. Lasswell, *Peasants, Power and Applied Social Change* (Beverly Hills, California: Sage Publications, 1964); and Helio Jaguaribe, *Economic and Political Development: A Theoretical Approach and a Brazilian Case Study* (Cambridge: Harvard University Press, 1968).

6. For a consistent development of Freud's analysis of female sexuality and its implications, see especially his lectures on female sexuality and reproduction and his analysis of the physical differences between men and women resulting from their functional specialization in reproduction, in *Standard Edition of the Complete Psychological Works of Sigmund Freud,* translated by James Strachey in collaboration with Anna Freud (London: The Hogarth Press and the Institute of Psychoanalysis, 1964). For the political implications of Freudian analysis and its role in Western political theory, see Juliet Mitchell, *Psychoanalysis and Feminism* (New York: Pantheon, 1974).

7. See C. K. Yang, *Chinese Communist Society: The Family and the Village* (Cambridge: M.I.T. Press, 1959); Marion J. Levy, *The Family Revolution in China* (London: Oxford University Press, 1949); and Clifford Kirkpatrick, *The Family as Process and Institutions* (New York: The Ronald Press Co., 1955), especially Part II, Chapter 7. See also "What Should a Mother Do About Her Career?" *The Wall Street Journal,* March 21, 1980.

8. Some writers, however, have emphasized that women can be either a major pillar of support for the traditional social order or a source of its disintegration. See Franz Fanon, *Studies of a Dying Colonialism: The Wretched of the Earth* (New York: Grove Press, 1966); and Jack Belden, *China Shakes the World* (New York: Harper and Brothers, 1949).

9. See Daniel Lerner, *The Passing of Traditional Society* (California: Glencoe Free Press, 1958); and Levy, *The Family Revolution in China.*

10. See Ester Boserup, *Woman's Role in Economic Development* (New York: St. Martin's Press, 1970). For an analysis of this in Britain see Ann Oakley, *Woman's Work: The Housewife, Past and Present* (New York: Vintage Books, 1974), especially Chapter 2.

11. See Rowbotham, *Hidden from History*; and Henry Rosovsky, *Capital Formation in Japan* (New York: Free Press of Glencoe, 1961). For the role of women in China's early industrialization, see Chesneaux, *The Chinese Labor Movement, 1919–1927*.

12. See Kuo Heng-shih, *China Enters the Machine Age* (Cambridge: Harvard University Press, 1944); Ivy Pinchbeck, *Women Workers and the Industrial Revolution, 1750–1850* (London: George Routledge and Sons, Ltd., 1930); and Rowbotham, *Hidden from History*. See also the case of Guangdong silk workers (women) in Marjorie Topley, "Marriage Resistance in Rural Kwangtung," in Roxane Witke and Margery Wolf, eds., *Women in Chinese Society* (Stanford: Stanford University Press, 1975), pp. 67–89.

13. This is true even in the United States. See "Gap in Earnings Between the Sexes Reported Up Threefold Since '55." *The New York Times*, November 30, 1976.

14. Boserup, *Woman's Role*, p. 195.

15. See Jacob Mincer, "Labor Force Participation of Married Women: A Study of Labor Supply," in *Aspects of Labor Economics* (Princeton: Princeton University Press [National Bureau of Economic Research], 1962), pp. 63–68; and Victor R. Fuchs, "Differences in Hourly Earnings Between Men and Women," *Monthly Labor Review*, No. 94 (Washington, D.C.: U.S. Department of Labor, Bureau of Statistics, 1971), pp. 9–15. Both works strongly suggest that while education is necessary for employment, in the case of women the impact of this variable is modified by cultural traditions and the organization of the economy to a much larger extent than it is with men.

16. For an analysis of the sexual division of labor in the U.S. labor force see Harry Braverman, *Labor and Monopoly Capital* (New York: Monthly Review Press, 1974).

17. In the U.S., while educational opportunities have increased over the past fifty years, proportionately fewer women hold masters degrees and doctorates today than did fifty years ago. See John J. Pietofesa and Nancy K. Schlossberg, "Counselor Bias and the Female Occupational Role," in Nona Glazer-Malbin and Helen Youngelson Wachrer, eds., *Women in a Man-made World* (Chicago: Rand McNally, 1972), pp. 219–222.

18. See Black, *The Dynamics of Modernization;* and Joseph LaPalombara and Myron Weiner, eds., *Political Parties and Political Development* (Princeton: Princeton University Press, 1966).

19. See Paul Baran, *The Political Economy of Growth* (New York: Monthly Review Press, 1957); and Raanan Weitz, ed., *Urbanization and the Developing Countries* (New York: Praeger, 1973). The recent literature questioning women's role in development generally is typified by by the following: Boserup, *Woman's Role;* and Irene Tinker, "The Adverse Impact of Development on Women," In Irene Tinker and Michele Bo Bramson, eds., *Women and World Development* (Washington, D.C.: Overseas Development Council, 1976). And see Hanna Papanek, "Implications of Development for Women in Indonesia," paper delivered at the Thirty-second Annual Meeting of the association for Asian Studies.

20. The supreme irony of this change is reflected in the attempted glorification of woman as chief consumer. See Betty Friedan, *The Feminine Mystique* (New York: Dell Publishing Co., 1963).

21. See Harriet Zellner, "The Determinants of Occupational Segregation," in Cynthia Lloyd, ed., *Sex, Discrimination and the Division of Labor*, Columbia Studies in Economics, No. 8 (New York: Columbia University Press, 1975), pp. 125–146.

22. See Jane S. Jaquette, ed., *Women in Politics* (New York: John Wiley and Sons, 1976).

23. See David C. McClelland et al., *Motivating Economic Achievement* (New York: Free Press, 1969).

24. See Mahmood Mamdani, *The Myth of Population Control: Family, Caste and Class in an Indian Village* (New York: Monthly Review Press, 1972).

25. See *Report: Part 1: The Critical Needs of Women,* Asian and Pacific Center for Women and Development of the United Nations.

26. The Percy Amendment to the Foreign Assistance Act led to the creation of the Women in Development (WID) Office in the Agency for International Development.

27. Karl Marx, *Capital,* 3 vols. (New York: International Publishers, 1947), 1:239–240; Frederick Engels, *Condition of the Working Class in England in 1844* (London: 1950).

28. Frederick Engels, *The Origin of the Family, Private Property and the State* (New York: International Publishers, 1942), p. 46.

29. Ibid. See also Braverman, *Labor and Monopoly Capital,* especially chapters 15, 16, 17.

30. Engels, *The Origin of the Family, Private Property and the State,* p. 66. This has often been misinterpreted by both Marxists and anti-Marxists to mean the abolition of the family in general.

31. See Norton Dodge, *Women in the Soviet Economy* (Baltimore: Johns Hopkins University Press, 1965); and Gail Lapidus, *Women in Soviety Society: Equality, Development and Social Change* (Berkeley: University of California Press, 1978).

32. See Barbara Wolfe Jancar, "Women and Soviet Politics," in Henry W. Horton and Rudolf L. Tokes, eds., *Soviet Politics and Society in the 1970s* (New York: The Free Press, 1974), p. 122.

33. Ibid., p. 126.

34. See Lapidus, *Women in Soviet Society.*

35. The term "noncapitalist" is less problematic than the term "socialist," so it will be used here.

36. See the essays in Zillah R. Eisenstein, ed., *Capitalist Patriarchy and the Case for Socialist Feminism* (New York: Monthly Review Press, 1979).

37. See, for example, Nancy Chodorow, "Mothering, Male Dominance and Capitalism," in Eisenstein, *Capitalist Patriarchy and the Case for Socialist Feminism,* pp. 83–107; Eli Zaretsky, "Socialist Politics and the Family," *Socialist Revolution,* No. 19 (January–March 1974), pp. 83–99; and Wally Secombe, "The Housewife and Her Labor Under Capitalism," *New Left Review,* No. 83 (January–February 1973).

38. See Carollee Bengdsdorf and Alice Hageman, "Emerging from Underdevelopment: Women and Work in Cuba," in Eisenstein, *Capitalist Patriarchy and the Case for Socialist Feminism;* Judith Stacy, "When Patriarchy Kowtows: The Significance of the Chinese Family Revolution for Feminist Theory," *Feminist Studies,* Vol. II, No. 43, 1975; and Nancy J. Hafkin and Edna G. Bay, *Women in Africa: Studies in Social and Economic Change* (Stanford: Stanford University Press, 1976).

39. See the debate in the *New Left Review,* 1973–1975, on whether housework does or does not create value in Marxist terms.

40. See Batya Weinbaum, "Women in Transition to Socialism," *The Review of Radical Political Economics,* Special Issue on "Women and the Economy," 1976; and Batya Weinbaum and Amy Bridges, "The Other Side of the Paycheck: Monoply Capital and the Structure of Consumption," *Monthly Review,* July–August 1976. The former analyzes the Chinese household as a unit of consumption and the latter the situation under American capitalism.

41. See Paddy Quick, "The Class Nature of Women's Oppression," *The Review of Radical Political Economics,* Third Special Issue on the "Political Economy of Women," Fall 1977, pp. 42–54. See also Lise Vogel, "Questions on the Woman Question," *Monthly Review,* June 1979, pp. 39–59.

42. See Nancy Chodorow, *Mothering: Psychoanalysis and the Social Organization of Gender* (Berkeley: University of California Press, 1978).

43. See Michelle Rosaldo and Louise Lamphere, eds, *Women, Culture and Society*

(Stanford: Stanford University Press, 1974); and Rayna Reiter, ed., *Toward an Anthropology of Women* (New York: Monthly Review Press, 1975).

44. See Quick, "The Class Nature of Women's Oppression," and Weinbaum, "Redefining the Question of Revolution," both in *The Review of Radical Political Economics* (Fall 1977) for two views on this issue.

45. See, for example, *Collection of Documents on the Women's Movement in the Liberated Areas (Zhongguo jiefang chu funü yundong wenxian)* (Shanghai, 1949), and Shi Songqiong, "Proletarian Dictatorship is the Life of Revolutionary Women" (Shanghai), *Wenhui bao* (June 27, 1968), in *Joint Publications Research Service* (JPRS), Translations on Communist China (CC), No. 29, among others.

46. See Mao Zedong, "Report of an Investigation into the Peasant Movement in Hunan," *Selected Works,* 5 vols. (New York: International Publishers, 1954), 1:45–49.

Chapter 1

1. See Chen Dongyuan, *A History of the Life of Chinese Women (Zhongguo funü shenghuo shi)* (Shanghai: Commercial Press, 1937); Levy, *The Family Revolution in China;* and Olga Lang, *Chinese Family and Society* (New Haven: Yale University Press, 1946).

2. Arthur H. Smith, *Village Life in China: A Study in Sociology* (New York: Fleming H. Revell Co., 1899), p. 264.

3. Martin C. Yang, *A Chinese Village* (New York: Columbia University Press, 1945), p. 106.

4. See Jean Chesneaux, ed., *Popular Movements and Secret Societies in China, 1840–1950* (Stanford: Stanford University Press, 1972); and Delia Davan, "Women in the Liberated Areas," in Marilyn Young, ed., *Women in China, Studies in Social Change and Feminism,* Michigan Papers in Chinese Studies No. 15 (Ann Arbor: University of Michigan Press, 1973), pp. 73–91.

5. Smith, *Village Life in China,* p. 304.

6. Martin C. Yang, *A Chinese Village,* p. 153. See also Margery Wolf's work on Chinese women in Taiwan, *Women and the Family in Rural Taiwan* (Stanford: Stanford University Press, 1972).

7. Levy, *The Family Revolution,* pp. 80–81, describes this kind of informal female gathering.

8. For a critical interpretation of China's imperialist experience, see Jean Chesneaux, Marianne Bastid, and Marie-Claire Bergere, *China from the Opium Wars to the 1911 Revolution* (New York: Pantheon, 1976). See also Dwight H. Perkins, ed., *China's Modern Economy in Historical Perspective* (Stanford: Stanford University Press, 1975).

9. See Chow Tse-tung, *The May Fourth Movement* (Cambridge: Harvard University Press, 1960).

10. See Mary Backus Rankin, *Early Chinese Revolutionaries* (Cambridge: Harvard University Press, 1971), pp. 40–46.

11. See Roxanne Witke, "Women as Politicians in China in the 1920's," in Young, ed., *Women in China,* pp. 33–47. Also Suzanne Leith, "Chinese Women in the Early Communist Movement," in Young, *Women in China,* pp. 47–73.

12. For graphic and detailed descriptions of factory conditions, see *Historical Materials on the South Seas Brothers Tobacco Company,* in *Chinese Sociology and Anthropology* (New York: International Arts and Sciences Press), Fall 1973 and Winter–Spring 1973–74.

13. See Elisabeth Croll, *Feminism and Socialism in China* (Boston: Routledge and Kegan Paul, 1978).

14. Chow Tse-tung, *The May Fourth Movement,* p. 259, bottom.

15. Xiang Jingyu headed the Women's Department of the Chinese Communist

Party in the 1920s. Cai Chang has been chairwoman of the Women's Federation of China since 1938. Deng Yingzhao has been vice-chairwoman of the Women's Federation of China since the 1940s.

16. Chesneaux, *The Chinese Labor Movement*, p. 42.

17. See "China's Industrial Workers," a series of articles in (Shanghai) *North China Herald*, April, 1923.

18. Chesneaux, *The Chinese Labor Movement*, pp. 73 and 75.

19. Ibid., p. 390.

20. See Chen Ta, *The Analysis of Strikes 1919–1926* (Shanghai, n.d.); and He Ganzhi, *The History of the Modern Chinese Revolution* (Peking, 1959).

21. See Chen Ta, *The Analysis of Strikes*.

22. See Helen Foster Snow [Nym Wales], *The Chinese Labor Movement*.

23. The Chinese consider this to have been a major event in the labor movement and have focused a great deal of historical study on it. See *The History of the Nanyang Brothers Tobacco Company*, in *Chinese Sociology and Anthropology*.

24. Levy, *The Family Revolution in China*, p. 333.

25. Topley, "Marriage Resistance in Rural Kwangtung," in Witke and Wolf, eds., *Women in Chinese Society*, pp. 67–89.

26. Agnes Smedley, *Chinese Destinies* (London: Hurst and Blacket, Ltd., 1954), p. 177.

27. Lang, *Chinese Family and Society*, p. 209.

28. Areas under Communist control before 1949.

29. For an excellent discussion of the Yanan base, see Mark Selden, *The Yenan Way in Revolutionary China* (Cambridge: Harvard University Press, 1971).

30. See Agnes Smedley, *China's Red Army Marches* (New York: The Vanguard Press, 1934).

31. See Conrad Brandt, Benjamin Schwartz, and John King Fairbank, *A Documentary History of Chinese Communism* (Cambridge: Harvard University Press, 1952), Document No. 17.

32. Ibid., Document No. 18.

33. Marinus Johan Meijer, *Marriage Law and Policy in the Chinese People's Republic* (Hong Kong: Hong Kong University Press, 1971), see Appendices I and II.

34. Brandt, Schwartz, and Fairbank, *Documents*, Document No. 17, Article 11.

35. Ibid., Document No. 18, Article 1.

36. See Helen Foster Snow [Nym Wales], in *Red Dust* (Stanford: Stanford University Press, 1952), pp. 199–202.

37. Mao Zedong, "Investigation into the Peasant Movement in Hunan," in *Selected Works*, 1:45.

38. Ibid., pp. 46–47.

39. Mao Zedong, "Investigation into Changgang District, 15 December 1933," cited in Delia Davin, *Woman-Work: Women and the Party in Revolutionary China* (London: Clarendon Press, 1976), p. 25 bottom.

40. See Kang Keqing's talk with Helen Foaster Snow, *The Chinese Communists: Sketches and Autobiographies of the Old Guard* (Westport, Conn.: Greenwood Publishing Co., 1972), p. 244.

41. See Mao Zedong, "Our Economic Policy," a report delivered to the Second National Congress of the Soviet Republic of China, 1934, in *Selected Works*, 1:142.

42. See Liu Chanxian talk in Helen Snow, *Sketches*, p. 244.

43. Mao Zedong, "Investigation into Caixi District," cited in Davan, *Woman-Work*, p. 32.

44. See Selden, *The Yenan Way*, for the most comprehensive analysis of this area.

45. Harrison Forman, *Report from Red China* (New York: Book Find Club, 1945), p. 70; and Belden, *China Shakes the World,* p. 126. Both note the difficulties of women with bound feet in agricultural production.

46. See John Lossing Buck, *Land Utilization in China* (Nanking, China: University of Nanking, 1937; reprinted, New York: Paragon Book Reprint Corp., 1968), p. 293.

47. See Selden, *The Yenan Way,* pp. 188–210; and Mao's "Talks at the Yenan Forum on Literature and Art," in Mao Zedong, *Selected Works,* Vol. 2:63–97.

48. See Edgar Snow, *Red Star Over China* (New York: Grove Press, 1961), p. 230; and Meijer, *Marriage Law and Policy.*

49. See Selden, *The Yenan Way,* p. 115.

50. The replacement of Liu Jianxian by Cai Chang as head of the Party's Women Department in 1938 illustrated the split within the women's movement at the time. See Liu's discussions with Helen Snow, *Sketches,* p. 193.

51. For a full discussion of the issue, see Merle Goldman, *Literary Dissent in Communist China* (Cambridge: Harvard University Press, 1967).

52. See our discussions on the post-Cultural Revolution period in chapter 6.

53. See "Decisions of the Central Committee of the CCP Regarding the Present Direction of Women's Work in the Anti-Japanese Areas," in *Collection of Documents on the Women's Movement in Liberated Areas,* pp. 1–5.

54. Ibid., p. 2.

55. See article by Deng Yingzhao, *Peoples China* No. 6, 1950, pp. 3–6.

56. Selden, *The Yenan Way,* p. 257.

57. *Xia-xiang* referred to a decentralization movement in which cadres were sent down to the villages.

58. A women's detachment did exist. See Nym Wales [Helen Foster Snow], *My Yenan Notebooks* (Madison, Conn.: 1961), p. 45.

59. One such women's corps was that of Nanguo County headed by Deng Zhengguo and consisting of unmarried young women. See Forman, *Report from Red China,* pp. 154–159.

60. See Belden's story of Gold Flower in *China Shakes the World,* pp. 275–308; Isabel and David Crook, *Revolution in a Chinese Village* (London: Routledge and Kegan Paul, Ltd., 1959), p. 107; and William Hinton, *Fanshen, A Documentary of Revolution in a Chinese Village* (New York: Monthly Review Press, 1966), pp. 396–399, for women's demands in China's Civil War period.

61. Deng Yingzhao, "New Tasks of Women's Work in Land Reform," in *Collection of Documents on the Women's Movement in the Liberated Areas,* pp. 27–35.

62. See *Chinese Women 'Fanshen' (Zhongguo funü da fanshen)* (Hong Kong: New People's Publishing House, 1949). *Fanshen* literally means "turn the body over." The Chinese use it to mean the act of committing oneself to the revolution.

63. Isabel and David Cook, *Revolution in a Chinese Village.*

64. See Hinton, *Fanshen,* pp. 397–398.

65. See Deng Yingzhao, "A Report on the Present Direction and Responsibilities of the Chinese Women's Movement," in *The First National Representative Conference of Chinese Women (Zhongguo funü diyice quanguo daibiao dahui)* (Shanghai, 1949), pp. 6–19.

Chapter 2

1. See Deng Yingzhao report in *The First National Representative Conference of Chinese Women,* pp. 6–19.

2. See Delia Davin, *Woman-Work.*

3. See, for example, "Guangzhou Women Organized for Agrarian Reform," (Guangzhou) *Nanfang Ribao,* 10 May 1951, trans. *Survey of the China Mainland Press (SCMP)* 103, p. 50; and see Zao Kuanjun article in *New Women of China (Xin Zhongguo Funü* [XZGFN]) No. 14, 1950, pp. 10–11.

4. Joint Economic Committee, U.S. Congress, *An Economic Profile of Mainland China,* 2 vols. (Washington, D.C.: Government Printing Office, 1967), 2:539. I suspect this number is too low, as it only refers to female employees in factories and shops and not, for example, in domestic service, in handicraft industry, or as peddlers, etc. See also *Ten Great Years* (Beijing: State Statistical Bureau), p. 180.

5. See *XZGFN* No. 14, 1950, pp. 14–15.

6. See the article on the directive of the State Council concerning labor, in *People's Daily (Renmin Ribao* [RMRB]), 4 August 1952.

7. The Federation directive "ACDFW Instructs Subordinate Organizations to Help Government Carry Out Decision on Labor Employment," (Beijing) *New China News Agency (NCNA)*, 10 August 1952, trans. *SCMP* 392, pp. 13–14.

8. See article by Yang Zhihua in *XZGFN* No. 8, 1950, pp. 10–13.

9. Ibid., p. 10.

10. See Yang Zhihua's discussion of these points in *XZGFN* No. 7, 1953, pp. 14–15.

11. See *XZGFN* No. 10, 1950, p. 14.

12. See editorial in *XZGFN* No. 10, 1953, p. 6.

13. *SCMP* 80, pp. 3–4, and *XZGFN* No. 14, 1950, p. 8.

14. See the editorial in *XZGFN* No. 14, 1950, pp. 6–7.

15. Editorial in *XZGFN* No. 14, 1950, pp. 6–7.

16. See article by Li Baoguang in *XZGFN* No. 15, 1950, p. 34.

17. See Norma Diamond, "Collectivization, Kinship and Status of Women in Rural China," *Bulletin of Concerned Asian Scholars,* vol. 7, no. 1, p. 26. See also Isabel and David Crook, *The First Years of Yangyi Commune* (London: Routledge and Kegan Paul, Ltd., 1966), p. 242.

18. See Shih Lu, "Chinese Farm Girls Prefer to Marry Workers," (Hong Kong) *Chou Mo Pao,* 18 October 1952, in *SCMP* 436, p. 34.

19. See article bi Li Liang in *XZGFN* No. 11, 1950, p. 10.

20. These included national campaigns focusing on reconstruction and eliminating corruption, waste, and inefficient management in preparation for the soon to be announced First Five-Year Plan for economic development.

21. See Zhang Yun article in *XZGFN* No. 1, 1953, p. 5.

22. See article by Li Chuyang in *XZGFN* No. 6, 1953, p. 8.

23. See "Beijing Women Deputies Meet Women Electors," (Beijing) *NCNA,* 10 March 1954, *SCMP* 764, p. 18.

24. See article by Mian Zhi in *XZGFN* No. 4, 1953, pp. 15–16. This district was particularly active during the Great Leap.

25. See article by Ji Fang in *XZGFN* No. 6, 1953, p. 23.

26. In Beijing, 98 percent voted. See *XZGFN* No. 3, 1954, p. 5.

27. See *XZGFN* No. 7, 1954, p. 4. Of a total of 5,699,144 delegates, 986,522 were women.

28. Christopher Howe, *Employment and Economic Growth in Urban China: 1949–1959* (Cambridge: Cambridge University Press, 1971), p. 97.

29. For the specific documents, see Chao Kuo-chün, *Economic Planning and Organization in Mainland China: A Documentary Study (1949–1957),* 2 vols. (Cambridge: Harvard University Press, 1963).

30. Chesneaux, *The Chinese Labor Movement,* pp. 42–43.

31. Howe, *Employment and Economic Growth,* p. 62. "The significance of these ma-

terials [Shanghai data on women workers] is that they suggest that by shortening hours, abolishing child labor and by limiting female participation to a lower share of employment than that in the prewar period, the labour administrators were able to mitigate substantially the effects of low employment absorption rates on open male unemployment—although in the nature of the case this was largely a once for all process" (p. 62).

32. See article by Song Ping in *Labor (Laodong)* No. 21, 3 December 1957, p. 2.

33. See *XZGFN* No. 4, 1955.

34. See *Women of China (Zhongguo Funü [ZGFN])* No. 1, 1956.

35. See the article by Zhang Yun in *ZGFN* No. 10, 1959, pp. 10–19. See also "Fully Promote the Positive Role of Business Women in Socialist Transformation," *RMRB* editorial, 9 April 1956, trans. *SCMP* 1276, pp. 2–4.

36. Mei Zheng, a Beijing housewife, Xuanwu district, but also an activist, "Support Women's Ardor in Socialism," in *RMRB*, 13 July 1958, trans. *SCMP* 1821, pp. 2–3.

37. "Regulations of Urban Organizations," (Beijing) NCNA, 31 December 1954, trans. in *Current Background (CB)* No. 310. See Article 7.

38. See *XZGFN* No. 5, 1955, p. 8.

39. See Janet W. Salaff, "The Urban Commune in Communist China," *China Quarterly*, No. 29 (January-March 1967), pp. 82–111.

40. See Chao Kuo-chün, *Agrarian Policies of Mainland China: A Documentary Study, 1949–1956* (Cambridge: East Asian Research Center, Harvard University, 1968).

41. Mao Zedong, *Socialist Upsurge in China's Countryside* (Beijing: Foreign Languages Press, 1957).

42. See article by Zhang Yun in *XZGFN* No. 3, 1954, pp. 7–10 and *XZGFN* No. 8, 1954, pp. 2–4.

43. Lie Huo, "Cooperation Comes to a Mountain Village," *Women of China* No. 2, 1956, p. 5. (This is an English language periodical.)

44. "Mobilize Women to Join the Cooperativization Movement," editorial *RMRB*, 5 November 1955, trans. *SCMP* 1170, pp. 14–17.

45. See Robert R. Bowie and John K. Fairbank, eds., *Communist China, 1955–1959, Policy Documents with Analysis* (Cambridge: Harvard University Press, 1962), p. 119, for the entire text of this document.

46. Trans. *SCMP* 1258, pp. 27–32.

47. Ibid., p. 27.

48. See *XZGFN* No. 9, 1950, p. 20. The article is written by the director of the Children's Bureau of the National Women's Federation.

49. "Safeguard the Health of Women and Children in Rural Areas," *RMBM* editorial, 16 May 1956, trans. *SCMP* 1299, p. 5.

50. See article by Zhang Yun in *XZGFN* No. 11, 1955, pp. 2–3.

51. See article by Li Jing in *XZGFN* No. 9, 1955, pp. 14–15.

52. See *XZGFN* No. 10, 1955, pp. 29–30.

53. "Vice-Chairman Chu Teh's [Zhu De's] Felicitations at Third All-China Women's Congress," (Beijing) NCNA, 9 September 1957, trans. *CB* 476.

54. Ibid.

55. See article by Zhi Wenjiao in *XZGFN* No. 5, 1955, pp. 10–12.

56. See article by Li Yimin in *ZGFN* No. 5, 1956, p. 9.

57. *NCNA*, Beijing, 3 March 1957.

58. See *Shi Shi Shouce (Current Events)* No. 5, 6 March 1957.

59. Ibid.

60. See article by An Zewen in *ZGFN* No. 2, February 1958.

Chapter 3

1. "National Conference on Women's Work Closes," (Beijing) *NCNA*, 31 July 1958, in *SCMP* 1830.

2. Mao Zedong, *The Upsurge of Socialism in the Countryside.*

3. See *RMRB* editorial, "Women of China, Put Up Skyrocketing Zeal and Make Greater Contributions," *RMRB*, 8 March 1959, in *SCMP* 1971.

4. Zao Guanjun, "Further Liberate Women's Labor Capacity and Channel This Force to Building Up Socialism in a Better Way," *RMRB*, 2 June 1958, in *SCMP* 1791.

5. See "Resolution of the Central Committee of the Chinese Communist Party on the Establishment of People's Communes in the Rural Areas," in Bowie and Fairbank, *Policy Documents*, p. 454.

6. "ACWF Holds Women's Work Symposium of Seven Provinces in Wuhan," *NCNA*, 17 April 1958, in *SCMP* 1766.

7. See *RMRB* editorial, 22 July 1958.

8. See, for example, *ZGFN* No. 8, 1958, p. 1; the article by Li Guang in *ZGFN* No. 11, 1958, p. 5; and that by I Nong in *ZGFN* No. 18, 1959, p. 4.

9. See *ZGFN* Nos. 5, 6, 12, and 20, 1959.

10. Wu Zhipu (Governor of Henan), "Achievements of Henan Province in 1958," *Henan Ribao*, 1 January 1959, in *SCMP* 1973.

11. See article by Li Guang in *ZGFN* No. 14, 1958, pp. 1–2.

12. See, for example, article by Yan Ruizhen in *Economic Studies (Jingji Yanjiu* [JJYJ]), No. 3, 1964, pp. 39–48.

13. Cai Chang, "The Party's General Line Illuminates the Path of Emancipation for Our Women," *ZGFN* No. 1, 1960, in *Extracts from China Mainland Magazines (ECMM)* 20.

14. "20,000,000 Women Emancipated in Central China Province," (Chengzhou) *NCNA*, 29 February 1960, trans. in *SCMP* 2210.

15. Ibid.

16. "Women Are Important Force in Socialist Construction," *Current Events (Shi Shi Shouce)* No. 5, 1959, trans. in *ECMM* No. 165.

17. Francis L. K. Hsü, "Chinese Kinship and Chinese Behavior," in Ho Ping-ti and T'ang Tsou, eds., *China in Crisis,* Vol. 1, Books 1 and 2 (Chicago: University of Chicago Press, 1968), Book 2, p. 606.

18. See Zao Guanjun, "Further Liberate Women's Labor Capacity."

19. Like Lu Yulan, a teenager from Hebei. See *China Pictorial*, June 1975, p. 15. See also Xing Yenzu in Mary Sheridan, "Young Women Leaders in China," *Signs*, Vol. 2, No. 1 (Autumn 1976), pp. 75–80.

20. See "Energetic Woman Commune Leader in Shanxi," (Daiyuan) *NCNA*, 21 February 1961, in *SCMP* 2451; and *ZGFN* No. 2, 1963, p. 8.

21. See article by Wu Zhipu in *ZGFN* No. 20, 1960, pp. 1–4.

22. "Women Play Important Part in East China Rural Areas," (Shanghai) *NCNA*, December 1959, in *SCMP* 2162.

23. "Safeguard the Health of Women and Children in the Rural Areas," *RMRB* editorial, 16 May 1958, in *SCMP* 1299.

24. David Lampton, "Health Policy During the Great Leap Forward," *China Quarterly* No. 60, December 1964, p. 675.

25. He Biao, "Health Unit Should Have the Aiding of Agriculture as Its First Duty," *Red Flag (Hong Qi)* No. 18, 16 September 1960, in *Joint Publications Research Service, Communist China Digest (JPRS CCD)* No. 31, pp. 49–53.

26. See article by Lin Xiao in *ZGFN* No. 2, 1959, p. 6.

27. "Measures to Protect Women Labor Adopted by Communes," *RMRB*, 22 June 1961, in *JPRS CCD* No. 51, p. 58.

28. *ZGFN* No. 3, 1959, p. 1.

29. Tong Fengdiao, "China's Planned Births and Population Increase," Beijing, *Renmin Baojian*, 1 May 1959, in *JPRS CCD* No. 6, p. 157.

30. See Wang Bocheng, "Premier Zhou's Talk With a Couple on Planned Parenthood," *Chinese Youth* (*Zhongguo Qingnian* [ZGQN]) No. 17, 1 September 1963, in *JPRS* 22, 301, pp. 31–35.

31. From September 11 to October 16, 1962, *Worker's Daily* (*Gongren Ribao* [GRRB]) published a series of letters regarding marriage and family problems. They are translated in *JPRS* 16, 813, pp. 43–45.

32. Cai Chang, "The Role of Women in Socialist Construction," (Beijing) *NCNA*, 17 April 1959, in *CB* 579.

33. See article by Gao Jian (Chairman of the Shanghai Women's Federation) in *ZGFN* No. 13, 1959, pp. 1–2.

34. *Facts About the Basic Levels in Paoan County* (Hong Kong: Union Research Institute, Vol. 27, No. 7, 24 April 1962). See discussion on Shangpu Brigade, p. 124.

35. Hu Jian, "Rural Household Handicraft Production," *Da Gong Pao*, 6 June 1962, p. 2, in *JPRS* 14809, p. 22.

36. Zao Guanjun, "Further Liberate Women's Labor Capacity."

37. See *ZGFN* No. 11, 1961, pp. 4–5.

38. "A Production Brigade in Guangdong Insists on Same Pay for Men and Women," *Nanfang Ribao*, 24 May 1961, in *SCMP* 2566.

39. Cai Chang, "The Party's General Line Illuminates the Path of Emancipation for Our Women," *ZGFN* No. 1, 1960, in *ECMM* 220, p. 30.

40. See "Questions Concerning the Establishment of Peoples' Communes in Urban Areas," in *Teaching and Research* (*Jiaoxue yu yanjiu*), in *ECMM* No. 163.

41. "There Are Boundless Advantages to Urban People's Communes," (Beijing) *RMRB*, 1 May 1960, in *SCMP* 2258, pp. 3–9.

42. "City Housewives Join Production Work," (Beijing) *NCNA*, 9 December 1958, in *SCMP* 1913, p. 9.

43. "100,000 Housewives in Shanghai Join in Social Labor," *RMRB*, 3 December 1958, in *SCMP* 1916, pp. 11–13.

44. "Substitution of Women for Men is Basically Completed in Commercial and Grain Departments in Xian," (Xian) *NCNA*, 18 November 1958, in *SCMP* 1899.

45. Zheng Xiaomei, "The Broad Masses of Housewives Take up the Posts of Social Labor," *RMRB*, 5 May 1959, in *CB* 579, p. 17.

46. "Urban Women Free from Family Chores and Join in Social Labor," *SCMP* 2234, p. 20.

47. See "100,000 Housewives in Shanghai Join in Social Labor."

48. Li Dongching, "Women Accomplish Miraculous Feats in the Leap Forward," *RMRB*, 27 April 1959, in *CB* 579, p. 14.

49. "Women Workers in the Great Leap Forward," *Peking Review*, 17 March 1959, Vol. I, No. 11, p. 14.

50. See "Women's Labor Power Liberated: Residential Industry Established on a Huge Scale in Heilongjiang," Harbin, *Heilongjiang Ribao*, 9 July 1958, in *SCMP* 1869, p. 30.

51. See "Growing Membership of Tianjin's First Housewives Cooperative," (Tianjin) *NCNA*, 7 April 1959, in *SCMP* 1970, p. 28.

52. See *ZGFN* No. 4, 1958, p. 8.

53. See article by Han Yin in *ZGFN* No. 4, 1963, p. 17.

54. "Women Take Part in Production in Anxun (Gueizhou)," Gueiyang, *Gueizhou Ribao,* 29 April 1960, in Supplement *SCMP*, No. 3, 1960, p. 39.

55. "An Urban People's Commune in Chongjing," *ZGFN* No. 4, 1960, p. 17.

56. See *ZGFN* editorial No. 18, 1959, pp. 1–3; and *ZGFN* editorial No. 12, 1959, p. 1.

57. See *ZGFN* Nos. 3, 5, 6, 9, 10, 12, and 15 during 1959.

58. "New Stage in the Women's Emancipation Movement in China," *RMRB* editorial, 8 March 1960, *Peking Review*, No. 11, 15 March 1960, p. 9. Ninety-five percent of the people in street industry in Beijing were women; the average for eleven of China's big and medium-sized cities was 76 percent.

59. "Beijing Announces Establishment of Thirty-Eight Urban Communes," *RMRB,* 9 April 1960, in *JPRS CCD* No. 21, p. 54.

60. "New Upsurge Appears in Urban Communes Movement in Beijing," (Beijing) *RMRB,* 9 April 1960, in *SCMP* 2260, p. 11.

61. Xiao Hua, "A Report on the Production of Small Commodities by Erlonglu People's Commune in Beijing Municipality," *RMRB,* 15 July 1960, in *SCMP* 2325, p. 9.

62. "Big Plants Help Former Beijing Housewives Master Trades," *NCNA,* 12 March 1960, in *SCMP* 2218, p. 19.

63. See "There Are Boundless Advantages to Urban Peoples' Commune."

64. Ibid.

65. "Inferior Food in Zhongjing Street Messhalls," *Da Gong Bao,* 13 January 1961, in *JPRS CCD* No. 47, p. 70.

66. See "Overhaul of Community Messhalls in Tianjin," *Tianjin Ribao,* 10 June 1960, in *JPRS CCD* No. 24, pp. 69–78.

67. "Beijing Commune Brings New Life to Former Housewives," *NCNA,* 20 April 1960, in *SCMP* 2245, pp. 15–16.

68. "Residents in Beijing Organize Collective Welfare and Social Service Work," (Beijing) *NCNA,* 17 March 1960, in *SCMP* 2224, p. 16.

69. See the important article by Liu Song, in *Study* (*Xuexi*), 10 September 1958, pp. 492–497.

70. "New Upsurge of the People's Commune Movement in Beijing."

71. See "Women Police Direct Beijing Traffic," (Beijing) *NCNA,* 20 April 1959, trans. *SCMP* 1999; "Women Taxi Drivers in Beijing," (Beijing) *NCNA,* 15 May 1959, trans. *SCMP* 2021; and *ZGFN* No. 12, 1961, pp. 2–4.

72. Barry M. Richman, *Industrial Society in Communist China* (New York: Random House, 1969), p. 303.

73. Ibid., p. 304.

74. See the story by Mao Meizu of a fitter in a clamp and pliers factory, in *Shanghai Women in the Leap* (*Yuejin zhong di Shanghai funü*) (Shanghai: Shanghai People's Publishing Company, 1958).

75. "Beijing Women Contribute to Science, Engineering, and Medicine," (Beijing) *NCNA,* 8 March 1960, in *SCMP* 2215, p. 24.

76. See chapter 6.

Chapter 4

This chapter is a revised version of an article published earlier. See "Politics of Chinese Development: The Case of Women, 1960–1966," *Signs,* Vol. 2, No. 1 (Autumn 1976), pp. 89–119.

1. See the "Communique of the 9th Plenum of the 8th CCP Central Committee" (Beijing), *NCNA,* 20 January 1961.

2. See Peter Schran, "Some Reflections on Chinese Communist Economic Policy," in Albert Feuerwerker, ed., *Modern China* (Englewood Cliffs, N.J.: Prentice-Hall, 1964), pp. 136–153.

3. See Mao's "Speech at the Lushan Conference," in Stuart Schram, *Chairman Mao Talks to the People* (New York: Pantheon, 1974), pp. 131–146.

4. See Stephen Andors, *China's Industrial Revolution: Politics, Planning and Management; 1949 to the Present* (New York: Pantheon, 1977), chapter 5.

5. See *ZGFN* No. 10, 1961, pp. 7–9, and *ZGFN* No. 6, 1961, p. 12.

6. The socialist education campaign associated with Mao began in the army and spread throughout rural China and was a forerunner of the Cultural Revolution. It emphasized collective production and development of socialist attitudes and patterns of behavior.

7. Report from Changsha Brigade, *Lianjiang Xian Documents* (a collection of documents captured by Taipei, Taiwan, Ministry of Defense in 1964; the documents are from Liangjiang Xian Fujian), p. 123.

8. See *GRRB*, 11 September to 16 October 1962, for a series of articles on marriage; *Liberation Daily (Jiefang Ribao)*, January 1963, for a criticism of dowries and gifts; *ZGQN*, January and July through November for a criticism of dowries and gifts; and *Beijing Daily (Beijing Ribao)*, March 1963, for criticism of betrothal presents. *Women of China (ZGFN)* throughout this period emphasized the compromised status of women resulting from these feudal practices.

9. See the League's publication, "Hunyin Jianghua" (Beijing: Youth Publishing House, 1964).

10. See *ZGFN*; see also Jan Myrdal, *Report From a Chinese Village* (New York: Pantheon, 1965), p. 215; and David and Nancy Milton, *The Wind Will Not Subside: Years in Revolutionary China, 1964–1969* (New York: Pantheon, 1976), pp. 46–80.

11. *RMRB*, 4 April 1962, in *JPRS* 14533, p. 105.

12. See *ZGFN* No. 8, 1962, pp. 16–17; *GRRB* articles by Wang Wenbin (China Medical University) in *JPRS CCD* No. 82, p. 98; and see "Family Planning, Main Topic of Discussion at Conference," *Chinese Journal of Gynecology and Obstetrics (Zhonghua Fuchan ke zazhi)*, Vol. 9, July 1963, in *JPRS CCD* No. 125, p. 104.

13. See article by Wan Rengceng (surgeon, Tongyi Hospital) in *Beijing Ribao*, 27 May 1963.

14. Leo Orleans, *Every Fifth Child* (Stanford: Stanford University Press, 1972), p. 47.

15. Bo Ling, "If There Is No Birth Control," (Guangzhou) *Yangcheng Cultural Daily (Yangcheng Wenbao)*, 21 August 1963, in *SCMP* Supplement 121, p. 24.

16. "It is Not a Blessing At All To Have Many Children," (Guangzhou) *Yangcheng Cultural Daily (Yangcheng Wenbao)*, November 1963, in *SCMP* Supplement 122, p. 5.

17. See article by Zheng Yuwu in *ZGFN* No. 5, 1 May 1964, p. 30.

18. See "Reform of Marital and Household System in China," *RMRB*, 13 December 1963, in *JPRS* 24, 180, pp. 98–100.

19. Yang Dawen and Liu Suping, "Our Nation's Marriage Law," *Political and Legal Studies* No. 2, 1963, in *JPRS* 24, 180, p. 94.

20. "Reform of Marital and Household System in China."

21. Ibid.

22. *ZGFN* No. 8, 1965, pp. 1–5.

23. Quoted from Mao Zedong conversation with Andre Malraux, in Andre Malraux, *Anti-Memoirs* (New York: Bantam, 1970), p. 465.

24. See Stephen Andors, "Factory Management and Political Ambiguity," *China Quarterly* No. 59 (July/September 1974), pp. 435–477.

25. "5,000 Women are Teaching in Beijing Colleges," *NCNA*, 6 March 1962, in *SCMP* 2694, pp. 20–21.

26. "Why Their Work Among Women Workers Is So Successful," *ZGFN* No. 12, 1961, p. 13, in *SCMM* 304, pp. 12–17.

27. See article by Liao Suhua in *ZGFN* No. 10, 1963, pp. 2–4.

28. See discussion "What do Women Live For?" in *ZGFN* No. 7, 1963.

29. See "What Shall I Do When My Wife Does Not Support Me In My Work," *ZGFN*, 23 June 1964, in *JPRS CCD*, No. 128 (1964), p. 43.

30. See Deng Yudang, *ZGFN* No. 6, 1963, p. 12.

31. Ibid., p. 14.

32. "Women's Status in Socialist China," (Beijing) *NCNA*, 4 March 1965, in *SCMM* 3412, p. 15.

33. "Beijing Woman At Leading Post," (Beijing) *NCNA*, 4 March 1965, in *SCMP* 3412, p. 17.

34. "Shanghai Factory Administrators Remain Good Members of the Working Class," (Shanghai) *NCNA*, 29 April 1965, in *SCMM* 3449, p. 23; and (Beijing) *NCNA*, 6 March 1966.

35. Richman, *Industrial Society*, pp. 754–756.

36. Marianne Bastid, "Economic Necessity and Political Ideals in Education Reform During the Cultural Revolution," *China Quarterly* No. 42 (April-June 1970), p. 21.

37. See article by Hu Xiuyin in *ZGFN* No. 5, 1965, p. 23.

38. See *Red Flag (Hong Qi)* No. 13, 6 December 1965, pp. 34–40.

39. See article by Zhang Yunching in *ZGFN* No. 8, 1964, and see the complaints of a middle-school graduate sent to the countryside, "Women in the Countryside Tied Down to Household Chores," *ZGQN*, 20 February 1964, in *JPRS CCD* No. 119, p. 80.

40. See *RMRB*, 20 July 1956.

41. See Christopher Howe, *Wage Patterns and Wage Policy in Modern China, 1919–1972* (Great Britain: Cambridge University Press, 1973), especially chapter 8; see also "Black Materials on Liu Shaoqi and the System of Temporary and Contract Labor," cited in Howe, *Wage Patterns and Policy,* p. 127.

42. See "Daxing Branch Commune Runs Collective Welfare Undertakings Better," *GRRB*, 20 April 1961, in *SCMP* 2494, p. 9; and see *The New York Times*, 15 February 1976, News of the Week in Review section, p. 3.

43. See "Beijing Housewives Introduce New Metallurgic Techniques," *RMRB*, 3 March 1964, in *SCMP* 3180, p. 13.

44. "Advances Made by Women Workers in North China City," (Tianjin) *NCNA*, 27 January 1965, in *SCMP* 3408, p. 20.

45. "Same Pay for Same Work in the Jingxi Production Brigade," *ZGFN* No. 11, 1961, in *SCMM* 291, pp. 13–15; and "A Production Brigade in Guangdong Insists on Same Pay for Men and Women doing the Same Kind of Job," *(Guangzhou) Nanfang Ribao*, 24 May 1961, in *SCMP* 2566, pp. 5–6.

46. "Women Play Increasingly Important Role in Chinese Countryside," (Wuhan) *NCNA*, 7 March 1963, in *SCMP* 2936, p. 16.

47. See Jack Gray and Patrick Cavendish, *Chinese Communism in Crisis* (New York: Frederick A. Praeger, 1968), chapter 8, and the *Lianjiang Documents,* p. 95.

48. "Production Team's Arrangement of Labor for Collective Production and Housework Cited," *RMRB*, 29 May 1962, in *JPRS* 15445, p. 16.

49. *Facts About the Basic Levels in Baoan County,* Guangdong, Baoan Bulletin, Issue 59, internal document published by General Office of CCP Baoan County Party Com-

mittee (Hong Kong: Union Research Institute, Vol. 7, No. 27, 1962), pp. 163–164. Henceforth cited as *Baoan Documents*.

50. See "Teaching Materials on Duties Relating to Work on Rural Women," *ZGFN* No. 2, 1 February 1962, in *SCMM* 318, pp. 12–28.

51. "Women Should Still Learn Needlework," *ZGFN*, 29 May 1962, in *JPRS* 151010, pp. 35–36.

52. Hu Jian, "Rural Household Handicrafts Production," *Da Gong Bao*, 6 June 1962, in *JPRS* 14809, p. 22.

53. Yen Ruizhen, "A Preliminary Study of the Agriculture—Animal Husbandry's Relationship in an Agricultural Enterprise with Grain Production As Its Principal Activity," in *JPRS* 1964, Translations from *JJYJ*, No. 3, pp. 69–89; and see Minister of Agriculture, Liao Luyan, "Collectivization of Agriculture in China," *Peking Review* No. 44 (1 November 1963), p. 7.

54. "Relying on Accumulated Labor for Capital Construction in Farmland," *Chinese Economic Studies* (White Plains: International Arts and Sciences Press), Vol. 1, No. 3, pp. 20–58, from *JJYJ* No. 9, 1965.

55. E. F. Jones estimates a 12 percent rise in the rural labor force. See his "The Emerging Patterns of China's Economic Development," in *An Economic Profile of Mainland China* (Joint Economic Committee of the U.S. Congress; New York: Praeger, 1968), p. 83.

56. (Beijing) *NCNA*, 6 March 1966.

57. Myrdal, *Report From A Chinese Village*, p. 10.

58. See Chu Li and Tien Chieh-yun, *Inside a Peoples Commune* (Beijing: Foreign Languages Press, 1973), p. 187, and *ZGFN* No. 3, 1965, pp. 6–14.

59. Fang Ping of the Changpu Brigade, *Baoan Documents*, p. 133.

60. See story of Peng Cejiu, a Women's Federation cadre, in *ZGFN* No. 7, 1963, pp. 3–5.

61. *Baoan Documents*, p. 124.

62. Ibid., p. 133.

63. Changsha Brigade Report in *Lianjiang Documents*, p. 207.

64. *Baoan Documents*, p. 120.

65. *Lianjiang Documents*, p. 206.

66. See Yen Ruizhen, "A Preliminary Study of Agriculture—Animal Husbandry's Relationship in an Agricultural Enterprise with Grain Production As Its Principal Activity," *JJYJ*, 17 March 1964, pp. 39–48, in *JPRS* 1964, Translations from *JJYJ*, No. 3, pp. 69–89.

67. *RMRB*, 21 May 1965, quoted in Frederick Teiwes and Richard Baum, *Szu Ch'ing: The Socialist Education Movement of 1962–1966* (Berkeley: University of California Press, 1968), p. 40.

68. See Jon Sigurdson, "Rural Economic Planning," in Michael Oksenberg, editor, *China's Developmental Experience* (New York: Praeger, 1973), pp. 68–80.

69. See *ZGFN* No. 3, 1963, pp. 11–13.

70. See article on Taozhu in *ZGFN* No. 8, 1965, pp. 1–5.

71. Discussion of militia women can be found in *ZGFN* No. 5, 1965, pp. 6–9; *ZGFN* No. 8, 1964, pp. 6–8; and in *Hong Qi* No. 3, 27 February 1966, in *SCMM* 517, pp. 12–17.

72. See article on Taozhu in *ZGFN* No. 8, 1965, pp. 1–5, and article by Zhao Shidang in *ZGFN* Nos. 1–2, 1965, p. 24.

73. See "Ideological Work Among the Family Dependents," *RMRB*, 10 December 1964, in *JPRS* Translations of Political and Social Information on Communist China, no. 231, p. 62.

74. See "The Women of Daqing Oilfield Play a Revolutionary Role," *NCNA*, 5 March 1966, in *SCMP* 3653, pp. 23–25.

75. For the story of the Dazhai Brigade, see Jin Wenling, "The Dazhai Brigade," in *The Seeds and Other Stories* (Beijing: Foreign Language Press, 1972), pp. 168–193.

76. See article by Xiang Hong in *ZGFN* No. 3, 1965, p. 14, and that by Xiao Ming in *ZGFN* No. 3, 1965, p. 12.

77. See *ZGFN* editorial, No. 3, March 1966, pp. 10–11.

Chapter 5

1. See "Decision of the CCP Central Committee Concerning the Great Proletarian Cultural Revolution," (Beijing) *NCNA*, 8 August 1966, in *SCMP* 3761, pp. 1–8.

2. See Mao's Tenth Plenum speech, in Stuart Schram, *Chairman Mao*, pp. 188–197.

3. See the discussion here in chapter 6.

4. For a discussion of the new mass organizations of the Cultural Revolution, see Victor Nee, "Revolution and Bureaucracy: Shanghai in the Cultural Revolution," in James Peck and Victor Nee, eds., *China's Uninterrupted Revolution* (New York: Pantheon, 1973), pp. 322–415; and David and Nancy Milton, *The Wind Will Not Subside*.

5. See "Class Nature of the Problems of Women Must Not be Written Off," *ZGFN* No. 6, 1966, in *SCMM* 547, p. 16; *ZGFN* No. 8, 1966, p. 35; and *ZGFN* No. 7, 1966, pp. 608, among others.

6. For an excellent discussion of the relationship between the Women's Federation and the CCP see Delia Davin's *Woman-Work*.

7. See An Zewen, "The Problem of Retirement of Women Cadres Must Be Understood Correctly."

8. Her big character poster (*dazubao*) was reprinted in *RMRB*, 2 June 1966, and is translated in *NCNA*, 2 June 1966.

9. See, for example, David and Nancy Milton's pictures of Red Guards in Tian Anmen Square and those of their own students in *The Wind Will Not Subside;* and Neale Hunter, *Shanghai Diary: An Eyewitness Account of the Cultural Revolution* (New York: Frederick A. Praeger, 1969).

10. See Marjorie Topley, "Marriage Resistance in Rural Kwangtung," in Witke and Wolf, eds., *Women in Chinese Society,* and see chapter 1.

11. See Stephen Andors, "Factory Management and Political Ambiguity, 1961–63."

12. For a good discussion of the student movement, see Victor Nee, *The Cultural Revolution at Peking University* (New York: Monthly Review Press, 1969).

13. See Stephen Andors, *China's Industrial Revolution,* chapters 7 and 9.

14. See *RMRB* editorial, December 1966, in *SCMP* No. 3852, pp. 1–4; and *NCNA* Beijing City Service, 26 December 1966.

15. Sources for this discussion come from my extensive files. They include information from the national press and national and local radio broadcasts as monitored by the Foreign Broadcast Information Service. The names of several factories will be cited.

16. Shanghai Cotton Mill #12, Shanghai Cotton Mill #22, Hangzhou No. 1 Cotton Textile and Dyeing Mill, No. 8 Cotton Mill in Shanxi.

17. The factory histories that date from the mid-1960s illustrate this. See Stephen Andors, ed., *Workers and Workplaces in Revolutionary China* (White Plains, N.Y.: M.E. Sharpe, Inc., The China Book Project, 1977), pp. 175–186.

18. See "Textile Workers Repudiate China's Khrushchev," in *China Reconstructs,* February 1968, p. 41.

19. Liu Shaoqi, former head of state, was considered the leader of the "capitalist roaders," i.e., those people who advocated policies which would lead to the restoration of capitalism in China.

20. The Textile Ministry put out a publication entitled *Hong Ying (Red Eagle)*. The only edition available focused on precisely the relationship between Liu's policies and that of the pre-1949 period.

21. See "Textile Workers Repudiate China's Khrushchev," pp. 40–41.

22. Ibid., p. 40.

23. For a discussion of the post-Cultural Revolution incentive system, see Carl Riskin, "Maoism and Motivation: Work Incentives in China," in *Bulletin of Concerned Asian Scholars,* Vol. 5, No. 1 (July 1973), pp. 10–25.

24. See, for example, "Urgent Notice: Stick to Production Posts," Shanghai City Service, 28 January 1967.

25. See the experience of Cotton Mill No. 8, Shenxi, Xian, Shenxi City Service, 7 December 1968.

26. See "Newspapers Hail Tibet Wool Record," *NCNA,* 17 April 1967.

27. "Liu Shaoqi is Chief Culprit Involved in Institution of System of Temporary Workers and Contract Workers," *Red Worker Combat News (Honggong Zhanbao)*, Shanghai, 6 February 1967.

28. For one of the few examples of public support for these workers, see "Thoroughly Abolish the System of Temporary Labor and Outside Contract Labor," *Wenhui bao,* 6 January 1967.

29. See David and Nancy Milton, *The Wind Will Not Subside,* pp. 187–190.

30. This is based on field research done in Shu Lu County, Hebei Province, in the summer of 1979.

31. See Stephen Andors, ed., *Workers and Workplaces,* pp. 139–217.

32. See "Textile Workers Repudiate China's Khrushchev," p. 42.

33. See "RMRB Features Revolutionary Changes in Textile Mill," (Beijing) *NCNA,* 31 August 1968, in *SCMP* 4252, p. 13.

34. See accounts in the Chinese press concerning the Tianjin and Shanghai mills, "The East Is Red" Silk Weaving Mill (Suzhou Jiangsu), Mutanjiang Cotton Mill (Heilongjiang), and the Yinchuan Woolen Textile Mill (Ningxia). For a more detailed account of how the issues evolved in one particular mill, Beijing General Knitwear, see Charles Bettleheim, *Cultural Revolution and Industrial Organization in China: Changes in Management and the Division of Labor,* trans. Alfred Ehrenfeld (New York: Monthly Review Press, 1974), pp. 13–45.

35. See (Shanghai) *NCNA,* 29 December 1967.

36. Daiyuan, Shanxi Provincial Service, 11 November 1968; (Beijing) *NCNA,* 10 October 1968; and Beijing City Service, *NCNA,* 26 October 1968.

37. See (Beijing) *NCNA,* 14 September 1968.

38. See Beijing *RMRB,* 23 April 1968, p. 2.

39. For a biographical sketch on Wu Gueixian, see Roxanne Witke, "Wu Gueixian" Labour Heroine to Vice-Premier," in *The China Quarterly* No. 64, December 1975, pp. 730–740.

40. See Stephen Andors, *China's Industrial Revolution,* p. 211.

41. Ibid., chapter 8.

42. See "Shanghai's Factory Administrators Remain Good Members of the Working Class," (Shanghai) *NCNA,* 29 April 1965, in *SCMP* 3449, pp. 23–25. Three hundred of a thousand newly appointed directors or deputy directors of Shanghai plants were women.

43. (Beijing) *NCNA,* 29 January 1967, and 8 June 1967.

44. Northeast State No. 1 Cotton Mill, Xian, Shenxi Provincial Service, 8 December 1968.

45. See Gueizhou Provincial Service, 14 June 1968.

46. See "The Workers in Shijiazhuang Printing and Dyeing Mill Fully Play Their Leading Role," *Peking Review* No. 40, 4 October 1968.

47. See Bettleheim, *Cultural Revolution and Industrial Organization,* pp. 35–37.

48. This was true until 1978 when revolutionary committees were replaced by management committees.

49. See "Cadres Must Be Treated Correctly." *Hong Qi* No. 4, February 1967, in *SCMM* 566, p. 1, and Tian Anmen (observer), "Unite More Than 95% of the Cadres, Make Revolution to the End," *Tian Anmen* (Red Guard Publication) No. 2, March 1967, in *SCMM* 576, pp. 8–10.

50. See Janet Salaff, "Urban Residential Committees in the Wake of the Cultural Revolution," in John W. Lewis, ed., *The City in Communist China* (Stanford: Stanford University Press, 1971), pp. 289–323.

51. See "The General Orientation of the Struggle Against the Neighborhood Cadres is Wrong," *Wenhui bao* editorial, Shanghai Domestic Service, 10 February 1967.

52. *Wenhui bao,* Shanghai City Service, 10 February 1967.

53. Ibid.

54. See especially *Wenhui bao,* 25 January 1967, and 11 February 1967.

55. See "A Letter to Revolutionary Parents," *Wenhui bao,* Shanghai City Service, 30 June 1968; and "Parents Urged to Send Youth to Countryside," Chingdao City Service, 1 November 1968.

56. See "A Residents' Revolutionary Committee in Shanghai Mobilizes Masses to Defeat Bad Elements Sabotaging Support for Xianjiang," *Wenhui bao,* Shanghai City Service, 26 May 1968.

57. See Che Gai, "A Small Cooperative with Big Ambitions Performs Miracles," *ZGFN* No. 13, 1966, in *SCMM* 564, p. 32, and Zui Yulan, "How We Women Won Equality," *China Reconstructs,* March 1974, pp. 2–5.

58. See "Street Industry in Beijing Municipality Have Become a 'Fresh Force' on the Industrial Front," (Beijing) *NCNA,* 31 March 1966. Beijing had more than 500 factories and 100 "production points."

59. See Ruth Sidel, *Families of Fengsheng: Urban Life in China* (New York: Penguin Books, 1974), especially chapter 4.

60. Canadian visitors reported in 1967 that at Sun Yat-sen Medical School in Canton 40 percent of the students were female. See Drs. Thomson, MacKenzie, and Peart, "A Visit to the People's Republic of China," *Canadian Medical Association Journal,* 12 August 1967, p. 10. See also Ruth Sidel, "Women in Medicine in the PRC," *The New Physician,* May 1973, pp. 299–305.

61. For a discussion on political labeling, see Gorden Bennett, "Political Labels and Popular Tension," *Current Scene,* Vol. 7, No. 4, 28 February 1969.

62. See "Let the Banner of Mao Zedong Thought Fly Over Every Street and Every Neighborhood," *Wenhui bao,* Shanghai City Service, 5 January 1957, and "Beijing Housewives have Study Courses in Mao Zedong Thought," (Beijing) *NCNA,* 15 January 1968. Zhengwen district reported an 85 percent attendance rate. This district was particularly active in the Great Leap Forward.

63. See "Neighborhood Committee Spurs Great Alliance," Shanghai City Service, 13 May 1967. In Beijing the revolutionary committees were not all formed until February 1968. See "Local Revolutionary Committees Set Up in Beijing," (Beijing) *NCNA,* 17 February 1968.

64. See "Three-in-One Residents' Revolutionary Committee Fortifies Red Political Power," *Wenhui bao*, Shanghai City Service, 4 May 1968.

65. See Stephen Andors, "Urbanization and Urban Government in China's Development: Toward a Political-Economy of Urban Community?" *Journal of Economic Development and Cultural Change*, Vol. 26, No. 3, April 1978, pp. 525–545.

66. See "The Orientation of the Revolution in Medical Education is the Growth of 'Barefoot Doctors'," *Peking Review* No. 38, 20 September 1968, p. 18. The number of barefoot doctors actually decreased in the Shanghai area.

67. "Actually Place the Key-points in Medical and Public Health Work in the Countryside," *RMRB*, 1 September 1965, in *JPRS CCD* No. 161, p. 18; and "Direct Focus of Medical and Health Work Toward the Countryside in Service of 500 Million Peasants," *Illumination Daily* (*Guangming Ribao* [*GMRB*]), 5 August 1965, in *JPRS CCD* No. 162, p. 142.

68. See Benedict Stavis, "How China Is Solving Its Food Problem," *Bulletin of Concerned Asian Scholars*, July-September 1975, pp. 22–39.

69. Jack Ch'en, *A Year in Upper Felicity: Life in a Chinese Village During the Cultural Revolution* (New York: MacMillan Publishing Co., 1973), p. 198.

70. See "Changing Undesirable Wedding Customs and Practices," *ZGQN* No. 2, 16 January 1966, in *JPRS CCD* No. 173, p. 134; William L. Parrish, "Socialism and the Chinese Peasant Family," *Journal of Asian Studies*, Vol. 34, No. 3 (May 1975), pp. 613–631.

71. See the discussion on family planning in chapter 7.

72. See, for example, "Guangdong Cooperative Medical System," Guangzhou City Service, 18 April 1969, which reported 50 percent of production brigades throughout the province had put into effect some form of cooperative medical service by March 1969. Deng County, Henan, had also set up a county-wide system by June 1969; see Chengzhou Henan Provincial Service, 18 June 1969, etc.

73. Arthur Galston, *Daily Life in People's China* (New York: Thomas Y. Crowell Co., 1973), p. 212.

74. See *ZGFN* No. 9, 1966, p. 25.

75. See article by Ding Mingjiao, *ZGFN* No. 1, 1966, p. 27; see also "Opposing Early Marriage, Promoting Late Marriage," *Wenhui bao*, 30 July 1968, Shanghai City Service, for a criticism of the Liuist position of *not* interfering in early marriages; and see discussion section "Hunyin jiating," *ZGFN* No. 1, 1966, pp. 26–28.

76. "A New Custom in Marrying Off Daughters," *GMRB*, 18 January 1969, in *SCMP*, pp. 10–11. This was a *joint* decision by poor peasants Zhang Chusheng and his wife.

77. See "How Should Young Women Handle Idle Rumors and Gossip When They Participate in Club Activities," *ZGQN* No. 8, 1966, p. 20, in *Chinese Sociology and Anthropology*, Vol. 1, No. 1 (Fall 1968), pp. 22–24. The clubs were Mao study groups.

78. See *ZGFN* No. 7, 1965, p. 6.

79. See Yang Zuohong, "I Prefer An Army Uniform to a Girl's Dress," *Hong Qi* No. 3, 27 February 1966, in *SCMM* 517; and see article by Zhou Jiusong in *ZGFN* No. 9, 1966, p. 20.

80. See "People's Cadre of a New Type Emerging in the Cultural Revolution," (Beijing) *NCNA*, 30 November 1967, in *SCMP* 4072, p. 14.

81. Jack Ch'en, *A Year in Upper Felicity*, pp. 144–145.

82. See article by Song Liying in *ZGFN* No. 3, 1966. Song is head of the Women's Federation at Dazhai. It appears that the poverty of Dazhai accounted for a great deal of the female labor participation.

83. For Liu Ling, see Myrdal, *The Revolution Continued*. For Yangdan, see *Peking Review*, 4 March 1966, pp. 8–11.

84. See Jon Sigurdson, "Rural Industrialization in China," in *China: A Reassessment of the Economy* (Joint Economic Committee of Congress; Washington, D.C.: Government Printing Office, 1975), pp. 411–438.

Chapter 6

1. The Gang of Four included Jiang Qing (Mao's wife), Zhang Chunqiao, Wang Hongwen, and Yao Wenyuan. All had played prominent roles in the Cultural Revolution.

2. See Elizabeth Croll, "The Anti–Lin Biao and Confucian Campaign: A New State in the Ideological Revolution of Women," *The Australian and New Zealand Journal of Sociology*, Vol. 12, No. 1, pp. 35–42.

3. "Revolutionary Women Should Make New Contributions in Struggle–Criticism–Transformation," Nanjing, Jiangsu Provincial Service, 14 March 1969.

4. "The Revolutionary Woman's Will is Strong," *Hong Qi* No. 2, February 1971, in *SCMM* 700, pp. 79–86.

5. The Chinese contend that both Liu Shaoqi and Lin Biao were revisionists and adherents to the traditional Confucian value system, thus making their policies fundamentally counterrevolutionary. We are not concerned here with the truth of these charges, but only with the implications of the alleged policies for women. Thus, for our purposes, it is not important that Liu or Lin actually espoused these policies, but that these policies and attitudes were obviously part of the political conflict involving women in China.

6. See article by Han Wen in *Hong Qi* No. 2, February 1971, pp. 63–66.

7. See *Hong Qi* No. 5, 1970, p. 81, and *Hong Qi* No. 10, 1973, p. 97.

8. Fu Wen, "Doctrine of Confucius and Mencius—The Shackle That Keeps Women in Bondage," *Peking Review*, No. 10, 8 March 1974, pp. 16–18. *Peking Review* was an especially good source for much of this material translated into English. See especially the issues of 15 February, 19 April, 19 July, 27 September, and 25 October 1974.

9. See, for example, Viana Muller, "The Formation of the State and the Oppression of Women: Some Theoretical Considerations and a Case Study of England and Wales," *The Review of Radical Political Economics*, Vol. 9, No. 3, pp. 7–22; Zillah Eisenstein, ed., *Capitalist Patriarchy and the Case for Socialist Feminism* (New York: Monthly Review Press, 1979), and Juliet Mitchell, *Women's Estate* (New York: Penguin Books, 1971.

10. See Workers Theoretical Group of Changzhou Railway Administration, "Working Women's Struggle Against Confucianism in Chinese History," *Peking Review*, 7 March 1975; and see the article by the Iron Girls' Team of the Dazhai Brigade in *Hong Qi* No. 3, 1974, pp. 37–39.

11. Xiang Jingyu and Yang Kaihui were early Communist leaders executed in 1928 and 1930 by the Guomindang. Yang was married to Mao Zedong at the time.

12. See the interview with Liu Gueiying in *China Reconstructs*, March 1972; Xu Guang, "Women's Liberation Through Struggle," and the experience of Fan Zhuhua in "The Life of Women is Entirely Different Before and After Liberation," (Hangzhou) *NCNA*, 5 March 1974.

13. Red Detachment of Women Squad, "Women Can Prop Up 'Half of Heaven,' " *GMRB*, 14 June 1974, cited in Elizabeth Croll article, p. 37.

14. "Safeguard the Health of Women and Children in Rural Areas," *RMRB*, 16 May 1956.

15. "Hail to Them for Shouldering Half of the Worldly Responsibilities," *GMRB*, 8 July 1973, Beijing City Service.

16. See *Hong Qi* No. 11, 1971, pp. 60–64.

17. "The Revolutionary Woman's Will Is Strong," pp. 82–83.

18. Ibid., and see Fu Wen, "Doctrine of Confucius and Mencius—The Shackle That

Keeps Women in Bondage"; see also Barbara Ehrenreich, "Democracy in China," *Monthly Review,* Vol. 26, No. 4, pp. 17–34.

19. See *Peking Review,* 30 April 1969, pp. 41–48.

20. See *Peking Review,* 7 September 1973, pp. 8–10.

21. "Sichuan Forum on Work Concerning Young People, Women," Chengdu, Sichuan Provincial Service, 1 July 1972.

22. "Marx, Lenin and Mao on Women's Participation in Revolution," *Peking Review,* 8 March 1974, pp. 13–14.

23. See article by Han Wen in *Hong Qi* No. 2, February 1971, pp. 63–66.

24. Parris Chang, "Political Rehabilitation of Cadres in China: A Traveller's View," *China Quarterly,* Vol. 54 (April/June 1973), p. 339.

25. "Pay Attention to the Expansion of the Female Party Membership," *RMRB,* 13 September 1971, in *SCMP* 4983, pp. 8–9.

26. "Guangxi Party Unit Seeks to Develop New Women Members," (Beijing) *NCNA,* 13 September 1971.

27. See *Hong Qi,* 1 July 1974.

28. "Pay Attention to the Expansion of the Female Party Membership."

29. Wuhan, Hubei Provincial Service, 31 May 1972. In Huangjiang county, Guangxi, a countywide effort to educate women and organize women's groups took place. See Nanning, Guangxi Provincial Service, 18 August 1972; see also article on CCP efforts in Chaojang County, Guangdong, "Conscientiously Train and Use Women Cadres Boldly," *GMRB,* in *SCMP* 1501, pp. 4–5, etc.

30. See article by Xia Bing in *Hong Qi,* December 1973, pp. 18–23; and Xiang Yanzu, "Training Women Cadres," *Peking Review,* 5 April 1974.

31. Zhaolu is a model commune with women secretaries or deputy secretaries in all seven commune Party branches and on all 223 production team Party committees. Women account for 35 percent of all commune cadres in Zhaolu. "Anhui County Women Criticize Liu-Confucius Slanders of Women," *NCNA,* 6 March 1974.

32. *NCNA,* 7 March 1975.

33. See Lu Yulan, secretary of brigade Party branch, Hebei, "Women Party Secretary Nurtured by Mao Zedong Thought," (Shijiazhuang, Hebei) *NCNA,* 8 March 1970; and Jiang Xuiying, secretary of Party branch of Yaojiahe Production Brigade in Hebei, "Woman Party Branch Secretary Praised by Poor and Lower-Middle Peasants," (Shijiazhuang, Hebei) *NCNA,* 6 March 1972.

34. "Woman Party Branch Secretary of North China Production Brigade," (Daiyuan, Shanxi) *NCNA,* 16 March 1972, in *SCMP* 5101, p. 62.

35. See "Revolutionary Committee of a Commune in Henan Pays Attention to Training and Using Women Cadres," *RMRB,* 15 November 1969, in *SCMP* 4546, p. 5.

36. See "Party Committee of Dancheng Xian, Henan, Seriously Trains and Educates Women Cadres," *GMRB,* Beijing, 5 March 1972, in *SCMP* 5094, pp. 131–132; on Shanxi Women Cadres, Daiyuan Shanxi Provincial Service, 7 March 1971; and "Lanshan xian Hunan Province Vigorously Trains and Uses Women Cadres," *RMRB,* 17 November 1971, in *SCMP* 5025, p. 128.

37. *GMRB,* 5 March 1972.

38. Guangzhou City Service, 24 March 1972.

39. *RMRB,* 17 November 1971.

40. "About Hubei County Women Cadres," Wuhan, Hubei Provincial Service, 8 January 1972.

41. Changsha, Henan Provincial Service, 30 August 1972.

42. See Kunming, Yunnan Provincial Service, 8 April 1972.

43. Even in Hainan Island the Party recruited women. See Haikou, Hainan Island Service, 7 March 1972.

44. See "Party Committee of Huaiyin Cigarette Factory of Chingjiang City Earnestly Promotes Women Cadres and Gives Full Play to Their Role," *GMRB*, Beijing, 17 March 1972, in *SCMP* 5101, p. 6, and "Zhangjiakou Municipal Rubber Factory is Mindful of Training Women Cadres," *RMRB*, 27 January 1973, in *SCMP* 5311, p. 109.

45. See "Party Committee of Chengdu Textile Mill Helps Female Cadres Raise Their Standard of Theory and Increase Work Ability," (Chengdu) *NCNA*, 7 March 1973, in *SCMP* 5338, pp. 90–92, and "Party Committee of Sanming Textile Mill Promotes Women Workers," (Fuzhou) *NCNA*, 25 August 1972, in *SCMP* 5210, p. 92.

46. See "Women Party Secretary of Northwest China Cotton Mill Carries Forward Revolutionary Tradition," (Yinchuan) *NCNA*, 15 April 1973, in *SCMP* 5362, p. 184; "Beijing Textile System Energetically Trains Women Cadres," *RMRB*, 27 January 1973, in *SCMP* 5311, p. 107; and "Cultivate Women Cadres to Re-enforce Leadership at Various Levels," *RMRB*, Beijing, 19 March 1972, in *SCMP* 5701, p. 93.

47. "Beijing Textile System Energetically Trains Women Cadres."

48. *RMRB*, 1 February 1973, p. 2.

49. "Party Committee of Chengdu Textile Mill Helps Female Cadres to Raise Their Standard of Theory and Increase Work Ability."

50. "Party Committee of Sanming Textile Mill Promotes Women Workers."

51. "Cultivate Women Cadres to Re-enforce Leadership at Various Levels."

52. See Sidel, *Families of Fengsheng*, p. 106. See also the Red Flag Embroidery Factory in Tianjin in Janet Goldwasser and Stuart Dowty, *Huanying: Workers' China* (New York: Monthly Review Press, 1975), pp. 142–145, and "Housewives Build Factory in Northeast China Xian," (Changchun) *NCNA*, in *SCMP* 5215, pp. 167–168.

53. See Charles Hoffman, *The Chinese Worker* (New York: State University of New York Press, 1974). Iron and steel, metals, electric power, coal, and other heavy industry accounted for only 36.8 percent of the total industrial employment. Barry Richman, *Industrial Society in Communist China*, pp. 630–631.

54. Richman, *Industrial Society*, pp. 734–735.

55. Goldwasser and Dowty, *Huanying: Workers' China*, p. 171.

56. Zui Yulan, "How We Women Won Equality," *China Reconstructs*, March 1974, pp. 2–5.

57. In Shanghai women were over one-third of the labor force. "Shanghai Women Workers Make Important Contributions," *Da Gong Bao*, Hong Kong, 6 March 1972, p. 1, in *JPRS* Translations on People's Republic of China #186, p. 24. In such advanced urban districts as Xijing, Beijing, women account for 46.4 percent of the full-time workers. See Pi-chao Chen, "China's Population Program at the Grassroots Level," *Studies in Family Planning*, Vol. 4, No. 8, p. 220.

58. For a discussion of the relationship between training and worker mobility, see Hoffman, *The Chinese Worker*, pp. 76–84.

59. See "Hundreds of Thousands of Women Workers in Shanghai's Industrial and Communications Fronts Forge Ahead Brimming Over with Vim and Vigor, Under Guidance of Chairman Mao's Proletarian Revolutionary Line," *RMRB*, 6 March 1972, in *SCMP* 5095, pp. 177–179.

60. See "Outstanding Chinese Women Surveyor," (Xian) *NCNA*, 7 March 1972, in *SCMP* 5096, p. 181, and "Women Train Crew in Northeast China," (Shenyang) *NCNA*, 7 March 1972, in *SCMP* 5096, p. 183.

61. See *RMRB,* 6 March 1972, for story on women in chemicals industry.

62. See "Outstanding Chinese Woman Technician," (Shanghai) *NCNA,* 7 March 1971, in *SCMP* 4859, p. 95.

63. Hu Jin, "Mobile Chairs for Spinners," *China Reconstructs,* Vol. 24, No. 3, March 1975, p. 7.

64. "East China Coastal City Develops Neighborhood Industry," (Fuzhou) *NCNA,* 14 July 1972, in *SCMP* 5180, p. 60.

65. "Housewives Build Factory in Northeast China Xian," (Changchun) *NCNA,* 2 September 1972, in *SCMP* 5215, pp. 167–168.

66. "East China Cotton Mill Turns Out Synthetic Fiber," (Nanjing) *NCNA,* 15 January 1971, in *SCMP* 4825, p. 176.

67. "Shanghai Develops Neighborhood Factories," (Shanghai) *NCNA,* 25 April 1972, in *SCMP* 5128, p. 18.

68. "New Prosperity of the Light and Chemical Industry in Lake Area," *RMRB,* 19 June 1973, in *JPRS* Translations on Communist China #234, p. 1; and "Housewives Start Factory From Scratch in Central China Province," (Changsha) *NCNA,* in *SCMP* 5096, p. 21.

69. See "No Difficulty Insurmountable for the Revolution," *Hong Qi* No. 1, 1970, in *SCMM* 671, pp. 9–19, and "Housewives Cooperative in Shanghai Makes Telecommunications Equipment," (Shanghai) *NCNA,* 19 March 1972, in *SCMP* 5096, p. 61.

70. See Zhong Chinggong, "Pay Proper Attention to Production of Small Commodities," *RMRB,* 12 June 1971, in *SCMP* 4927, p. 122; "Changes Come to Beijing Neighborhood," (Beijing) *NCNA,* 22 February 1972, in *SCMP* 5086, pp. 25–28; "Housewives Cooperative in Shanghai Makes Telecommunications Equipment"; etc.

71. See "East China Cotton Mill Turns Out Synthetic Fiber." Production was increased by supplementing cotton textiles with synthetic fibers made from local materials. These textile industries were to become an important component of rural industrialization.

72. See Zhou Enlai, Report to the Fourth National People's Congress, January 1975, in *NCNA,* 22 January 1975.

73. "Beijing Municipality Develops Light, Heavy Industry," (Beijing) *NCNA,* 22 September 1972.

74. Pi-chao Chen, "China's Population Program at the Grassroots Level," p. 220.

75. Ibid.

76. Ibid., p. 122.

77. See "Industrial Cities Must Also Carry Out Farming Successfully," *RMRB,* 2 January 1971, in *SCMP* 4818, pp. 65–70; and Ji Weiwen, "Rousing Workers' Dependents to Take Part in Collective Productive Labor," *RMRB,* 1 September 1970, in *SCMP* 4739, pp. 55–57.

78. "Women in Daqing Oilfield Take Part in Production," (Beijing) *NCNA,* 5 March 1972.

79. Ji Weiwen, "Rousing Workers' Dependents to Take Part in Collective Productive Labor."

80. "Cadre Dependents Also Must Take the 'May 7' Road," *RMRB,* 23 August 1970, in *SCMP* 4732, p. 97.

81. "70,000 Dependents in Fushan Municipality Participate in Production, Put Over 500 Small Factories into Operation Within Two Years," *Wenhui bao,* 3 March 1972, in *JPRS* Translations on People's Republic of China, #192, p. 7.

82. In regard to agricultural developments, see Benedict Stavis, "How China Is Solving Its Food Problem." For local small-scale industrial strategy, see Carl Riskin, "Small Industry and the Chinese Model of Development," *China Quarterly* No. 46, 1971, pp. 245–273.

83. See *Hong Qi* No. 10, 1971, pp. 60–64.

84. See *Hong Qi*, especially 1971 and 1972.

85. "A Plan Suggested by the Old Leader of a Production Team," *RMRB*, 29 November 1971, in *SCMP* 5029, pp. 69–72.

86. "Men and Women Must Receive Equal Pay for Equal Work," *RMRB*, Beijing, 6 March 1972, in *SCMP* 5096, pp. 8–13.

87. See Jin Jizu and Hong Song article in *Hong Qi* No. 2, 1972, pp. 59–63.

88. See *Hong Qi* No. 3, 1974, pp. 37–39.

89. Zhou Kezhou, "How Our Village Got Equal Pay for Equal Work," *China Reconstructs*, Vol. 24, No. 3, March 1975, p. 8.

90. See the case of Dao Jigeng Commune, Wu County, Zhejiang, in Hangzhou, Zhejiang Provincial Service, 8 April 1972.

91. See article by Jin Jizu and Hong Song, p. 59.

92. Investigation Report on Chenjiafang Brigade, Xuanhua xian, Hebei, "How to Realize Equal Pay for Equal Work for Men and Women," *Hong Qi* No. 3, 1 March 1972, in *SCMM* 725–6, p. 133. See also, "Men and Women Must Receive Equal Pay for Equal Work." In this brigade 80 percent of the able-bodied women were working.

93. See article by Zhong Xiangzu in *Hong Qi* No. 10, 1969, p. 76.

94. See Chen Yongguei speech on the role of women, Beijing City Service, *NCNA*, 10 March 1974.

95. See Song Liying of the Dazhai Brigade; Fu Jingdai of the Zaizhuang Brigade, Anhui, Hefei, Anhui Provincial Service, 25 October 1971; Xiao Zhang and Bien Xiuying of the Marco Polo Brigade Commune, in Galston, *Daily Life in People's China*, p. 89; Dong Daozhong of the Chiliying Brigade in Chiu Li and Tien Chie-yun, *Inside the People's Commune*, pp. 185–186; etc.

96. Jiang Chun, "Seriously Tackle the Problem of Girls' Schooling," *RMRB*, 6 January 1972, in *SCMP* 5055, p. 96.

97. See Lo Yu, "Pay Attention to Selected Girl Students," *RMRB*, Beijing, 22 August 1970, in *SCMP* 4730, p. 46.

98. "Women Students From Among Workers, Peasants, and Soldiers in Beijing University," (Beijing) *NCNA*, 14 March 1971, in *SCMP* 4864, pp. 108–110. Changes in university recruitment at the national level resulted in women constituting one-third of the students of worker-peasant background entering Beijing University in 1971.

99. See article by Jiang Weifu, *GMRB*, 21 September 1973.

100. See "Let More Women and Girls Receive Schooling," *RMRB*, Beijing, 6 January 1972, in *SCMP* 5057, pp. 94–95; and "Liaonan 'May 7' Middle-School Runs an Additional Class for Young Women and Girls," *RMRB*, 6 January 1972, in *SCMP* 5057, pp. 97–98.

101. In Yuankou Brigade, Hebei, before the brigade took over, only 37 percent of the children attended class. Under brigade management, all attended some school, some full time and the rest part time. See "How Universal Primary Education is Brought About in Yuankou Production Brigade," *RMRB* 20 April 1972, in *SCMP* 5127, p. 175.

102. During the summers of 1978 and 1979, talks with officials in China, including local commune and industrial cadres, confirmed this impression.

103. John Gardiner, "Educated Youth and Rural-Urban Inequities, 1958–1966," in John Wilson Lewis, Ed., *The City in Communist China*, pp. 268–276. Pi-chao Chen, "Over Urbanization, Rustification of Urban Youth, and the Politics of Rural Transformation: The Case of China," *Comparative Politics*, April 1972, pp. 361–386. David Gordan White, "The Politics of Hsia-hsiang Youth," *China Quarterly* No. 59, July/September 1974, pp. 491–518.

104. "Pay Attention to the Selection of Cadres from Among Young Female Workers," *RMRB*, 4 March 1973, in *SCMP* 5334, pp. 128–130, and "Educated Young Women from Beijing in Yanan," (Xian) *NCNA*, 8 March 1973, in *SCMP* 5337, p. 63.

105. Concerning the *xia-xiang* girls' construction team which built a five-arch concrete bridge across the Xilinshi River in the Daxinganling area of Heilongjiang, see *RMRB*, 27 February 1971, p. 4; "YCL Girls in Heilongjiang Build Highway Bridge," *NCNA*, Beijing City Service, 22 February 1971. Also see "Educated Nanjing Girl Matures Quickly in Countryside," (Nanjing) *NCNA*, 12 May 1970, in *SCMP* 4660, p. 84; and "School Graduate from Shanghai Settles Down in Countryside and Revolutionizes Her Thinking," Hefei, Anhui, *NCNA*, 11 January 1971, in *SCMP* 4822, p. 62.

106. Shenyang, Liaoning Provincial Service, 20 August 1973.

107. See the case of Bai Jixian, who married a "common commune member." She was a college graduate and her marriage was criticized by local commune members as well as by her own family. *RMRB*, 7 February 1974, p. 1, and *NCNA* report on 6 March 1974.

108. *RMRB*, 22 March 1975.

Chapter 7

This chapter is a revised version of an article published earlier. See "Women in the Post-Mao Period," *Bulletin of Concerned Asian Scholars*, No. 3, 1981.

1. For typical examples, see "Guangxi Women's Rally Denounces Jiang Qing," Nanning Guangxi Regional Service, 11 November 1965; "Gansu Women's Group Condemns Jiang Qing," Lanzhou, Gansu Provincial Service, 27 January 1977; and "Anhui Women's Federation Criticizes Former Leader," Hefei, Anhui Provincial Service, 9 December 1977.

2. See Xue Muqiao's articles, "Observe Economic Laws, Speed Up the Four Modernizations," *Peking Review*, 10, 17, 24 November.

3. See Kang Keqing, "Chairman Mao Leads Us To Take the Road of Complete Emancipation of Women," *RMRB*, 22 September 1977.

4. Throughout the 1950s, *Women of China* devoted a section to child care. Kang was a frequent contributor.

5. "Give the Reins to the Tremendous Role of Women in Achieving the Four Modernizations," *Hong Qi* No. 3, 1978, (Beijing) *NCNA*, 7 March 1978.

6. See, for example, "Beijing Housewives Labour, Men Do Housework," (Beijing) *NCNA*, 9 April 1976.

7. "Top Leaders Attend Opening," (Beijing) *NCNA*, 8 September 1978.

8. See Wang Dong speech, (Beijing) *NCNA*, 9 September 1978.

9. Kang Keqing, "Four Modernizations Discussed," (Beijing) *NCNA*, 11 September 1978.

10. See the reports of Kang's speech in (Beijing) *NCNA*, 9 and 11 September 1978; and "Lofty Tasks of the Women's Movement in China in the New Period," (Beijing) *NCNA*, 18 September 1978.

11. (Beijing) *NCNA*, 18 September 1978.

12. (Beijing) *NCNA*, 12 September 1978.

13. "People's Daily Praises Women's Congress," (Beijing) *NCNA*, 17 September 1978. For similarities with the Five Goods campaign of the 1950s, see chapter 2.

14. See chapter 4 for similar approach to these matters in the early 1960s.

15. (Beijing) *NCNA*, 12 September 1978.

16. Women constituted 26 of the 223 members of the Praesidium, 14 of the 201 members of the Central Committee, and 23 of the 132 alternate members of the Central Committee. *Peking Review* No. 35, 26 August 1977, pp. 14–16.

17. See (Beijing) *NCNA*, 7 March 1978.

18. See "Inner Mongolia Planned Parenthood," Huhehot, Inner Mongolia Regional Service, 21 July 1978; "Sichuan Planned Parenthood Meeting Opened," Chengdu Provincial Service, 20 August 1978; "Fujian Holds Meeting on Planned Parenthood," Fuzhou, Fujian Provincial Service, 3 September 1978; and "National Planned Parenthood Conference Held in Beijing," (Beijing) *NCNA*, 26 January 1979; among others.

19. See "Shanghai Holds Planned Parenthood Meeting," Shanghai City Service, 16 September 1978, and "Hunan Opens Congress on Planned Parenthood," Changsha, Hunan Service, 11 November 1978.

20. See Marina Thorberg, "Chinese Employment Policy in 1949-78 with Special Emphasis on Women in Rural Production," in *Chinese Economy Post-Mao*, Vol. 1, *Policy and Performance*, Joint Economic Committee of Congress (Washington, D.C.: Government Printing Office, 1978).

21. See David Lampton, "Economics, Politics and the Determinants of Policy Outcomes in China: Post-Cultural Revolution Health Policy," *The Australian and New Zealand Journal of Sociology*, Vol. 12, No. 1, February 1976, pp. 43–50.

22. See E. Gray Diamond, "Medical Education in China," *Asia* No. 26, Summer 1972, p. 68. He remarked, "Almost 50% of the students in medical school are women."

23. See Victor Sidel, "Serve the People: Medical Care in the People's Republic of China," *Asia* No. 26, Summer 1972, pp. 3–30.

24. Pi-chao Chen, "China's Population Program at the Grassroots Level," p. 219; Chen claims Premier Chou stated: "For the past two years, the government has provided free planned birth services of all kinds, in order to facilitate the practice of planned birth."

25. "Jiangsu Municipality Coordinated Planned Parenthood Work," (Beijing) *NCNA*, 10 September 1973.

26. See Tameyoshi Katigori, "A Report on the Family Planning Program in the People's Republic of China," *Studies in Family Planning*, Vol. 4, No. 8, p. 217.

27. See Han Su-yin, "Family Planning in China," *The New York Times* editorial page, 1 September 1974.

28. "Actively Prevent and Cure Women's Diseases, Protect the Women Labor Force," *RMRB*, 13 March 1973, in *SCMP* 5340, pp. 173–76.

29. See *Hong Qi* No. 3, 1973, pp. 43–45. The 10th Brigade in Judong xian, Jiangsu, was commended for paying attention to women's needs by training midwives and barefoot doctors specializing in women's illnesses. See Chu Li and Tien Chieh-yun, in chapter 13, "Medical and Health Services," in *Inside a People's Commune*, pp. 194–208.

30. See Mao Zedong, "Instructions on Public Health Work," February 1970, *JPRS* Translations on Communist China, No. 49826, No. 90, p. 24; "Fight for Women's Better Health," *RMRB*, 3 March 1971, in *SCMP* 4859, pp. 86–90; "Medical Network Protects Health of Women and Children," (Beijing) *NCNA*, 8 March 1973; etc.

31. *GMRB*, 29 September 1971, p. 3.

32. See Carl Djerassi, "Some Observations on Current Fertility Control in China," *China Quarterly* No. 57, January–March 1974, pp. 40–63.

33. See "Fogang Xian, Kwangtung Province, Strengthens Leadership Over Women's Work," *RMRB* 24 September 1971, in *SCMP* 4991, pp. 150–151; see article by Bian Fenging in *RMRB*, 5 October 1970.

34. "Bring the Role of Women into Full Play in Revolution and Construction," *Hong Qi* No. 10, 1971, in *SCMM*, pp. 73–78.

35. See the practical results of actress Shen Ping's efforts in "Educating Young People to Practice Late Marriage and Family Planning," *RMRB*, 20 November 1972, in *SCMP* 5268, pp. 14–15.

36. "Vigorously Encourage Late Marriage for the Revolutionary Cause," *RMRB,* 30 January 1971, in *SCMP* 4831, pp. 122–123.

37. See Norma Diamond, "Collectivization, Kinship and the Status of Women in Rural China," pp. 27–28.

38. See "Gueizhou Conference on Birth Control Cites Gains, Policies," Gueiyang, Gueizhou Provincial Service, 19 March 1977; "Zhejiang Holds Meeting on Planned Parenthood," Hangzhou, Zhejiang Provincial Service, 16 January 1977; and "Fujian Holds Meeting on Planned Parenthood," Fuzhou, Fujian Provincial Service, 3 September 1978.

39. "National Planned Parenthood Conference Held in Beijing," (Beijing) *NCNA,* 26 January 1979.

40. See "Sichuan Adopts Family Planning Measures," (Beijing), *NCNA,* 14 March 1979. And see "Gueizhou Officials Punished for Ignoring Birth Control Regulation," (Beijing) *GMRB,* 7 September 1979.

41. I spent two weeks in Shulu County as part of a five-member research team studying county-level government in the summer of 1979. All of the data on Shulu were provided by county officials.

42. *Information Concerning the Question of Planned Births (Jihua shengyu zhishi wenti)* (Renmin Weisheng Chuban she, Gulin sheng). This was first published in 1972 and reissued in 1979, and *Planned Births (Jihua shengyu)* (Renmin chubanshe, Beijing), 1975. Both of these were purchased in Shulu County, Hebei, in the summer of 1979. I was told they had been available for several years.

43. Information on Wuxi was obtained from county officials during a field research trip in the summer of 1979.

44. These are specially constructed fields in some Wuxi County communes that can yield one ton of grain (rice). They were built by the local population with the help of the county.

45. Xu Dixin, professor at Beita and vice-president of the Chinese Academy of Social Sciences, in a visit to Columbia University in 1979, stated that national policy favored single-child families and indicated that a good deal of pressure is being exerted on local areas to tighten up their population control programs. However, recent policies involving the development of the "responsibility system" in rural areas threaten to compromise birth control policy.

46. See "Beijing Maternity Hospital Makes Good Progress," (Beijing) *NCNA,* 7 March 1972.

47. See "Beijing Obstetrics Hospital: A Modern Gynecological Hospital," *Wenhui bao,* 22 March 1972, in *JPRS* Translations on People's Republic of China, No. 229, p. 15.

48. See the remarks of Vice-Minister of Health Jian Xinzhong on the question of the modernization of the medical field in China. (Beijing) *NCNA,* 30 December 1978.

49. See "Shanghai Holds Meeting on Educated Youth Guidelines," Shanghai City Service, 4 January 1979. "They [Shanghai's youth] will no longer be sent to settle in the countryside." See also "Zhejiang Stresses Shift of Emphasis in Educated Work," Hangzhou, Zhejiang, 1 January 1979, and "Shanxi Holds Conference on Educated Youth," Taiyuan, Shanxi Provincial Service, 8 January 1979.

50. See "Further Reportage on Leaders' Meeting With Educated Youth," (Beijing) *NCNA,* 29 August 1979; and "Anhui Holds Conference on Educated Youth," Hefei, Anhui, 26 March 1979.

51. (Beijing) *NCNA,* 14 December 1978.

52. Xu Dixin, vice-president of the Chinese Academy of Social Sciences, has stated that more than twenty million people were waiting for job assignments in China's major urban centers.

53. "Zhejiang Stresses Shift of Emphasis in Educated Youth Work." And see "Zhejiang Labor Bureau Director Discusses Jobs for Youth," Hangshou, Zhejiang Provincial Service, 3 March 1979.

54. See "Shanghai Arranges Jobs for Returned Educated Youth," Shanghai City Service, 19 February 1979.

55. See the *RMRB* editorial, "There Should Be a Big Growth of Foreign Trade," *RMRB*, 4 December 1978.

56. That there was a potential if not actual substitution of youth for married women in the urban labor market seemed to be acknowledged by Xu Dixin, who noted that many "former housewives" were ready to retire anyway!

57. See *GRRB*, 13 March 1979, for a discussion of the textile industry's role in earning foreign exhange. See also "Light Industry Minister Discusses Accomplishing Modernization," Beijing City Service, 3 February 1979.

58. See "NCNA Commentary Calls for Advanced Sideline Production," *NCNA*, 13 October 1977.

59. Discussions at the Chinese Academy of Social Sciences with Xuan Xiang, its president in 1979, and others confirmed the policy that the production team was considered the basic unit of accounting and also confirmed the new effort to develop rural free markets and have private plots managed by individual families.

60. See Jon Sigurdson, "Rural Industrialization in China," in *China: A Reassessment of the Economy*, Joint Economic Committee, Congress, of the United States (Washington, D.C.: Government Printing Office, 1975).

61. See the stories of Wang Yunying and Liu Xiumin, both of Honan, in "Women in Central China Mountains Make Progress in Revolutionary Struggles," (Chengzhou) *NCNA*, 27 March 1972, in *SCMP* 5110, p. 71. See also paper delivered by William Hinton at 1980 Association for Asian Studies conference in which he talks of Longbow, Shenxi women's participation in rural industry.

62. In Shulu County some of the larger factories in the city provided dormitory facilities for workers.

63. Taiyuan, Shanxi Provincial Radio, 6 March 1972.

64. In Foshan, outside of Guangzhou, the textile industry was almost entirely staffed by female workers. This observation was made in the summer of 1978.

65. See Hu Qiaomu, "Act in Accordance with Economic Laws, Step Up the Four Moderizations," (Beijing) *NCNA*, 5 October 1978.

66. See "College Graduates to be Assigned to Key Projects," (Beijing) *NCNA*, 16 August 1978, and "Accelerate the Training of Middle Grade Technicians," *GMRB*, 19 August 1978. See also the series of articles on education appearing throughout 1977 and 1978 in the Chinese press.

67. See "Guangdong Schools to Use New Teaching Materials," Guangzhou, Guangdong Provincial Service, 1 September 1978; "Guangzhou Abolishes Rural Branches of Urban Middle Schools," Guangzhou, Guangdong Provincial Service, 29 July 1978, and a *GMRB* editorial, "One Cannot Be Indifferent to Not Making Use of What One Has Learned," *GMRB*, 13 July 1978.

68. For an analysis of the 1979 to 1982 period see Phyllis Andors, "The Internationalization of Capital and the Development of the Female Labor Force in China," unpublished paper delivered at the "China in Transition Conference" held at Oxford University, September 1982.

INDEX

Abortion, 158: in Soviet Union, 7
Agrarian society. *See* Agriculture, Rural areas
Agricultural economy. *See* Agriculture, Rural areas
Agriculture, 2, 16, 25, 33, 36, 40, 47, 76: women's role in, 7, 50, 55, 90, 95, 98, 147; development of, 30, 39, 165; policies on, 40, 95; collectivization of, 41, 45, 54, 57; cooperative movement in, 45, 48, 49, 52, 58; increasing production in, 48, 67; 1961 crisis in, 89; capitalism in, 90; diversification of, 92; industry and, 94, 98, 139; mechanization of, 94, 142, 144, 166; peasant-worker inequalities in, 141
"Agriculture as the base," slogan, 94
All-China Federation of Labor, 30
All-China Women's Federation. *See* Women's Federation
Ance Xian, 44
Anhui, 132
Anshan Iron and Steel Works, 70
"Anti-Duhring," 132
Anti-Japanese War, 24, 34, 41
Army, 23, 26. *See also* Red Guard

Banks, 16
Baoan, 94
Beidaihe Resolution, 49
Beijing, 137, 161: prominent women of, 35, 70, 83; communes of, 66, 69; Cultural Revolution Group of, 109; Junshu neighborhood, 132; light industry in, 139; Fengsheng district, 139–40; cadres in, 141; population growth in, 160; committees in, 193n63
Beijing Bus Company, 69: refuses to hire women, 84
Beijing General Knitwear, 110, 111, 113
Beijing Hat Factory, 62
Beijing Municipal Bureau of Textile Industry, 135
Beijing Silk and Satin Factory, 135

Beijing State No. 2 Cotton Mill, 110, 113
Beijing Steel Wire Plant, 87, 136
Beijing Union Medical College, 70
Beijing University, 70, 105
Beijing Woolen Textile Mill, 135
Beixinjiao Commune, 66
Beiyuan Chemical Factory, 67
Biology, and women's role, 1, 2, 72, 126
Birth control, 71, 120, 148, 152, 154, 168: in Soviet Union, 7; forms of, 7, 56, 78, 158; education in, 54, 78, 156; policies on, 56, 77, 156, 163, 202n45; in rural areas, 120, 155, 158; acceptance of, 155, 163; Red Guard and, 156; Dazhai approach to, 157–58; rewards and punishments and, 160, 161–62
Birth rates, 19, 155, 156
Bolsheviks, 6
Bourgeoisie, 38, 152, 153
Brigades, 92, 94, 96, 104: women's role in, 51; and women's wages, 144
"Bumper crop maidens," 57
Bureaucracy, 15, 47

Cadres, 30, 80, 110, 111, 114, 117, 141: women in, 32, 33, 46, 102, 104, 118, 133, 134; in Shanghai, 116; and birth control, 157
Cai Chang, 17, 151
Cai Huabo, 59
Caixi, township in Fujian, 23
Capital: and competition with West, 15–16; creation of, 37; labor as substitute for, 48; investment, 71, 154
Capitalism, 16, 82: development of, 1, 12; exploitation of women under, 6; in agriculture, 90; and industrialization, 106; denunciations of, 107, 115; American, 179n40
CCP. *See* Chinese Communist Party
Changan Residents' Committee, 63
Changchun, 138